Unconditional LOVE

Good news for all creation

Mike Parsons

Unconditional Love

Copyright © 2025 Mike Parsons,
Freedom Apostolic Ministries Ltd.

Cover Design: Jeremy Westcott and Beth Lane,
Freedom Apostolic Ministries Ltd.

The right of Mike Parsons to be identified as the author of this work has been asserted by him in accordance with the Copyright, Designs and Patents Act 1988.

All rights reserved. No part of this publication may be reproduced or transmitted in any form or by any means, electronic or mechanical including photocopying, recording or any information storage or retrieval system, without prior permission in writing from the publishers.

First published in the United Kingdom in 2025 by
The Choir Press
in conjunction with
Freedom Apostolic Ministries Ltd.

ISBN: 978-1-78963-545-4

Contents

Introduction to Unconditional Love 5
Part I God is Love 7
  1. Being, not doing 9
  2. God is love, BUT 29
  3. No Record of Wrongs 45
  4. Repentance, confession and forgiveness 65
  5. Faith 83
  6. God-breathed Writings 103
  7. Pleasing God 123
  8. The Extent of Love 141
  9. Relationship is All God Desires 159
Part II Consuming Fire 175
  10. The 'Hell' Myth 177
  11. Parables of 'Hell'? 197
  12. The Consuming Fire of God's Love 215
  13. Hellfire Preaching 231
  14. More Adventures in the Fire 251
  15. Worm Theology 269
  16. Deconstruction 293
Part III Immortality 323
  17. Embrace Immortality 325
  18. Jesus Abolished Death 343
  19. The Chariot of Ascension 359
  20. Transcending Time and Space 375
  21. Time Miracles and Immortality 393
  22. Unlocking Our Identity as Sons 407
Further resources 429
Bible Versions 431

Introduction

The God I believed I knew 20 years ago, or even 12 years ago, has become a distant memory. He is not what religion had led me to believe. He is far better than that. He is profoundly good, loving, kind, thoughtful and passionate beyond my wildest expectations – as I have come to know through face-to-face encounters and personal experiences. Fortunately, He did not reveal all this at once, or it might have been too much for me.

None of this came from studying or attempting to understand God from an intellectual standpoint. The true nature of God can only be grasped through an intimate, experiential relationship, not through intellectual knowledge. It is all about relating to God and understanding our true identity as His children. My own journey has been one of deepening intimacy, in which God has been revealed as my Father, Mother, Brother and Friend.

This book came out of the teaching sessions I did live with our Patreon patrons over almost two years, and it quickly became clear that God's unconditional love is an immense topic, and one for which this is a *kairos* moment. I continue to be thrilled by the increasing number of people joining us on this journey of uncovering our identity as children of God and our relationship with Him – both the relational and governmental facets of this connection. And this is indeed a journey, not a fixed destination. It is about our ongoing walk with God, staying closely connected, without rushing ahead or lagging behind, avoiding detours, and maintaining an intimate connection that will help us outwork our destiny.

The path we tread is anything but linear. Sometimes it leads left, sometimes right, up and down. The road ahead is not always clear, but God is our guide. We are headed towards a place of restoration, deepening intimacy and increased creativity in our role as children of God. For me this has been an adventurous ride, and I have witnessed and participated in wonders I could never have imagined. What is even more

INTRODUCTION

exciting is that it shows no sign of slowing down. There is so much more to explore and experience as we continue.

I believe you are reading this because you are hungry for more, for something greater. You recognise that there is more than you currently know, and I am truly grateful for that because it implies you have higher aspirations and are willing to push boundaries. I do not believe God wants us confined in any way. Thus, there are challenges along the path, challenges that transform our perspectives, redefining what we thought we knew about Him and about ourselves. He desires to remove all the limitations and restrictions that religion has imposed on us, releasing us to become all He designed us and intends us to be.

Part I

God is Love

1. Being, Not Doing

Over the past several years the Father has deconstructed my thinking and expanded my consciousness beyond anything I could have ever imagined or thought possible. And God has shown Himself to be so much bigger, better, further, greater; He far surpasses any preconceived notions I might have had. Many of the beliefs I held about God had been ingrained in me through religious instruction and theological teachings in my years passing through the Methodist and Brethren to charismatic churches. For example, like most people, I thought that you could only go to heaven when you die. When God opened up that realm to me, it conclusively proved that belief false. Now I realise that many of the beliefs I held were never true, even though I once believed they were. Any theological argument pales in comparison to engaging with God in the realms of heaven face-to-face or connecting with God within ourselves in a place of deep intimacy.

Experience

I now recognise that all the doctrines that had been ingrained in me, presenting God as an angry deity, a God requiring appeasement, the Old Testament God distinct from the New Testament God, and all the other confusing notions I harboured, were founded on intellectual beliefs because neither I nor those who taught me had ever truly met Him. One day, God posed a question to me: "How much of what you know about me comes directly from Me, and how much have you picked up from reading, listening to sermons, and other people?" I had to admit that probably 99% of what I thought I knew was not based on personal experience. It was mere information, not genuine knowledge. It became evident that all of us have been conditioned, programmed by the teachings we have received, whether from religious or non-religious sources. You could be raised in an atheist household and be conditioned to believe that God does not exist, or you could grow up in a legalistic religious setting that shapes your beliefs about God and the Bible.

For me, this has been a long and sometimes challenging journey toward discovering the truth and realising that God is indeed love. His love is unconditional, and experiencing that love is what He desires for us. This way, we can enter a reality where we love as He loves.

Understanding unconditional love is a daunting task for many because of the way we have been conditioned. In terms of God being love, if His love is not unconditional, then it is not love at all. Love, by its very nature, cannot be conditional. You cannot earn love. Recognising and grasping the nature of unconditional love and why it causes offence to the religious mind is of paramount importance. I firmly believe that this is the one truth that has made the most impact in my life over the last 10-12 years.

The truth that God's love is unconditional has come under attack and has been distorted in numerous ways, precisely because understanding and experiencing it is so essential. When we experience unconditional love, it brings freedom. It liberates us to be ourselves, eliminating the need to perform to earn or deserve it. You may be familiar with a phrase I often use, which the Father said to me: "Live loved, love living, and live loving." He reiterated this message countless times as a source of encouragement and motivation. This is simply how we can live our lives. We can live knowing that we are loved. It does not entail striving to be loved, or attempting to earn or deserve love, or prove ourselves worthy of it. It is about accepting that we are already unconditionally loved. This understanding and experience are the keys to leading a life full of love.

When we live from that place of feeling unconditionally loved, we can genuinely love living. Life becomes a joyous journey, and each day brings new experiences and opportunities to explore, rest, and simply be. We can also live loving, and this is where the rubber meets the road. To live loving means that we demonstrate the love we have received to others, just as Jesus instructed His disciples to do. This can be challenging, especially when people are unkind or hurt us. If you have been involved in church life, or indeed any kind of human interaction, you know how easily people can cause hurt, whether intentionally or inadvertently. Maintaining a loving attitude towards others, even when they have wronged us, is undoubtedly difficult. Nevertheless, it is possible, as that is precisely how God has loved us. If God's love to us is unconditional, then our love towards others should likewise be unconditional.

Should

I used the word 'should,' but in fact, that word is one I aim to remove from my vocabulary when it comes to God, relationships, and living life. I do not want to do things because I should do them. Who decrees that I 'should' do them? God? If so, that sets a condition, but I know His love is unconditional. So, what are the repercussions of not doing what I 'should' do? "What will God do, if I do not do what He wants?" This prompts us to reflect on what kind of God we believe in and what He does when our actions do not align with His wishes.

Are there really a multitude of things we 'should' do? "I should go to church, I should pray, I should read my Bible, I should witness." It seems like an endless list of 'shoulds.' Why should I do them? It is because I am conditioned to, and because I think it is the right thing to do. God challenged me about whether I should be obedient. Initially, I thought, "Of course, I should." But then He revealed that my thinking was deeply rooted in an Old Covenant mindset. Obedience implies adherence to a law, and God does not want us to obey Him. Instead, He desires a relationship where we cooperate with Him; where we do things because we see the Father doing them, not because we should, but because we desire to. It becomes the desire of our hearts to be in a relationship with God who loves us in such an extraordinary way.

So, do we have an obligation or a duty to perform certain actions? Are we striving to please God through our behaviour? If so, we are operating within that same Old Covenant mindset. The Father posed a question: "Are you trying to please Me?" Initially I replied, "Yes," because I was! But He responded, "You are already pleasing to Me. Why are you trying to become something you already are?" This exchange revealed how my mind had been conditioned with 'should.' God does not want that kind of obligation-driven vocabulary in our lives. He desires a deep, intimate relationship where heart-to-heart sharing reveals how we can just be, enabling us to move away from constant doing.

Religion often emphasises doing, doing and more doing to please God, which leads to exhaustion. So, why not simply rest and be ourselves? God accepts us as we are, yet we often struggle to accept our own acceptability because we have been accustomed to believe we need to change. Do we desire change? Certainly, we do. We want to become more like Him, not because we need to change to be acceptable to Him, but because we are unconditionally loved. Our motivation for transformation is not negative; it is positive. We love that we are becoming more like Him whom we behold.

When we are face-to-face with Him, living in the light of His presence, transformation and change occur without our strenuous efforts. I used to be systematic in addressing issues because that is how I am wired. Over the years, I have become less so, and more relational. Rather than trying to fix myself, renew my own mind, sort myself out, or change my genetic and generational lines, I simply allow God to take the lead. He sets the agenda for what He wants to address and when He wants to address it. My role is to agree and cooperate with Him, most often by getting out of the way. As God once told me most succinctly, "I do not require your help, just your surrender."

If we live in a state of being loved by God, we can find complete security in our identity within the relationship we share. We are part of the *perichoresis*, the circle of conversation among the Father, Son and Spirit. They engage in continuous dialogue about us, and are conversing about us right now, all of us, including you. This conversation is invariably positive. They are smiling, enjoying talking about you, because They are discussing the 'you' They know you to be, not the 'you' you might think you are. Sometimes we are concerned that if we open up, God might get to know something about us that we would not want anyone else to know. The fact is, He already does. He knows everything, and He loves us unconditionally.

I would like to share a few profound statements that God shared with me, which deeply resonated with me and ignited my pursuit of understanding their significance.

"I have laid a true foundation that can carry the weight of all mankind, so all can become fully mature sons of God." This statement intrigued me, and it made me ponder the nature of this foundation. What foundation has He laid? It is a foundation that existed before the foundation of the world, and it is meant to allow all of humanity to become fully mature sons, not just a select few. God's unconditional love leaves no one out.

"The ages to come ought to be times of wonder and awe, where I will take my sons on an amazing journey of creative discovery." I believe this journey entails discovering just how creative we are. We understand that we are co-heirs, but how well do we realise that we are co-creators? What creative abilities lie within us? The Father encouraged me to be attentive to the extraordinary things that are unfolding.

"Knowing the depth, height, breadth and length of My unconditional love multi-dimensionally is what this age is designed to accomplish. There are 12 ages of man and 12 ages within each age. All are opportunities to become mature sons in relationship and responsibility." Whilst I have not delved too deeply into this statement yet, I am familiar with the idea that God operates in cycles and seasons, and that ages are overlapping processes that lead us to maturity as sons.

"The ascent of man is a slow process from a creative perspective, hindered by the false images of me that religion has known." Recognising the true nature of God is essential. Are we truly seeing Him for who He is or are we filtering Him through our preconceived notions? I have found it quite a challenging endeavour to unveil the truth of God's love, as so many attempts to reveal it are twisted into lies and deception.

Online interactions, for instance, are often marred by individuals misrepresenting what is said. Some folk are genuinely seeking answers, whilst others are only seeking confrontation. I have learned to discern between those genuinely inquiring and those looking for a fight. Fighting is not productive; it often digs a deeper trench between us. Some just assume they know what I believe and want to disabuse me of error. However, I do not want to be labelled with any one particular set of beliefs because that is so limiting and restricting; God invites us to understand Him in diverse and expansive ways. Religion has placed veils over the eyes of many, including those who do not profess any faith. Believers and atheists alike may be sheltering behind veils that prevent them from seeing God as pure love, whose desire is to bless everyone and everything.

"Even the attempts to show the extent and power of our consuming, fiery love that reaches beyond the grave has been twisted into a chamber of horrors: the 'hell' illusion and delusion." I visited a fiery realm on a number of occasions between 2005 and 2010, and at the time I described it as 'hell' due to a lack of a better frame of reference. I was going into a supernatural dimensional reality where there was fire and a whole lot of unhappy people. What else was I supposed to think? So people ask me quite often. Well, what about these testimonies of these people who went down and came back? Firstly, it is obviously not an inescapable place, because they came back (as did I). That is a good thing to start with. But like me, they will have had a prior understanding of what that place was, and our conditioning can be extraordinarily strong. On my journey of enlightenment and deconstruction, that was probably one of the most difficult things for God to challenge and to break. Eventually, He showed me what was going on there, and that I could have a part to play in it, which then totally changed my whole understanding.

Never give up

God cannot deny himself because He is love. The Father said, "Son, We will never give up on even one of those who are Our sons, as We cannot deny Ourselves. Love cannot and will not fail, as We will never give up and cannot be denied or resisted forever. Love wins. If love does not win at all, in the end, then We cannot be love. For love can never be forced, just continually demonstrated again and again until it eventually overcomes every obstacle, objection, excuse and reason."

This is why I am such a firm advocate for the restoration of all things, because God's love is unwavering. It persists because it is intrinsic to His being. His love endures eternally. God and love will never falter. As He said, "Our love never fails, never gives up, and can never be escaped because it is filled with age-enduring grace and mercy. Our grace and mercy will never cease to be a vehicle for love to be expressed and demonstrated abundantly, lavishly, with extreme desire and intent; without limits. If love is limited, it is not love. Love must be extreme or it is not love. Love must seem wasteful and undeserved, or it is not love. Our love cannot be stopped by sin, rejection or death. It has experienced all there is and yet has conquered and overcome all things."

Thus, all things can be restored to face-to-face relational innocence, which is the nature of what God has done. He has made us innocent. That is how He sees us, but do we? Or do we constantly feel 'less than'? Have we experienced unconditional love, or do we struggle with the very concept?

Romans 8 contains a wealth of insights on love, particularly in the context of the impossibility of separation from it:

Who will separate us from the love of Christ? Will tribulation, or trouble, or persecution, or famine, or nakedness, or danger, or sword? Just as it is written: "For Your sake we are killed all day long; we were regarded as sheep to be slaughtered." But in all these things we overwhelmingly conquer through Him who loved us. For I am convinced that neither death, nor life, nor angels, nor principalities, nor things present, nor things to come, nor powers, nor height, nor depth, nor any other created thing will be able to separate us from the love of God that is in Christ Jesus our Lord (Romans 8:35-39).

This love is unwavering and immutable. There is nothing we – or anyone, or anything – can do that can separate us from the love of God. Religion will tell you the complete opposite, even though it might teach on that Bible verse. It will tell you that there is something that can separate you from the love of God: your choice. But it cannot. It can only separate you in your own thinking. It cannot separate you from a God who loves you unconditionally.

What will it take to distance us from the love of Christ? You name any potential calamity: intense pressure of the worst possible kind; claustrophobia, persecution, destitution, loneliness, extreme exposure, life-threatening danger or war... This is my conviction: no threat, whether it be in death or life, be it angelic beings, demon powers or political principalities, nothing known to us at this time, or even in the unknown future; no dimension of any calculation in time or space, nor any device yet to be invented, has what it takes to separate us from the love of God demonstrated in our Lord Jesus Christ (Romans 8:35, 38-39 Mirror).

That is really good news. And for those who think they can separate themselves, or feel separated because of their past life or what they might have done: God takes no notice of what we think, or what others think. He just takes notice of who He is – and He is unconditional love.

One thing is essential for us to recognise our true identity as sons and daughters of God: that we experience unconditional love personally and intimately; a cardiognosis, a heart knowing that goes beyond mere intellectual knowledge. Whilst I have always believed that God is love, my understanding of that love is very different now because of experience. I have had many experiences of the nature of that unconditional love, both personally and in how God has expressed and shown His love to others, and I am absolutely convinced that this is the key everyone needs to know. All of us would probably say we know that God is love, but the question is, do we just know it as a concept, a theory, or have we experienced that love as unconditional in practice?

To become true sons and daughters of God, I believe that the foundation of our lives must be firmly rooted in the unchanging nature, character and essence of God as I AM, constant and never changing. God is unconditional love; He is limitless grace; and He is triumphant mercy. These three attributes combine to create a rock-solid foundation upon which our lives can be built and mature; and they are intended to be experienced, not just asserted, studied or discussed. God is working in our lives constantly to enable us to experience the reality of who He is – and so discover who we are.

"Son, never cease dwelling in the reality of unconditional love, limitless grace, and triumphant mercy." Some religious people have raised concerns about so-called 'hyper-grace'; the fact is that grace extends far beyond hyper; it is truly limitless. His grace can handle and conquer anything, as His mercy has already achieved victory over every obstacle and hindrance. This is far more than anything religion has to offer.

State of 'being'

To live in this reality means to abide, dwell, or remain in a state of 'being'. It is about finding rest in the conscious awareness of being unconditionally loved, with no need for any additional effort on our part. It is utterly free and unconditional, yet not without its challenges: our conditioned perceptions of love and God are what can make it difficult. This state of 'being' is complete immersion in unconditional love, limitless grace and triumphant mercy. It expands our consciousness and awareness, forming the basis for our thoughts, emotions and actions. Ultimately, it empowers us to just be – no small feat in a world that emphasises doing. Our programming, derived from the tree of the knowledge of good and evil, pushes us toward independence and the need to do. Our true identity and consciousness of that identity, however, revolve around being rather than doing. Embracing this truth can liberate us to lay hold of the astonishing power and significance of our sonship.

Most of us have likely been part of (or at least encountered) some form of religious system in our lives. These systems often demand a level of performance or adherence to specific behavioural standards for acceptance. Each religion or Christian denomination tends to impose its own set of norms onto God, and these norms are quite potent because our inherent human desire for connection and family makes us susceptible to their influence. It becomes challenging when the systems we have lived under condition us to believe that God expects certain things from us. Such laws, duties and obligations can drive us to seek acceptance by performing certain works, adopting particular behaviours, or something else we believe will earn us approval. Worse, we may equate obedience to our religious tradition with obedience to God. This dynamic is closely tied to the curse of the do-it-yourself tree of independence, a path that many have unwittingly found themselves on.

Romans 12:2 warns us not to conform to the patterns of this world; in context, not yielding to the pressures of whatever religious or political moulds seek to shape and form us within the systems we live under. Instead, we can be transformed by the renewing of our minds. However, renewing our own minds is a task we cannot accomplish independently, despite our best efforts. I personally made a diligent effort to renew my mind by repeatedly confessing Bible verses, making declarations, and issuing decrees, often to convince myself of the truths I declared. Whilst this helped me memorise many Bible verses, it did not actually renew my mind.

True renewal of my mind only occurred through a profound experience that altered my perspective. I came to know a truth that was different from my previous understanding, and I chose to align myself with God's viewpoint. This *metanoia*, misleadingly translated 'repentance', is essentially agreeing with God, embracing His thoughts, and has nothing to do with 'saying sorry' or other religious notions. True repentance involves God revealing something to us, our agreeing with it, and the resulting renewal of our minds. The process is quite straightforward, but the issue is our tendency to intervene. We often believe that we must take action ourselves, which is not what the verse is saying at all. When it comes to breaking free from the constraints of religious and political moulds, we are incapable of doing it on our own. We cannot fix a problem with the same elements that created it in the first place. Thus, attempting to use our own minds to mend our minds is ineffective. Only God can transform our minds by revealing truths that will bring about the change.

Immortality

God is undeniably good. The true understanding of God's good, acceptable and perfect will, as mentioned in Romans 12, is realised through experience. Unfortunately, we have often taught people that this can only be known through faith. Faith is about believing in things not yet seen. Personally, I do not want to solely rely on faith. Instead, I desire to live in the tangible reality of experiencing everything God intends for me to see and have. I do not want to be like those in the Old Covenant promises described in Hebrews 11 who all died without witnessing their fulfilment. In fact, I do not want to die at all, because I believe God never intended for us to die.

...but now has been revealed by the appearing of our Savior Christ Jesus, who abolished death and brought life and immortality to light through the gospel (2 Timothy 1:10).

The gospel has revealed the concept of immortality. It challenges the conventional belief that we are all destined to die one day. Jesus Himself taught that we do not have to die: by partaking in His life, symbolised by His flesh and blood in communion, we gain not only a life without end but a life of extraordinary quality that flows from eternity. All of this belongs to us now, and it is part of God's will for us.

Blameless and innocent

... just as He chose us in Him before the foundation of the world, that we would be holy and blameless before Him. In love He predestined us to adoption as sons through Jesus Christ to Himself, according to the kind intention of His will, to the praise of the glory of His grace, which He freely bestowed on us in the Beloved (Ephesians 1:4-6).

He associated us in Christ before the fall of the world. Jesus is God's mind made up about us. He always knew in his love that he would present us again face-to-face before him in blameless innocence (Ephesians 1:4 Mirror).

This statement is truly profound. When we have experienced being face-to-face with Him, we come to realise how blameless and innocent we truly are, unless we still struggle with this concept due to our minds not being fully renewed. God's love transforms us into innocence in His eyes. Ask yourself whether you feel unconditionally loved and innocent. If not, it might suggest that you believe you need to meet certain conditions to be loved, that you are not good enough because you do not feel innocent. When we reflect on our lives, we can usually recognise our imperfections. However, when He looks at us, God does not zero in on our self-perceived shortcomings; His focus is on who He says we are, His beloved children. He loves us, and we are blameless and innocent in His eyes.

So, who can call themselves blameless? I can, because I am simply repeating God's words. If I were to rely solely on the evidence of my own actions, I would not dare claim to be blameless. But God looks beyond our deeds; He looks at what

He has done and what Jesus has accomplished. He sees us as He says we are. His love enables us to stand face to face with Him without fear, because perfect love casts out all fear (see 1 John 4:18). His love has chosen us to be His children. His love is His will, and His will is His love. His love, expressed through His will, has chosen us to be restored to a state of blameless innocence. Even before we took on our human form, before creation itself was spoken into being, in God's heart we were already restored. We just need to catch up with what is already true rather than trying to make it true. God's limitless grace and triumphant mercy ensure that we will come to know His unconditional love, one way or another, regardless of how long it takes. His patience far exceeds our own, and His love never fails.

Path of independence

Why do people find it difficult to accept that God is love and that His love is unconditional? This struggle stems from the deep-seated programming of humanity towards the path of independence. This DIY path, chosen by Adam, has fundamentally altered our thinking, leading us to believe that we can go it alone. This pushes us toward self-effort and striving for acceptance through our own hard work. Unfortunately, all this endeavour leaves us weary, frustrated, and trapped in what the Bible describes as 'evil,' meaning hardships, toil, and the often-fruitless labour of self-effort.

The entire human race has lost touch with its identity as God's children, having become independent and opting to do things in our own strength. As a result, many can no longer bring themselves to embrace the grace-filled benefits of being a child of God. They have forgotten their true identity and feel alienated or separated from God, even though nothing can truly separate us from His love. We have changed mankind (made in the image of God) into humanity (made in its own image); and humanity has been deceived into feeling orphaned by its own independent, alienated mind. So we feel separated, although that is not the truth. However, when we view it as the truth, it is the truth that we live in, even though it is false. And God wants that truth to be changed for us so that we know what is really true.

The problem lies in the fact that most people do not realise they are already loved. They work tirelessly to earn love as if it were a reward for obedience, fulfilling duties, or meeting obligations. This deception adds to the weariness and the heavy burden of trying to earn God's favour, appease His anger (because that is the other side of the 'god' that we have created in our own image), and make up for past wrongdoings. That is a heavy burden to bear.

Thankfully, Jesus offers relief to those who are weary and burdened. He invites them to come to Him and find rest, because His yoke is easy and His burden is light. Religious systems, on the other hand, are man-made constructs designed to make people feel they must earn God's approval through their own efforts. They are essentially systems of self-improvement – and even the 'Christian religion' falls into that category. Christianity from a religious perspective is very different from the simplicity of the relationship God wants us to enjoy. Religious systems often employ fear, guilt, shame and condemnation to make people feel unworthy of being accepted as they are, pushing them to strive for change. This is a deception.

God is love, and His love is inherently unconditional. In other words, there are no conditions you must meet for God to love you. No conditions whatsoever. It is worth taking a moment to reflect on the conditions you might have been taught or somehow come to believe that you must fulfil to be accepted and loved by God. Perhaps you were told you had to pray a specific prayer, 'repent', get baptised, or participate in certain religious rituals. Many belief systems have their requirements for building a relationship with God. However, the way we often present the good news, particularly in evangelical circles, tends to distort the essence of what has already been accomplished into something that is only achieved through our actions, through works.

Whilst the evangelical wing of the church identifies itself with justification by grace through faith, it often teaches a form of religious law. It instructs you to pray a certain prayer and admit you are a sinner, creating the impression that God's love and forgiveness are contingent on these actions. This conditional perspective, despite proclaiming itself as a gospel of grace, conditions us to rely on our own works for salvation.

The truth is that God has already done everything necessary. There is nothing more for Him to do. There is certainly nothing that we can add to it. We simply need to acknowledge what He has already accomplished. This realisation can free us from the burdens of imposed conditions and allow us to embrace the unconditionally loving nature of God. In reality, there are no 'not-yet-Christians' as I used to believe; there are simply those who have yet to discover and appreciate the depth of God's unconditional love.

I accept that there are individuals who do not identify as Christians, but that does not imply they are unsaved. My perspective on salvation aligns with the belief that God has already completed this work for all of humanity. I am not particularly inclined to encourage people to adopt the label 'Christian' because that would entail unravelling some of the religious ideas associated with it, which may not even be possible. Instead, my focus is on inviting people to follow Jesus, and through Him to enter into relationship with the Father, who embodies unconditional love.

The truth is that everyone has already been born from above, living in a state of resurrection life. The 'all' who are made alive in Christ are the same 'all' who were dead in Adam (see 1 Corinthians 15:22). We all shared in Christ's death, burial and resurrection. When Jesus breathed upon His disciples, they received the Holy Spirit on behalf of all mankind, just as Adam had received life when the Father breathed into him. The choices made by Adam led to us being dead in Adam, but now, through Christ, we are all alive in Him. This is incredible news. If we could share this message with the world in a way that does not involve threats of eternal punishment, perhaps people would more readily realise that God is love.

The essence of unconditional love is what underlies the restoration of all things. Through Jesus, everything that was created by Him, through Him, and for Him has already been reconciled through the blood of the cross. This is truly good news.

An amazing aspect of God's love is that it is extended equally to all His children, whether they are aware of it or not. The full experience of this love may only come when we enter into a relationship with Him and delight in it, yet God is good to everyone all the time, and He works to bring about good in every situation, regardless of how poor or misguided our choices may be.

I recall a remarkable experience I had in heaven a few years ago. I was standing under a waterfall of the river of life, and as I looked up, I witnessed a multitude of colours cascading down over me. Each colour represented God's love for various groups of people or individuals. I could feel God's profound love for those who had suffered, those who were victims, and those who were hurt, broken, abused and damaged by others. I was in awe of God's immense love for them. Then, the colours changed, and I began to experience God's love for those who had caused the pain and harm, the victimisers, traffickers and abusers. Initially, I struggled with this and questioned the fairness of it all. How could God love these individuals in the same way? But then I received a deep revelation that if God did not love me that way and did not love them that way, then He could not love anyone that way. 'God is love' became not merely a statement from scripture but a truth I fully embraced. This experience shifted my perspective on people, even those who had committed terrible deeds. Instead of anger or revulsion, I feel a desire to reach out to them with love.

Whether we are 'religious' or not, we have been programmed by religion that we have to do something to deserve or earn love or appease anger. This is the fundamental deception. It deceives people into believing that they must earn what is rightfully theirs through inheritance (because we are all His children and coheirs, whether we are aware of it or not). We are all loved unconditionally by our loving Father, abounding in loving kindness. Experiencing and understanding this truth can be truly life-changing.

Consider for a moment the conditions you might believe apply to God's love for you or His acceptance of you. Think about those 'buts.' God is pure love, unconditional love, but what makes it challenging for you to fully believe and embrace this truth? What obstacles are preventing you from knowing that you can simply be, live loved, and love living, without any 'buts'?

Perhaps it is the way you perceive yourself, the projections others have placed on you, or your past actions. Do you genuinely know that you are entirely forgiven? Unconditional love goes hand in hand with unconditional forgiveness. While some may argue that repentance is a prerequisite for forgiveness, please understand that *metanoia* is not about doing penance but rather agreeing with God's perspective. Belief and agreement play a significant role in experiencing God's truth.

So, what are those 'buts'? Are there any hindrances or obstructions preventing you from receiving and experiencing unconditional love as God intends? Please take a moment to reflect.

I believe the Father desires you to let go of all those things as if you are shedding a set of clothes, clothes that are not the ones He wants you to wear. These are garments of thoughts, beliefs and feelings that do not align with the reality of God's unconditional love. He wants you to surrender them so that you are no longer clothed in your past, false beliefs or anything that contradicts the truth: that God loves you unconditionally, and you have no conditions to fulfil. Perhaps you have an Old Covenant mindset, thinking that in order to be acceptable you need to be obedient, you need to please God, and you need to offer your own types of sacrifices and offerings to Him.

In these activations you may choose to read the text or listen to the audio which will open on your phone or tablet when you scan the QR code at the head of each one. Links to the audio files are also included on the additional resources webpage which accompanies this book: freedomarc.org/UCL-resources

Activation #1
The Prodigal

To stream the audio, scan the QR code or visit freedomarc.org/ UCL-resources.

> Relax, close your eyes
> and start thinking on living loved.
>
> Begin to slow down your breathing.
> Just slow down.
>
> Picture the Father
> with welcoming arms.
> And picture yourself
> like the prodigal son.
> And picture yourself coming to the Father.
>
> But all those things
> that may be hindrances and obstructions to you,
> obstacles to you feeling and knowing
> that you are loved unconditionally
> are like all the dirty clothes that the prodigal was wearing,
> having worked in a pigsty.
> And he must have been feeling smelly
> and sweaty and stinky himself.
>
> But he came to the father
> and the father welcomed him with open arms
> in the state that he was in.
> The father gave him a ring of sonship to put on his finger.
> The father gave him new clothes to wear.
>
> So I just encourage you to take all of those dirty clothes,
> whatever those things are,

beliefs, mindsets, past experiences,
unworthiness, unbelief,
anything that is a hindrance that you may know
and anything you do not know,
hand everything over to Him.

I'd encourage you to take everything off
and stand naked before the Father.
I know that might feel really, really uncomfortable.
But the Father does not see you naked.
The Father sees you clothed in righteousness,
clothed in glory.

And as you remove all of the things
that you have clothed yourself in or been clothed in,
let the Father now clothe you in glory,
clothe you in light,
clothe you in love
so that you can celebrate how good the Father is,
how loved you are, unconditionally.

Start to breathe in
the unconditional love of the Father.
And as you breathe deeply, love starts to fill you.

Be still
and let God love on you.
Let Him whisper in your ear
something significant that He wants you to know.

Be still and know that God is love.
Look deep into those eyes
which are pools of unconditional love.
Feel the Father's heart welcoming you,
accepting you, loving you, affirming you,
revealing how deep, how high, how wide His love is.

Overwhelming love.

Overwhelming love.

Rest in overwhelming love.

2. God is Love, BUT...

Many religious people accept that God is love because the Bible says so, but there is always a 'but'. Why is that 'but' there? Because it is too good to be true for an independent, alienated mind to accept – and many of us have been alienated or separated from God within our own minds because of our religious programming.

"Yes, God is love, but He is also holy." How many times have I heard that? As if His holiness contradicts His love! "Yes, God is love, but He is also righteous." As if His righteousness contradicts His love! "Yes, God is love, but He is also just." As if His justice contradicts His love! I admit, all these are all religiously-programmed statements that I used to believe, because I had never experienced the contrary. I had never experienced the truth, so that made it easy to believe the lies.

"Yes, God is love, but He is also a judge." As if that makes Him a bad judge? A judge who is going to find us guilty? Love never finds us guilty because love keeps no record of wrongs (see 1 Corinthians 13:5), so how can He find us guilty?

"Yes, God is love, but He cannot look upon sin." By 'sin' they normally mean certain behaviours, but in reality, sin is lost identity. If God cannot look upon sin, if He cannot look at a lost world, how could Jesus ever have come? And God is not just looking at this world, He is engaged within each and every person to bring us all into the reality of our relationship and inclusion in Christ. So the fact is that we have already been reconciled in Christ, we have already been made righteous in Christ, we have already been made holy in Christ. We did not need to do anything, He did it all!

Religion always adds a 'but', but none of those 'buts' refutes the fact that God is love, other than in the false religious doctrines that create a god who seems to be two-faced, a god who in the Old Testament seems to be angry and needs to be appeased in some way but in the New Testament seems to be loving – though even in the New Testament there seems to be wrath and anger. In reality, the word translated 'wrath' can equally well be rendered as 'passion.' God is passionate about anything that hinders our coming into relationship with Him. He is passionate about making available that relationship for us and therefore His wrath is going to be poured out on anything that hinders our coming into relationship; not the kind of 'wrath' that we have tended to believe, but rather God passionately outworking His love to bring about change and transformation for our good.

That kind of religious deception alters and denigrates God's character and makes love able and willing to punish us – not to discipline or correct us, but to bring retribution upon us. What loving Father would ever eternally punish His children like that! These religious concepts have created a god that people find it difficult to trust, a god who says he loves us and yet threatens to torment us forever if we do not do things the way he wants us to do them.

None of that is the reality of who God is. Religion twists God's holiness and righteousness through a wrong understanding of the concepts of judgment and justice. This deception is what creates the false 'hell' narrative in which such a god would torture his children eternally. No, God will love His children eternally, and will never stop and never give up until they experience that love. Yes, His love is a purifying, refining fire, a consuming fire: it will consume every hindrance and objection and anything that comes in the way of us entering into the depth of unconditional love.

So holiness, righteousness, judgment and justice do not contradict unconditional love:

Holiness expresses it
Righteousness reveals it
Judgment is its result
And justice enforces it.

Justice brings about the judgment – and the judgment that has been made by God on behalf of the whole of humanity, the whole of mankind, and the whole of creation, is "not guilty!" We are innocent; and if we would only think of ourselves the way God thinks about us, as innocent, then we might begin to operate out of that understanding and experience of innocence.

Always love

God cannot be a contradiction. He is either love or He is not, and He definitely is! He can never deny Who He is. He cannot both love and punish, despite what the Hebrews thought and wrote in their scriptures. Their version of God was someone whom they feared, because they were writing from an understanding that was not experiential. They had mediators who experienced God and went to Him on their behalf, but the people themselves only had a system of religious beliefs, with sacrifices, offerings and all the things they thought they had to do to keep God happy and avoid Him punishing them.

God never changes. He was not different in the past and He will never be different in the future. He is faithful; His nature and character are unchanging and unchangeable. Nothing can change Him: He is love. He will never be anything other than love, and that love is never-ending and always unconditional. If what you read or hear about God seems to contradict love, whether in the Old or New Testament, or in anyone's writings or teachings, then either what was said or written is wrong, or you have a flawed understanding of it, most likely because of your religious or cultural programming.

Religion twists the concepts of holiness and righteousness, which are indeed characteristics of God, so that in some way they are understood to outstrip His grace and mercy. His holiness and righteousness are in no way stronger or greater than His grace and mercy: they are equal. His holiness and righteousness are outworked in His grace and mercy and in

His unconditional love. God's grace and mercy are attributes of unconditional love and unconditional love affirms them.

All religion is the fruit of the do-it-yourself tree, and it is a deception. I was deceived by it for much of my life, and I missed the reality of who God was because I accepted an image of Him programmed into me by the various churches and streams of thought I was involved with. God took me on a journey to change my whole understanding of who He was, is, and will be: and that is always love. He wants us to experience the reality of that love. Only when it is real can it change and transform us; if we are trying to make it real, striving for it to be real, then we are not at rest.

"Be still and know that I am God" (see Psalm 46:10). To know in this context is not an intellectual endeavour but an experiential journey, delving deeper into the profound reality of God's essence. A sense of lost identity renders humanity susceptible to this terrible deception. God certainly is holy and righteous; however, these are fundamentally expressions of His boundless love. They do not entail God ever forsaking any of His children or abandoning any aspect of His creation.

We are holy

It is humanity that has distanced itself from God as Father, shaping a deity in our own image to be feared and appeased through religious works. It is because of God's holiness and righteousness that we stand acquitted. In His justice, we are declared the righteousness of God in Christ, and so become righteous and holy ourselves. God, in His holiness, has fashioned all His children in His image, adorning them with glory. He has clothed us in holiness, and the essence of our being bears the weight of godliness and holiness which is our true identity. This is who we genuinely are.

The entire creation will eventually attain the glorious freedom that comes with being the children of God. Some might object, saying, "I cannot say I am holy; that would be pride." In reality, it is an act of humility to acknowledge and agree with what God calls us. God longs for us to comprehend our true identity; that we are indeed holy. The epistles are consistent in affirming this truth:

... just as He chose us in Him before the foundation of the world, that we should be holy and without blame before Him in love (Ephesians 1:4 NKJV).

His love envelops us, making us holy and blameless.

... that He might present to Himself the church in all her glory, having no spot or wrinkle or any such thing; but that she would be holy and blameless (Ephesians 5:27).

Replace 'church' with '*ekklesia*,' and you will better grasp what Paul is referring to, distinct from religious institutions associated with the word 'church,' which are far from having no spot or wrinkle. God has created us to be one in Him, as the *ekklesia* of God.

... yet He has now reconciled you in His body of flesh through death, in order to present you before Him holy and blameless and beyond reproach (Colossians 1:22).

Do you feel it? Do you know it? Have you genuinely embraced the reality that you are holy, blameless and beyond reproach? Some may baulk at this, considering their past actions and personal history. Yet from God's perspective, that is precisely who you are. That is how He perceives you. That is how He sees you. And if we will look into the mirror of His face, if we will see that reality reflected back and embrace it, that will again change and transform our whole lives.

For He made Him who knew no sin to be sin for us, that we might become the righteousness of God in Him (2 Corinthians 5:21).

... because it is written, you shall be holy, for I am holy (1 Peter 1:16).

'Sin' relates to lost identity and a consequently distorted self-image, not just behavioural flaws. Religion often focuses on the idea that improved behaviour leads to acceptance, whereas God accepts us already because He refers back to our true identity. He sees who He created us to be, and seeks to show us how our perception of ourselves has been fashioned out of lost identity in our own minds.

We need to start embracing the renewal of our minds, allowing Him to renew our thinking so that we think the way He does. This process encapsulates the true meaning of *metanoia*, often misrepresented as 'repentance.' *Metanoia* describes a shift towards a mindset in agreement with God, accepting who He declares us to be.

... and these whom He predestined, He also called; and these whom He called, He also justified; and these whom He justified, He also glorified (Romans 8:30).

'Justified' is not merely a religious term but a legal declaration that signifies we bear no sin – 'just as if I'd never sinned,' as some have put it. Those He justified, He also glorified, elevating us to a state of full awareness of our identity as His children, as His sons, and seating us in heavenly realms.

God is a righteous judge and embodies true justice. The issue for many people lies in the religious conditioning that equates judgment and justice with wrath and punishment. God, our loving Father, does not pass judgment according to human notions of justice. His judgment is rooted in His kindness and His reconciliation of the world to Himself, not counting anything against anybody. He has nailed every accusation against all of us to the cross. His verdict is always informed by love and is 'not guilty.' You stand acquitted and innocent of all allegations. If accusations arise within your mind, reject them; recognise their origin, whether from within yourself or an external source that seeks to burden you with guilt and condemnation. Believing yourself guilty and condemned when God sees you as innocent will hinder the quality of life you experience. You will live a 'less than' kind of existence.

John 3:16 reminds us of God's profound love as demonstrated through Jesus. However, that love extends even further and deeper, beyond the cross. Jesus offered Himself even before the foundation of the world to ensure love's ultimate triumph. Justice decrees us innocent; and that verdict was brought in before we were even created. Jesus, the lion, fully identified with humanity as a lamb – we all, like sheep, have gone astray, and each of us has turned to our own way – and He did so in order for mankind to be brought back into relationship.

So whilst we may be lost and gone astray in the independence of humanity (a term which reflects our humanistic perspective of doing it in our own strength rather than reflecting the nature and character of God), His identification with us through Jesus is a profound act of love. That is why, on the cross, He cried, "My God, my God, why have you forsaken me?" He chose to become one with us, assuming the fallen nature of our world, fully engaging with our fallen condition and representing us entirely. In reality, God never forsook Jesus, because in Christ He was reconciling the world to himself. He never abandoned or turned away from us; it only seemed that way to us because of our guilt and the loss of our true identity, which occurred when we chose the path of independence. Jesus became one with us to restore us to the original divine plan. We now live in a new era, under a New Covenant forged between Jesus and the Father, which encompasses all of mankind.

Jesus warned us about the influence of the religious and political spirit, comparing it to leaven that spreads throughout the entire batch of dough. Indeed, through all the churches and streams in which I have been involved, my understanding of the New Covenant has invariably been tainted with Old Covenant concepts. Unconditional love is an incredibly powerful force that requires no sacrifices or offerings. It stands in stark contrast to the Old Covenant mindset, which always demands something – our obedience, our obligation, our duty – which are all dead works. None of them have any value whatsoever before God. The Father does not and never did require them, which will be a shock to many people. We have to be really careful that we are not operating under an Old Covenant works-based, performance-orientated mindset towards God because it will wear us out. We will never be at rest if we think we have to earn God's love and favour. There is no guilt, shame or condemnation whatsoever within unconditional love. They are just religious concepts which keep us coming back for more religion. It is time to set aside such outdated beliefs and fully embrace the New Covenant of love.

Not laying again

Therefore leaving the elementary teaching about the Christ, let us press on to maturity, not laying again a foundation of repentance from dead works and of faith toward God, of instruction about washings and laying on of hands, and the resurrection of the dead and eternal judgment (Hebrews 6:1-2).

This is a very much misunderstood passage. I totally misread it for most of my life and actually taught these principles as foundations of the New Covenant. I thought they were the elementary principles of Jesus and that we needed to lay them. They are the exact opposite. The writer clearly says 'Let us press on to maturity, not laying again a foundation of repentance..." So the Old Covenant was immature; and the New Covenant will bring us to maturity only if we do not lay another foundation of all those Old Covenant understandings and mindsets listed, which have no place in the New Covenant. Yet still today we teach repentance, faith, baptisms, laying on of hands, resurrection and judgment – and they are part of many churches' foundation courses (as they were part of ours). Do not lay that Old Covenant foundation in the New Covenant: the only foundation of the New Covenant is love.

This is from the Mirror Bible:

Consequently, as difficult as it may seem, you ought to divorce yourselves from your sentimental attachment to the foreshadowing doctrine of the Messiah, which was designed to carry us like a vessel over the ocean of prophetic dispensation into the completeness of the fulfilled promise. A mind shift from attempts to impress God by your behavior, to realizing the faithfulness of God, is fundamental. There is no life left in the old system. It is dead and gone; you have to move on. (Romans 3:27.) (Hebrews 6:1 Mirror).

And yet, for most of my life, I tried to live in that same Old Covenant system, by doing the very things that were better left behind. Verse 2 continues:

All the Jewish teachings about ceremonial washings [baptisms], the laying on of hands (in order to identify with the slain animal as sacrifice), and all teachings pertaining to a sin consciousness, including the final resurrection of the dead in order to face judgment, are no longer relevant. (All of these types and shadows were concluded and fulfilled in Christ, their living substance. His resurrection bears testimony to the judgment that he faced on mankind's behalf and the freedom from an obstructive consciousness of sin that he now proclaims... (Hebrews 6:2 Mirror, with translator's note).

Are you free from 'an obstructive consciousness of sin'? Every church I have ever been in has always focused on sin. And the more you try not to do something, the harder it is not to do. The Old Covenant system was based in sacrifices and offerings associated with the Law, instituted by Moses and never God's idea (I do not mean the so-called Ten Commandments[1], which describe how amazingly good a relationship with God can be. They are not really 'thou shalt not' but 'you do not need to'. "You do not need any gods but Me. You do not need to steal. I have everything you need within this amazing relationship of safety and security, inside My hedge of protection").

---

[1] See my previous book *Into The Dark Cloud* for a discussion of the 'Ten Commandments' as God's marriage proposal to Israel.

The Law, or grace and truth?

For the Law was given through Moses; grace and truth were realised through Jesus Christ (John 1:17).

They sent Moses to meet with Him because they were afraid of Him, and so set up a mediatorial system called 'the Law.' There were 613 parts of 'the Law' that they supposedly had to keep. Jesus made it very clear that it was impossible, and if you failed in one thing, you failed in it all, which is why we need to realise that 'the Law' is not something we have to try to abide by. From the very beginning of the birth of the church, there were recurring attempts to get believers back under 'the Law'. The religious spirit operating through the Judaizers in Jerusalem and within the early church tried to get them back under the Law of Moses. Paul took the Galatian church to task about this issue in no uncertain terms.

God never really wanted any of those sacrifices and offerings, as the prophets clearly realised:

"What are your multiplied sacrifices to Me?" says the Lord. "I have had enough of burnt offerings of rams and the fat of fed cattle; and I take no pleasure in the blood of bulls, lambs or goats" (Isaiah 1:11).

"For I did not speak to your fathers, or command them in the day that I brought them out of the land of Egypt, concerning burnt offerings and sacrifices." (Jeremiah 7:22).

Sacrifice and meal offering You have not desired;
My ears You have opened;
Burnt offering and sin offering You have not required.
Then I said, "Behold, I come;
In the scroll of the book it is written of me.
I delight to do Your will, O my God;
Your Law is within my heart."
(Psalm 40:6-8).

So if God never really wanted or asked for any of those sacrifices and offerings, we might wonder why He accepted them. The truth is, God accepts us. He meets us where we are and works with us in our brokenness. The law He writes on our hearts is not about restrictions, but about permission to live as sons of God and co-creators with Him.

One of the scribes came and heard them arguing, and recognizing that He had answered them well, asked Him, "What commandment is the foremost of all?" Jesus answered, "The foremost is, 'Hear, O Israel! The Lord our God is one Lord; and you shall love the Lord your God with all your heart, and with all your soul, and with all your mind, and with all your strength.' The second is this, 'You shall love your neighbor as yourself.' There is no other commandment greater than these."

Note that Jesus was specifically speaking to a member of the religious elite, a Jewish scribe, and specifically about commandments in the Old Covenant. He was not talking to us. If we try to love Him with all our heart, understanding and strength in our own power, we are guaranteed to fail. We love because He first loved us; and it is only when we experience that unconditional love that we are able fully to love others.

Every priest stands daily ministering and offering time after time the same sacrifices, which can never take away sins; but He, having offered one sacrifice for sins for all time, sat down at the right hand of God, waiting from that time onward until His enemies be made a footstool for His feet. For by one offering He has perfected for all time those who are sanctified. And the Holy Spirit also testifies to us; for after saying,

*"This is the covenant that I will make with them
After those days, says the Lord:
I will put My laws upon their heart,
And on their mind I will write them,"*

He then says,

*"And their sins and their lawless deeds
I will remember no more."*

Now where there is forgiveness of these things, there is no longer any offering for sin (Hebrews 10:11-18).

He has perfected and sanctified every single one of us and only wants us to come into the realisation of that astounding truth. The laws He writes on our hearts and minds are again not prohibitions on doing this or that. He has not written that sin consciousness on our heart, but love; and He wants us to fully embrace the reality of that love, the freedom and the joy of that love.

All is already forgiven and no sin-offerings are necessary. We do not have to try to make amends for the things we have done towards God. Of course we can make amends to each other, and be genuinely sorry if we have hurt or damaged anyone. But towards God, it is already forgiven; and if we become aware and conscious of the reality that we are already forgiven, we will not live in sin consciousness. Forgiveness is as unconditional as love.

Look at the previous few verses, this time in the Mirror Bible:

So when Jesus, the Messiah, arrives as the fulfillment of all the types and shadows, he quotes Psalm 40:6-8, and says, "In sacrifices and offerings God takes no pleasure; but you have ordained my incarnation. None of the prescribed offerings and sacrifices, including burnt offerings and sin offerings, were your request. Then I said, I read in your book what you wrote about me; so here I am, I have come to fulfill my destiny."

Having said what he did in the above quote, that the prescribed offerings and sacrifices were neither his desire nor delight, he condemned the entire sacrificial system upheld by the law. (These only served to sustain a sin-consciousness and were of no redemptive benefit to anyone.) *Also by saying, "I am commissioned to fulfil your will," he announces the final closure of the first in order to introduce the second.* (Grace replaces the law; innocence supersedes sin-consciousness.) *So, by this fulfilled will, in the mind of God and by his resolution he declares mankind immediately sanctified through one sacrifice; the presentation of the body of Jesus Christ* (Hebrews 10:5-10 Mirror, with translator's notes).

Mankind is declared innocent. You are innocent. Let that sink in. The verdict of the judge, in the light of the victory of Jesus through the cross, is that all mankind is innocent, 'not guilty', justified and righteous. That is unconditional love in action. That is God in action. The cross was an amazing love transaction that dealt with the legal consequences of man's lost identity. Jesus conquered sin and death with love; and love releases full and total unconditional forgiveness.

All that I have experienced and discovered about the unconditional nature of God's love has systematically deconstructed my mind, my thinking, my beliefs and my life. This profound transformation of my worldview unlocked my identity as a son, revealing my inherent creative sonship abilities. It unveiled the reality that I am seated in heavenly places, with access to the very face-to-face light of God's presence. I can dwell in the realm of perfection within the realm of light, functioning not only as a son but as a co-heir and co-creator, with unrestricted access to all the realms of heaven, to every dimension and aspect of my destiny.

All this is true for you too. All these privileges become readily available to us when we grasp the knowledge of who we are – when we live in the reality that we are wholly loved, accepted, approved of and affirmed. And He has done it all without us having to do anything. It is wonderful to come to that realisation and enter into the fullness of it.

We are all on this collective journey of discovery which will draw us beyond every barrier, restriction and limitation, into limitlessness. Then we can fully and actively participate in our sonship and in the restoration of all things. God is inviting us on a wild joyride, going further and deeper. No doubt it will challenge our belief systems, especially if we are still holding onto any Old Covenant mindsets or beliefs. However, the potential for transformation and the richness of the experience make it a journey worth embarking upon.

Activation #2
Experiencing Unconditional Love

To stream the audio, scan the QR code or visit freedomarc.org/UCL-resources.

I encourage you to close your eyes
and come to a place of rest.
In that place of rest,
begin to fix your eyes on the Father,
on His love,
on the light of His presence.

    Begin to breathe slowly.
    Just begin to fill your mind
    and think about God
    as unconditional love.

    Breathe in slowly
    breathe in unconditional love.
    Breathe in.
    Let it flow into you
    fill your mind
    fill your heart
    fill your emotions
    fill every fibre of your being
    every particle and every cell.

    Be saturated with unconditional love.
    Let the frequency and the energy
    and the living strength of unconditional love
    fill you.

    And if you struggle with acceptance
    if you struggle with rejection
    if you struggle with your identity
    if you struggle with Old Covenant mindsets
    of trying to appease an angry God
    hand all of that baggage over to Him.
    Hand it all over.
    Hand it over and be still.

Be weightless
float in an atmosphere
of complete, unconditional love and acceptance.
Be filled with love and joy and peace.

Just rest
so that you can truly know
the reality of who God is.

Be still and know unconditional love.

Let the frequency of love go around you.
Rest in limitless grace
triumphant mercy
and unconditional love.

In that safe place, open up your heart.
Open up every area of your life
that unconditional love would touch you
would heal you
would restore you
would make you whole
spirit, soul, body, completely whole –
one, in union, in love.

Engage in the realm of light.
Let the Father take you into that realm
face to face in that place of perfection
where everything is as it was always intended to be
where you can rest.

Where you can live loved
free from guilt, shame and condemnation;
where you can be filled with joy
the joy of life
and love living.

Where you can live loving and be merciful
choosing to forgive and release
and live in that place of peace
resting in love and joy and peace.

Stay in that place.
Let the Father open up your heart
maybe whisper into your heart
truth and life
the light of love and truth.

Look deeply into the Father's face
look deeply into His eyes
and let Him take you
deeper and deeper and deeper into His heart.

Feel free to stay in that place as long as you want
and just allow Him to take you
and go deeper and deeper and deeper
into that place of intimacy and love.

3. No Record of Wrongs

Everything was created by Jesus, for Him, through Him, and for the purpose of relationship. God's overarching desire is to restore everything back to that relational position; not only all people, but the whole of creation.

God's love is unconditional and for everyone. There really are no conditions. Unconditional love knows no boundaries or limitations: it expresses itself through limitless grace and triumphant mercy. These are not just facets of God; they embody His very essence, and His mercy triumphs over every barrier hindering our relationship with Him.

I have believed in God for the majority of my life. Yet it was only when I encountered God face-to-face as Father that I realised the extent of the deception caused by religious programming. The God I thought I knew did not really exist: I am an atheist to that version of God. What I once believed to be true about Him was a distortion, and in some cases an outright lie.

The good news is that the true God, the Father, Son and Spirit that I encountered, surpassed my wildest expectations in terms of goodness, kindness, love, tolerance, patience, grace and mercy. My experiences and encounters with God's love have systematically deconstructed the deeply ingrained belief systems in my mind. Numerous assumptions I never questioned were profoundly challenged during such encounters with the Father.

Nine pillars

On one occasion, we strolled through a dimly lit space, and He directed me to look up. Above, there was a network-like construction framed by nine pillars. He revealed that we were walking within my mind, and that these were the pillars which upheld and sustained my beliefs. Six were religious, ingrained from my extensive engagement with Christianity, and three were cultural pillars supporting my worldview.

Honestly, when the Father unveiled what these pillars represented, I had to look up some of them. These pillars that sustained my belief systems had been imprinted during my upbringing in a predominantly Christian background. They had been absorbed subconsciously; some I had rarely (if ever) even contemplated, whilst others I held firmly by conviction. Your pillars might differ from mine, but their subconscious nature renders them mostly invisible to our conscious minds. Unbeknown to us, they frame our beliefs, and the Father was revealing that if I were to discern the truth, these pillars needed addressing in my mind.

Ezekiel mentions nine fire stones, initially meant to reflect the knowledge, wisdom or understanding from Lucifer as the light bearer in the Father's garden. These stones were intended to facilitate mankind's ascent to maturity. However, Lucifer, after receiving this revelation, chose not to share it, turning these stones into counterfeits that framed our distorted minds. The nine pillars that arose from this perversion were deeply rooted in my consciousness.

Each pillar acted as a support for a veil of lies, filtering God's light and distorting His image within me. These veils controlled how my mind interpreted incoming data, leading inescapably to wrong conclusions. Confirmation bias further complicated matters, because existing beliefs influence how we perceive things. Even when we examine it closely, there is a tendency to interpret information in a way that aligns with our pre-existing beliefs.

These pillars represented mindsets mostly originating from beliefs imparted by others. Some were shaped by religious thinking, drawn from outdated Old Covenant theological ideas. They seemed to form a consistent system, providing a logical framework, yet the Father's revelations challenged their truth and accuracy. We are now in a new era of truth revelation, a time to uncover the reality of God and our role in creation.

My six religious pillars were:

- Evangelicalism, a strong influence from my various church settings.
- *Sola scriptura*, Bible alone, the doctrine that everything has to be in the Bible, which is to be taken literally.
- Protestantism, as much a construct as Catholicism might be for others.
- Augustinianism, a term I had to look up, encompasses such doctrines as human depravity and God's sovereign role in salvation, commonly linked with Calvinism.
- A Hebrew mindset.
- A Greek mindset. Despite not having learned Hebrew or Greek, these mindsets existed within the religious and cultural systems that shaped my upbringing.

The cultural pillars were:

- Cultural relativism, another concept I had to look up for clarification. Our upbringing immerses us in a specific cultural context, causing us to perceive truth in relation to that culture. Therefore, different cultures might hold conflicting beliefs about identical subjects.
- Scientific rationalism, influenced by my training and 18 years working in biochemistry.
- Humanism, following the path of the Tree of Knowledge.

At times inevitably these clashed, with religious programming usually prevailing over cultural influences due to the strength of my beliefs.

The Father revealed these pillars, exposing how my mind was veiled from the light of truth, living in the deception of darkness but thinking it was light. In His kindness He allowed me the choice to cooperate, and He asked if I wanted Him to remove those pillars and deconstruct my beliefs. I hesitated, fearing the loss of my reasoning and my ability to 'know', but on condition that He would remove them one at a time, I ultimately agreed.

So the first area of deconstruction was evangelicalism, particularly my understanding of the nature of God, the cross, and the atonement. The doctrine of penal substitutionary atonement (PSA) was ingrained in me, asserting that God punished or killed Jesus in place of punishing us for our sins. I knew of no other atonement theory (and many still mistake it for the Gospel). Encountering God's unconditional love revealed the flaws in this theology: love, by its very nature, does not kill or punish; and God never required sacrifice in the first place. This realisation led to the collapse of many interconnected misguided beliefs. I began to question everything I believed, discovering that God did not punish Jesus, and that the crucifixion was orchestrated not by God but by an unlikely alliance of warring religious and political leaders who perceived Him as a threat.

Jesus clearly told his disciples who would kill Him, and it was not His Father:

"Behold, we are going up to Jerusalem; and the Son of Man will be delivered to the chief priests and scribes, and they will condemn Him to death, and will hand Him over to the Gentiles to mock and scourge and crucify Him, and on the third day He will be raised up." (Matthew 20:18-19).

It was the result of human choices manipulated by the religious and political spirit. His judicial murder was a tragedy, yet became an avenue for God to bring all mankind into union, a state of oneness with Father, Son and Spirit.

Why have You forsaken Me?

I also came to reject the idea that the Father was separated from Jesus on the cross, as I was brought up to believe. It was based on the idea that God could not look at sin, so when Jesus took on our sin, the Father supposedly had to turn away. In reality, Jesus took our lost identity and fully identified with us to overcome obstacles to our reconciliation with the Father. The Father never turned away from Jesus; that was a teaching that derived from penal substitution theory and a false doctrinal system.

Now all these things are from God, who reconciled us to Himself through Christ and gave us the ministry of reconciliation, namely, that God was in Christ reconciling the world to Himself, not counting their trespasses against them, and He has committed to us the word of reconciliation (2 Corinthians 5:18-19).

Most of my life, what I had was the word of separation, not reconciliation! Yet we have all been reconciled to God. True, many people live in the alienation of their own mindsets, not realising this truth. They believe they are separated from God, which diminishes the scale of what Jesus accomplished. When I engaged with Jesus on the cross, I saw Him with eyes filled with the deepest love. This experience challenged my understanding and began my journey of realising the truth.

About the ninth hour Jesus cried out with a loud voice, saying, "Eli, Eli, lama sabachthani?" that is, "My God, My God, why have You forsaken Me?" (Matthew 27:46).

Does that verse not destroy my argument? No. On the cross, Jesus identified with our lostness and cried our cry of lost identity. And when Jesus quoted the beginning of Psalm 22, His hearers would have known the whole psalm. Later, in verse 24, it affirms that God never despised the afflicted, nor did He hide His face from him. God never did forsake mankind; it was humanity who turned away.

Atonement theories

There are seven major theories of atonement:

- Moral Influence Theory:
  - Jesus' death brings positive change to humanity.
  - The early church strongly held this view, which emphasises transformation into our true identity.
- Ransom Theory:
  - Adam and Eve sold humanity to the devil at the fall.
  - Justice required God to pay the devil a ransom, and Christ's death was accepted.

- Christus Victor:
    - Jesus died to defeat powers of evil such as sin, death and the devil, freeing mankind from their grip.

The early church held a mixture of the above views. But in more modern times, other ideas began to take over.

- Satisfaction Theory:
    - Postulated by Anselm of Kent in the 11th century.
    - Jesus' death satisfies the justice of God, meaning restitution and debt payment.
    - Based on Augustinian forgiveness concepts.
- Penal Substitution:
    - The reformers introduced this theory.
    - Jesus died to satisfy God's wrath against human sin.
    - Jesus was punished in place of sinners to fulfil the justice and legal demands of God.
- Governmental Theory:
    - Jesus' suffering and death served as a substitute for the punishment of sinners, allowing God to forgive humans whilst still maintaining divine justice.
    - This theory suggests Jesus died for the church, limiting salvation to the faithful.
    - Associated with Methodism.
- Scapegoat Theory:
    - Jesus dies as the scapegoat of humanity.
    - Killed by a violent crowd who deems Him guilty.
    - Jesus, as the true Son of God, is proven innocent, implicating the crowd in guilt.
    - Rooted in an understanding of scapegoats in the law and sacrificial practices.

These theories offer diverse perspectives on the meaning and purpose of Jesus' death, and reflect the complexity (some might say futility) of theological argument throughout history.

My encounters and conversations with the Father have led me to see the cross as an expression of God's unconditional love. It signifies victory over death and redemption from lost identity. Jesus, in identifying with us, experienced death, crucifixion and resurrection. The cross represents Jesus' triumph over our enemies: sin, lost identity, and death (which is the 'wages of sin', that is, the consequence of turning away from our true identity and from its source).

Choosing independence, humanity walked away from eternal life, seeking to derive life from themselves. The Father has always considered all mankind as His children. Throughout history, He consistently reached out to humanity, but each time, humans turned down the offer out of self-induced guilt and condemnation, transforming His desire for relationship into a religious duty.

Driven by lost identity, humanity created a 'God' in their own image out of guilt and shame, who required appeasement through religious sacrificial systems. I once lived under the burden of continually trying to please God, which led to a perpetual sense of failure, since the religious system always sets unattainable standards. I never matched up to the standard I had set myself, a standard which God did not apply.

God did not sacrifice His Son. Jesus willingly identified with humanity in order to restore all that was lost, a plan established from the beginning by love. Jesus overcame sin, our lost identity, by restoring relationship with the Father. He overcame death by conquering it and defeating it in the grave through the power of resurrection life. As a result, we can now walk in the newness of that same resurrection life and its transforming power. Therefore death does not mark the end of the opportunity to accept Jesus, contrary to what I have been told repeatedly (and insistently) by online critics.

My continuing journey of deconstruction revised my perspectives on death, hell, judgment, resurrection, salvation, being born again, faith, the role of the Bible, and more. As I delved deeper into my relationship with God, gazing into the

Father's eyes and experiencing His love, I began to question how the beliefs I held matched up to the Father I was getting to know.

Jesus is the living Word of God, not the Bible, which is a compilation of writings by various authors and only called the 'Canon of Scripture' by men. The Bible itself reveals Jesus as the living Word, as the Way, the Truth and the Life; the Resurrection, and the Door to our relationship with the Father. He is the only way to the Father: Jesus opens that door for people to access – but not necessarily only in the way I had been told. Jesus is always looking to awaken people to the truth that He is operating within them to reveal Himself to them.

In all I write, I aim to dispel religious myths that held me captive and to share the liberating truth of unconditional love. Future chapters will encompass such topics as forgiveness, repentance, confession, faith, being born again, salvation, mixing covenants, the growing trend towards deconstruction, and the truth about immortality; but in the remainder of this chapter I will focus on how God views sin.

God cannot look upon sin

One of the most prevalent clichés you will hear is that "God cannot look upon sin." This is a falsehood that generates guilt and condemnation, causing individuals to feel shameful and unworthy so that, rather than approaching God, they run away from Him. I distinctly recall feeling that way. Particularly during my teenage years, I repeatedly messed up, made decisions, did things and said things that I knew were not what God wanted from me or for me. I was constantly burdened by guilt, thinking it was a normal state, until I came across a book entitled *The Normal Christian Life*. In it, Watchman Nee described a normal Christian life that entailed freedom rather than guilt and condemnation. That was the beginning of my journey: instead of turning away, I wanted to turn towards God.

This idea that He cannot look at sin or sinners was programmed into my thinking. For years, I never questioned it, but it makes no sense. God is omnipresent and omniscient, so He knows and sees everything and is present everywhere. He sees all sin (all lost identity) and any actions that result from it. If we behave in a way that contradicts our identity, He notices it. He does not ignore it or turn a blind eye to it; He sees it all. His response is what matters. God sees our sin, our lost identity, and does not turn away in disgust, but uses it as an opportunity to demonstrate His loving nature to us.

His loving kindness to us is all contained in His unconditional love, His limitless grace, and His triumphant mercy. Whatever we do, His grace is sufficient to overcome and His mercy is triumphant, victorious; so nothing can ever separate us from His love. Except, perhaps, in our own thinking, which will not be that way forever because our minds are being renewed to the Father's love, His grace, and His mercy. God is at work, overcoming all the obstacles and barriers to our restoration. He is not passive and He does not turn away. He seeks to bring good out of everything we do, even the most ridiculously stupid things and the most heinous misdeeds: He still loves us enough to be at work to bring good out of them.

If God could not see man's lost state, how could He save us from it? The authors of the Old Testament scriptures describe God from the perspective of their own lost identity and tradition. That is why there was such an uproar when Jesus came as the express image of God to fully display who God was and challenge how people thought about Him. "If you have seen me, you have seen the Father. I and the Father are one." Of course He was called a heretic and they wanted to stone Him to death on the spot, but instead plotted how to kill Him in a way that would be most advantageous for them. That did not deter Jesus from coming and it did not deter the Father from sending Him because love was His only motive. So what evidence is there that God seeks us out in our lostness rather than turning away from us? Jesus is the proof. Jesus is the proof of unconditional love.

Perishing?

For God so loved the world, that He gave His only begotten Son, that whoever believes in Him shall not perish, but have eternal life (John 3:16).

That word 'perish': what picture does it bring to your mind? To me the picture it brought was of being consigned to the punishment of hell forever, because I 'knew' that was what it meant. I loved that verse and could quote it from memory, but although it was remarkable that God loved the world so much that He sent Jesus, it still said that if you do not believe, you will be going to hell forever.

It does not say that.

Bible translation is framed from pre-programmed theology and is not always faithful to the original meaning of the Greek or Hebrew. When you think about it that is no surprise. *Apollymi*, the word translated here as 'to perish,' is usually rendered as 'to be lost' elsewhere in scripture, which would totally change the meaning (or at least, it would if many Christians were not equally convinced that 'lost' also means 'condemned to hell forever'). A single misunderstood word can utterly compromise our impression of what God is about. To the religious, that verse says if you do not believe, you will be sent to hell. The real meaning is that if you are familiar with God's love as evidenced by Jesus, you will no longer live in a state of lost identity. Only those who remain unfamiliar with God's love as evidenced by Jesus will continue in their state of lost identity.

Even then, He will not leave them that way. I love John 3:16 in the Mirror Bible, which beautifully conveys the extent of God's love:

The entire cosmos is the object of God's affection, and he is not about to abandon his creation. The gift of his son is for humanity to realise their origin in him who mirrors their authentic birth, begotten not of flesh, but of the Father. In this persuasion, the life of the ages echoes within the individual and announces that the days of regret and sense of lostness are over (John 3:16 Mirror).

The parables of the lost (*apollymi*) sheep, lost (*apollymi*) coin, and lost (*apollymi*) son in Luke 15 convey a powerful message – and all are eventually found safe and sound. You cannot be lost unless you belong in the first place. If some of God's children have lost sight of this truth, He seeks them out. As Jesus said:

"The Son of Man has come to seek and to save that which was lost (apollymi)" (Luke 19:10).

The audaciousness of His response reflects the magnitude of His desire for a restored relationship. The Good Shepherd leaves the many to search for the one that went astray, showing the depth of His love and commitment to bringing us back from our lost state.

The practical evidence of God's unwavering love, even in the face of sin, is evident in the story of Adam and Eve. Despite their act of independence, God did not turn away from, hide from or abandon them. He did not say "Tough luck!" and turn around to go back to heaven. He actively sought them out, asking "Where are you?" and found them hiding, without their glory covering. The Father did not view them as irredeemable sinners that He could not even look at anymore, but as His children who had temporarily forgotten their true identity. He still wanted to have a relationship with them and He offered them a path to follow through the fire to the Tree of Life. But they chose the path of independence and of self.

Contrary to a common religious myth, God did not kill an animal to provide new clothes. They lost their covering of glorious identity, so the Father clothed them in skin to physically preserve them; saving them so that they could live, not die. In the same way, God does not see mankind as sinners, but as His children who need to rediscover their true selves. Rather than inducing guilt or fear, the true gospel is about helping people remember who they are and realise that God loves them and is already reconciled with them.

Jesus identified with humanity from before the foundation of the world in order to reveal and restore our identity as sons of God. God's love was unconditional throughout, and Jesus came not to change God's mind about us but to change our mind about God. God's love has never changed. Jesus exemplifies that love; all we have to do is let Him love us, and that will inspire us, motivate us and empower us to love others in the same way.

From God's perspective, mankind was always righteous, but following Adam led to a lost identity, self-condemnation and alienation in our own minds. Mankind, made in God's image, created a god in its own image. With its misguided attempts at humanistic solutions (through religions or non-religious systems), lost humanity imagines itself incapable of facing God because of shame. In that sense, it is humans who cannot look on God, not the other way round.

Seeking relationship

Throughout history, the Father, in His boundless love, sought out humanity. His unwavering desire was to restore relationship; every time it was He who initiated the first step and made the initial move towards individuals like Adam and Eve, Noah, Abraham, Moses, Joshua, David, and the prophets. In each of these encounters, God was seeking relationship; but often, people constructed their own systems – typically religious or works-based systems – around their meeting with Him. They opted for religious mediation through a specialised priesthood, and various sacrificial systems, not feeling worthy to directly engage with a God they falsely perceived as intimidating.

Then came Jesus, fully revealing the Father, in His image. The Father in Jesus forgave us unconditionally, reconciled us, justified us, and wiped out any record of perceived wrongs. The work on the cross was complete, and accomplished everything necessary for a restored relationship with God. All that remains is for us to grasp the reality of this truth. As Paul wrote:

Blessed be the God and Father of our Lord Jesus Christ, who has blessed us with every spiritual blessing in the heavenly places in Christ, just as He chose us in Him before the foundation of the world, that we would be holy and blameless before Him. In love He predestined us to adoption as sons through Jesus Christ to Himself, according to the kind intention of His will, to the praise of the glory of His grace, which He freely bestowed on us in the Beloved (Ephesians 1:3-6).

It is even more striking in the Mirror Bible:

Let's celebrate God! He lavished every blessing heaven has upon us in Christ. He associated us in Christ before the fall of the world. Jesus is God's mind made-up about us. He always knew in his love that he would present us again face to face before him in blameless innocence (Ephesians 1:3-4 Mirror).

The power of these words only truly comes alive through experience. When we reach that place of being face-to-face with Him in blameless innocence, the reality of what He has done becomes tangible. Transformational encounters begin to change and renew our minds and unveil our sonship. I have learned to dwell continually in this place, enabling me to live in unconditional love: simply being, and letting Him love me.

I do not need to do anything to earn His love. Whilst I have learned to love Him back and trust in His good intentions, the real power lies in His faithfulness. When I look into His eyes, feel His heartbeat, and grasp the ongoing revelation of His heart, it takes me ever deeper into the experience of unconditional love. 5 or 6 years ago now, I wrote about my experiences of encountering God in love that I never imagined could be surpassed. And yet, time after time after time, He takes me deeper and deeper and deeper into that experience of unconditional love, deeper into revelation of Himself.

He is the architect of our design, his heart dream realised our coming of age in Christ. His grace plan is to be celebrated: he greatly endeared us and highly favored us in Christ. His love for his son is his love for us. [The Gospel is not about telling people how lost they are but reminding them of how loved they are.] (Ephesians 1:5-6 Mirror, with author's note).

And hope does not disappoint; because the love of God has been poured out within our hearts through the Holy Spirit, who was given to us. For while we were still helpless, at the right time Christ died for the ungodly... But God demonstrates His own love toward us, in that while we were yet sinners, Christ died for us (Romans 5:5-6, 8).

God desires that we grasp the reality of His love and immerse ourselves in the experience. He did not wait for us to be good enough: He came when we were completely lost. Even when we were alienated from Him in our own minds, God loved us. While all mankind was still in bondage to lost identity, He demonstrated His love to free us and restore the relationship. That is unconditional love.

God has no personal enemies; His unconditional love extends to all He has made. Jesus' death addressed mankind's enemies – sin (lost identity), and its consequence, death – overcoming and defeating them. He triumphed over death, conquered the grave, and rose again, bringing new life and restoration to all of mankind.

Love-consciousness

*Put me like a seal over your heart,
Like a seal on your arm.
For love is as strong as death,
Jealousy is as severe as Sheol;
Its flashes are flashes of fire,
The very flame of the Lord.*
(Song of Songs 8:6).

I resonate with the love message of the Song of Songs, and particularly with that verse. It vividly encapsulates what I have experienced – the intensity of His passion for us.

Who will separate us from the love of Christ? Will tribulation, or distress, or persecution, or famine, or nakedness, or peril, or sword...? For I am convinced that neither death, nor life, nor angels, nor principalities, nor things present, nor things to come, nor powers, nor height, nor depth, nor any other created thing, will be able to separate us from the love of God, which is in Christ Jesus our Lord (Romans 8:35, 38-39).

Nothing – not even we ourselves – can sever us from the love of God.

Jesus holds the ultimate authority in our lives, guiding us to live in a consciousness of love, not in the consciousness of sin or lost identity. He reminds us to live loved, love living and live loving. Embracing awareness of His unconditional love transforms our perspective on life. Set free from the burden of trying to adhere to the Law or earn God's favour through duty, a life of love brings joyful expectation, turning each day into an opportunity to freely give the love we have received.

Religion tends to impose conditions on love and acceptance, but God's love is entirely unconditional. It is essential for us to break free from these religious mindsets and obligations. As Paul tells us, love does not keep score of the sins of others; it keeps no record of wrongs. God does not keep a record of our wrongs or score our actions out of 10. Jesus came to take away the sins of the world, not to punish us for them. Love forgives unconditionally, based on what Jesus accomplished in eternity and on the cross.

Since God is love then the words 'love' and 'God' can be used interchangeably. Any discrepancy between them raises questions about the validity of the source, whether the Bible or any other. If the concept presented does not align with God as pure love, let us beware. God is unequivocally love, and any teaching that suggests otherwise is at best either a misunderstanding or a misinterpretation.

Love is patient, love is kind. It does not envy, it does not boast, it is not proud. It does not dishonour others, it is not self-

seeking, it is not easily angered, it keeps no record of wrongs. Love does not delight in evil but rejoices with the truth. It always protects, always trusts, always hopes, always perseveres. Love never fails... (1 Corinthians 13, 4-8a NIV).

So if God as love keeps no record of wrongs, why is religion so sin-focused? Every church that I was brought up in was always focused on sin and behaviour, and you had to maintain a certain standard to be acceptable. If people keep focusing on sin and misbehaviour, it only serves to reaffirm their lost identity. It keeps people who see themselves as sinners coming back for more religious help to make them feel better. That never works – in fact they probably feel worse, because religion is an addiction: you always need more.

When you were dead in your transgressions and the uncircumcision of your flesh, He made you alive together with Him, having forgiven us all our transgressions, having canceled out the certificate of debt consisting of decrees against us, which was hostile to us; and He has taken it out of the way, having nailed it to the cross (1 Corinthians 2:13).

That is a powerful statement. We can now be love-conscious, not sin-conscious, because all sin is already dealt with, already forgiven. His forgiveness is as unconditional as His love. That is not a licence to go about doing terrible things to people: that would be contrary to love. Love wants the best for others; it never desires harm to anyone. Having received love, we can love in the same way we are loved. If we perceive the love we receive as conditional, then what we demonstrate to others will be conditional: so it is that forgiveness becomes conditional for most people, based on the other person apologising (or 'repenting'). We have been unconditionally forgiven; every debt has been cancelled, and God holds nothing against us.

Our religious upbringing may focus us continually on feelings of guilt and shame, but God's focus is always on reconciliation and restoration of relationship. Sin and lost identity are placed as far as the east is from the west; they are completely removed by God. He wants us to know the reality of that forgiveness. God has forgiven unconditionally because God is love, and love is unconditional. As always, love wins.

When we know we are loved and forgiven unconditionally, we can be free from all religious manipulation, guilt, shame, and condemnation. We can also be free from religious slavery to obedience, duty and obligation, which many religions impose to keep people aligned with their rules.

We can be free. As sons of God, we are not slaves, servants or stewards. We are co-heirs and co-creators, seated in places of honour in the heavenly realms and included in the decision-making of heaven. This is when we mature and come into the realisation of who we are and what we are called to do.

No end to love

The Father said, "Son, my overwhelming love will conquer all things; it will not fail and will never give up. My overwhelming love is stronger than death, more jealous than the grave. Nothing can quench its fierce passion and burning desire for restored relationship, face to face innocence. My love for each of my children cannot fail; it can never stop, any more than I can cease to be I AM. Love is the atmosphere of glory, the frequency of heaven, the timeless now within the circle of the dance. There can be no end to love; it is eternal and infinite, expanding throughout creation with my Kingdom government and peace. My love has no beginning, no end; it is the Alpha, Omega, the Aleph and the Tav, the living word and truth. Love is the fullest expression and intrinsic essence of I AM that I AM. So learn to just be loved, living in the rest of love, joy and peace."

Love is who you are. You are not defined by your gifts or deeds. (Love gives context to faith. Moving mountains is not the point; love is). *Love is not about defending a point of view... love does not have to prove itself through acts of supreme devotion or self-sacrifice. Love is large in being passionate about life and relentlessly patient in bearing the offenses and injuries of others with kindness. Love is completely content and strives for nothing. Love has no desire to make others feel inferior and has no need to sing its own praises. Love is predictable, and does not behave out of character. Love is not ambitious. Love is not spiteful, and gets no mileage out of another's mistakes; it bears no record of wrongs. Love sees no joy in injustice. Love's delight is in everything that truth celebrates. Love is a fortress where everyone feels protected rather than exposed. Love's persuasion is persistent. Love believes. Love never loses hope, and always remains constant in contradiction.* (1 Corinthians 13:2-7 Mirror, with translator's note).

The Greek word for love in this passage, *agape*, stems from *agoo* meaning to lead like a shepherd guides his sheep and *pao* meaning to rest. This calls to mind Psalm 23, the Shepherd leading us to rest beside still waters, where our souls remember our true identity. We can cease striving and working to earn His love, and rest in the assurance of who we are as His children.

He wants us to intimately experience this unconditional *agape* love in every moment, transcending time and space. It is not theoretical or an intellectual idea: experiencing this unconditional love will transform us, freeing us from the religious version of the angry God – if we will just allow God to love us. It sounds so simple, yet it is a long journey from all the false religious constructs and wrong understandings about God to the truth of our face-to-face innocence. In that place, the motives of God's heart motivate me; His passion causes me to be passionate; and His burning desire creates in me a burning desire to only do what I see Him doing. That too, unconditional love can do for all of us, but only if we truly experience it.

Activation #3
Washed in Unconditional Love

I encourage you to close your eyes
and begin to rest.

> Fix your eyes,
> your thinking, your desire,
> on engaging face to face,
> heart to heart,
> with unconditional love.
> Rest.
> Be still.

> As the unconditional love of God surrounds you
> Where love is poured out, lavished upon you
> Where every bit of guilt, shame or condemnation
> that you have felt
> that people have made you feel
> that religion has made you feel
> that right now,
> the unconditional love of God
> as it's flowing all over you, around you, and in you
> just washes you –
> washes you clean
> so that you see yourself the way that the Father sees you.
> Forgiven.
> Reconciled.
> Justified.
> Innocent, not guilty.
> Pure and holy.
> Just let the truth come...

> As the Father begins to speak words into your heart,
> words of love
> words of affirmation
> words of approval,
> He is affirming you as His child.
> He is approving of you as His child.
> He wants you to feel completely, unconditionally loved.

Let that love wash over you, flow through you:
rivers of living water, rivers of love,
unconditional love,
flowing through your spirit, soul and body.
You are cocooned in unconditional love,
soaking in unconditional love.

You are forgiven for everything from your past.
Completely innocent.
Every stain completely removed.
Every black spot in your DNA restored and made whole
in unconditional love.

Let the frequency of love be all around you right now.
Let the sound of love penetrate.

You are in a completely safe place, cocooned in love.
Just be open to whatever the Father wants to show you,
whatever the Father wants to say to you
wherever the Father wants to take you.

As you are resting in that safe place,
open up your heart, open up your mind,
open up your whole consciousness.
And just experience the light of His presence,
the light of love and truth
as you rest in that place of love.

4. Repentance, Confession and Forgiveness

God is awakening people around the world to the reality of His unconditional love.

One such example is that of Riaan Swiegelaar, the co-founder and leader of the South African Satanic Church. During an interview on the CapeTalk radio station, Riaan expressed his disbelief in Jesus Christ. After the interview, an employee at the radio station approached him and hugged him in a way that he had never experienced before. This simple act of love stayed with him, and he later discovered that the lady who had hugged him was a Christian. Not long after, during a satanic ritual, he challenged Jesus: "If you are Jesus, you need to prove it." Jesus flooded him with love and energy, which he recognised immediately as what he had experienced in the woman's embrace. He resigned from his role in the satanic church and posted several videos on YouTube testifying to the transformational power of this love.

When discussing this with a friend in South Africa, he told me that the typical response from South African evangelicals to this story was, "He did not say he was sorry and repent, so it cannot be real." It is sad that people cannot rejoice when someone meets God because they think there are conditions to be met first. Why would someone just experiencing unconditional love for the first time want to even think about their past and what they have been forgiven from? They are looking forward, rejoicing in the amazing love they have begun to experience.

This is what the Father said to my good friend, Lindy Strong: "I offer you my unconditional love. All I ask is for your heart, not for my sake but yours. When you give me your heart, My unconditional love has a place to land; and yes, only then can you begin to fully trust me and walk in the fullness of what I have for you." God simply seeks our hearts; He is not interested in our attempts at obedience or to prove or earn anything, as we will never be good enough in our own strength. All He desires is for us to come to Him, and He is willing to go to any lengths to encounter and engage us, showing us what unconditional love truly means.

Again, a video circulated on the internet featuring Creflo Dollar, a well-known preacher of the prosperity gospel, renouncing tithing and emphasising that we are under grace, not under law. His subsequent teachings on intimacy with God reflect a shift in his message, as he delves deeper into the concept of unconditional love.

Encountering unconditional love has challenged my own previously unquestioned beliefs. Doctrines concerning sin, forgiveness, repentance and confession have often hindered people from experiencing unconditional love, as they focus on works rather than God's unconditional love and acceptance. Understanding this truth does not require us to do anything; it simply invites us to experience it fully. This is the foundation. Until we experience God's unconditional love, we will never truly know ourselves nor effectively engage with creation as sons of God. When we grasp our identity rooted in unconditional love, creation will respond to us.

The evangelical perspective on salvation, which I was raised with, certainly included the concept of grace, yet also implied that it required works. Salvation necessitated believing in your heart and confessing with your mouth, and that troubled me. All the while I was deeply entrenched in this evangelical mindset, I struggled with uncertainty, constantly questioning whether my efforts were sufficient.

I now understand that belief is a result of experiencing God's love and grace; we do not have to believe before we can experience it. This is what shifts the focus from works to grace. Had I understood this earlier, my journey with God would have been revolutionised. These last fourteen years or so have brought me to a place I could not have even imagined, but I wonder how different my life would have been if I had grasped this truth twenty-five years ago.

I envy anyone who enters into a profound relationship with God immediately, like Riaan when freed from Satanism. It took me 25 years to feel confident conversing with God, and he experienced it on day one. If only everyone experienced such a relationship with God, free from religious falsehoods, without the need for deprogramming and renewal of the mind!

Forgiveness

It really is all about relationship. It is all about us experiencing who God is and Him revealing who we are in a pure relationship of love, without any of the religious trappings of having to fit in and be accepted. So we believe we are forgiven. We do not believe in order to be forgiven, because we already are forgiven; forgiveness is unconditional. God has reconciled the whole world to Himself through Jesus, not counting anything against anybody, so there is nothing more to forgive. He does not see us through anything we are doing; He sees us through the lens of who we are. We have been made the righteousness of God in Christ, so all the religious works we do produce no life. They are independent of God's grace, and it is only the grace of God that empowers us. Grace is the divine enabling power of God to live in a relationship with Him, not having to 'try' to be in a relationship with Him, which was what I did for so much of my early Christian life.

Did Jesus wait for those who were crucifying Him to be sorry or to confess their sin in order to forgive them? No, He had obviously forgiven them already and asked the Father audibly to forgive them because He was proactive, choosing to forgive without conditions. No one was sorry amongst those who crucified Jesus but He forgave them anyway. It is a misunderstanding of forgiveness to wait for the other person to say sorry before we forgive them. We forgive others because we have been forgiven: that is what real forgiveness is all about.

Jesus did a lot of teaching about forgiveness. Some was in the context of the Old Covenant, under which His hearers were living at that point. But some of it was pointing to what it would be like in the New Covenant. He taught about the importance of forgiving from the heart, not just saying words. It can be easy to say the words, "I forgive you," whilst in the heart, you really have not. And when you see or think of the person, you are still conscious of what they have done and therefore you may be angry, frustrated, bitter or resentful. That means you have not forgiven them. And there are consequences for not forgiving: not God punishing us, because He keeps no record of wrongs, but it still affects us.

At the end of Matthew 18 we find a parable about forgiveness in which Jesus describes how if you sow unforgiveness, you reap unforgiveness. Unforgiveness is toxic to the soul and the body, and it can be torture. Someone said it is like drinking poison and expecting someone else to die. Unforgiveness binds you to the memory of the event and to the perpetrator: you are not free because they are not free: you have not released them, and they still owe you. Some people even get sick and die from living in the toxicity of unforgiveness. So it is important that we do not just say the words because we think we ought to, but that we truly settle the accounts.

It is not about wanting to, or even thinking the person deserves anything: it is about understanding that we have been forgiven everything. You can reflect on your own life and recognise what you have been forgiven for, even the things that no one else knows about, so you can understand the power of that forgiveness within you. Forgiveness calculates the cost of the offense and acknowledges the debt owed. Then, it chooses to release the person from any future reckoning, letting them off completely scot-free. Our humanistic idea of justice cries out against this: it is not fair – they should not just get away with it! But that is exactly what has happened. God has not counted anything against us and has kept no record of our wrongs, so why would we then keep a record of someone else's wrongs? Jesus forgave every offense and empowers us to forgive as well.

Forgiveness is the ability to genuinely bless and want the best for the person who has committed an offence against you, even if they never say sorry. And that really is the acid test. Can you genuinely want the best for and truly bless the person who has never said sorry to you? If you cannot, I suggest you take that back to the Father and ask Him to help you; to show you how to make that choice.

Forgiveness is the heart and power of the good news, it is the gospel. God has forgiven everyone, and the power of that forgiveness can bring people into a relationship with God that they never imagined they could possibly have. When we know we are forgiven, we are empowered by grace to forgive. If we do not, we may feel disconnected from God's forgiveness, not because He has abandoned us, but because we are not operating in that forgiveness. This can lead to feelings of guilt, bitterness and resentment, robbing us of the joy of life.

When I first grasped the power of forgiveness, I realised that no one had ever taught me how to forgive. I had a long list of people I had not forgiven, even if they did not often surface in my conscious mind. It is vital that we rid our lives of this burden.

Repentance

There is a kind of mantra among evangelical Christians that you cannot be forgiven unless you repent. The true meaning of the Greek term *metanoia* gets lost in translation: it signifies a shift into alignment with God's thoughts, a transformative process of renewing the mind. 'Repentance' is a misleading translation, linking forgiveness with sorrow and penance, implying that we must prove our remorse through repeated actions to deserve forgiveness. This has even led to extreme practices such as self-flagellation in an attempt to demonstrate sorrow.

The Hebrew equivalent, *teshuva*, literally means to return to one's true self, to destroy the self-made construct and return home to the original intention God had for us. It is about shedding the false identities we have constructed and returning to our true identity as children of God. The meaning, therefore, is not focused on negative behaviour but about aligning our minds with God's truth. Ultimately, both *metanoia* and *teshuva* lead us back to our true identity, which is only found in relationship with God the Father.

Forgiveness was freely given to all creation once and for all time, and there is no need for us to earn it through remedial actions or doing penance. Whilst it is natural to feel sorry for our actions and seek reconciliation, it is not that this sorrow earns forgiveness; rather, forgiveness changes our perspective and empowers us to live righteously.

This has completely and radically changed my life. It enables me to interact with people in a different way because I no longer hold grudges, and forgiveness has become a way of life for me. I make the choice to forgive immediately when I notice something wrong, regardless of what it is or whether it is even directed towards me. I have even found myself forgiving people for terrible acts I saw on the TV news, because I knew God had forgiven them. The same applies today with the current events in Ukraine and Gaza, and around the world. Despite the terrible things happening, I choose to forgive those who commit such acts; otherwise, I would only tie myself to bitterness, anger and resentment. It is challenging to forgive when harm is done to us; but even more so when done to others, especially to the most vulnerable. However, God has forgiven us, and embracing forgiveness is essential to demonstrate to the world that we operate differently.

Anything that requires penance or a change of behaviour to be accepted is a deception: it is based on works rather than grace. We need to return to the simplicity of grace, where the realisation of God's unconditional love motivates our transformation. We do not need to change our behaviour to be accepted or acceptable; rather, agreeing with God's mind releases the power for transformation and the renewal of our minds, which is incredibly powerful. All we need to do is walk in relationship with the Father and surrender to His guidance: He will transform us and align our thinking with His. It is not about us trying to fix ourselves or prove our worthiness; it is about surrendering daily and allowing God to work in us.

Confession

Confession is another area ripe for misunderstanding. The concept of confession in the Catholic religion, with the confessional and the priest absolving sins, focuses solely on behaviour, makes people sin-conscious and entraps them in religious duty and obligation. Instead, confession should align with what God says about us.

If we confess our sins, He is faithful and righteous to forgive us our sins and to cleanse us from all unrighteousness (1 John 1:9).

That appears to say we have to 'confess our sins' before God can forgive us. But read the same verse in the Mirror Bible:

Our conversation takes on a brand new dynamic when we take sides with what God believes about us. So, instead of telling God about the details of your sin, you remind yourself about the details of your redemption. God does not need the information, you do. God's faithfulness and righteousness is the basis of our forgiveness and cleansing from every distortion. Jesus removed every bit of condemning evidence against us. (The word traditionally translated "confession" is the word *homologeo* from *homos*, the same, and *logos* the Word. The context of verse 7 suggests that we say what God says about us...) (1 John 1:9, Mirror; with translator's note).

In this sense, confession does not focus on listing our sins and feeling guilty. Instead, it is about going along with what God says about us, acknowledging our forgiven, redeemed and restored identity as sons and daughters of God. We confess God's truth about us, not our shortcomings. This perspective aligns with God's love and grace, rather than religious conditioning that focuses on sin and guilt. Confession is affirming our true identity in Christ and acknowledging all that God has already provided for us. We can declare that we are not guilty but innocent and justified. Confessing our righteousness and new identity as sons of God shapes our thinking and actions: as a man thinks in his heart, so is he.

Religion often argues that unlimited grace is a dangerous licence to sin: without the threat of punishment, people will continue in wrongdoing. Religion operates under the law, and does not want people to operate in grace, because then they will be free from the law – and from religion. Grace is not permission to live from our old identity but the power to live from our new identity as sons of God.

The Bible says that without the Law there would be no sin. So grace is totally anti-law: it is the absolute antithesis of the law. The mixture of law and grace is absolutely lethal, and it is this mixture of covenants that is present in so much of the religious teaching I hear. Being lukewarm is mixing hot and cold together: a lukewarm cup of water is not very nice to drink. Let's not mix these things. Let's live in grace. Religion calls this kind of grace by derogatory terms like 'hyper grace' or 'greasy grace,' out of fear of not being able to control people. Grace is the divine enabling power. That is why I say that it is not only hyper, it is limitless: any limitation to grace would bring us back under the law.

And sin, from *hamartia* (*ha*, not having, and *miros*, image) is not just wrong actions but a state of lost identity which causes us to live in a manner contrary to God's intention for us. God desires us to live in our new identity in Christ as included and blessed sons of God.

Paul addresses the issue of grace as a licence to sin in his letter to the Romans:

It is not possible to interpret grace as a cheap excuse to continue in sin. It sounds to some like we are saying, "Let's carry on sinning so that grace may abound." How ridiculous is that. How can we be dead and alive to sin at the same time? What are we saying then in baptism, if we are not declaring that we understand our union with Christ in His death? (Romans 6:1-3, Mirror).

And of course, we have been raised from the dead.

Another religious meaning of sin is failing to reach a standard of behaviour. I remember people told me "The pass mark is 100%; so even if you get 99%, you failed." True, you are never going to be good enough in your own strength. But they then went on to say, "So you need to accept Jesus." And what do you do to accept Jesus? You need to repent. To be sorry. They wanted to take everyone through a whole list of things they have to do to attain a standard so they can be forgiven – when they are already forgiven. Religion has turned the noun 'sin' into a verb and linked it to bad behaviour, to make people fearful, feel guilty and condemned enough to repent and confess their sin so that they can then be forgiven, which is a total twisting of the truth. We already are forgiven. Religion will keep getting people to identify as sinners so that they continually feel guilty, keep struggling with behaviours and therefore keep coming back for more penance and more absolution.

When you identify with the truth that you have already been made righteous and are not a sinner, then you know you are not guilty. Instead of a sin-consciousness, you then have a forgiveness-consciousness, a grace-consciousness, a mercy-consciousness, and a love-consciousness. You do not think about sin at all, because you now know who you are in the context of His love. Now of course, wrong actions do carry consequences. But those consequences are not God's punishment. He desires us to always receive mercy, which can triumph over the consequences of what we do; and His grace is always sufficient for us if we turn to Him to receive it.

Or maybe someone told you that the Bible says that if you look into God's face, you will die? Well, the reality is that many biblical characters looked into God's face and did not die. It is more religious nonsense. We can have a face-to-face relationship with the Father through Jesus the Son. Therefore we can look into the wonderful eyes of God and know the deep pools of love and the amazing grace and mercy He has for us.

Guilt tends to make people hide away from God. Where were Adam and Eve, immediately after they chose to operate independently from God? Hiding away from Him. And what was God doing? Trying to find them, not hiding away from them. God never turned from them: they turned from Him. I recommend you search out an excellent YouTube video, *The Gospel in Chairs*, by Brad Jerzak[2]. He uses two chairs facing away from each other to represent what religion says about God and sin, and two chairs facing each other to represent what grace says.

Relationship will draw us back to God. When we come boldly to the throne of grace, we receive grace and mercy. Sin has a wage or a payback, but grace does not, and mercy triumphs over man's ideas of justice. There is no payback when you come to the throne of grace. When you try to please or appease God, when you try to earn your way back to God rather than just returning to Him, there will always be something you have to do, and there will always be consequences for failing to do it.

Jesus defeated death and its consequences. We are included in the New Covenant made by the Father with Jesus, and any works we try to do under the Old Covenant Law are dead, producing no life. Abundant life flows from the spirit within us, not from our own efforts. God's unconditional love ensures that we can never be separated from Him, and immortality (as we shall see) is a manifestation of this love.

Modern evangelical theology will tell you that you will only be forgiven if you fulfil certain conditions: repent, confess your sin, believe and be baptised; be born again; have faith in God; believe in your heart and confess with your mouth. All that makes forgiveness and salvation dependent on what you do and therefore how good your works are. That is why so

---

[2] Brad Jersak - The Gospel in Chairs - Session 1 (FGC 2016)
https://www.youtube.com/watch?v=N7FKhHScgUQ

many people are insecure about their salvation; thinking they can lose it, thinking that God will take it from them.

We do not need to allow confirmation-biased programming to condition our understanding. If we read 1 John 1:5-10 remembering that God is love, God is light and Jesus is the truth, I believe we will come to a completely different conclusion and become free from religious bondage. Let us take it verse by verse:

This is the message we have heard from Him and announce to you, that God is Light, and in Him there is no darkness at all (1 John 1:5).

We are in Him, illuminated and enlightened to know our true identity as sons of light. Darkness in context is therefore our lost identity, not knowing unconditional love (by experience).

If we say that we have fellowship with Him and yet walk in the darkness, we lie and do not practice the truth (1 John 1:6).

Our lost identity is a lie, from the Father's perspective. How the Father sees us is the real truth.

but if we walk in the Light as He Himself is in the Light, we have fellowship with one another, and the blood of Jesus His Son cleanses us from all sin (1 John 1:7).

True fellowship is walking with others in the light of our true identity, honouring each other. We are cleansed from lost identity not by re-penance but by agreement with the truth that we are already cleansed, from the Father's perspective; our agreement brings that truth into our experience, and our minds are renewed from the lies of lost identity.

If we say that we have no sin, we are deceiving ourselves and the truth is not in us (1 John 1:8).

We do not need to be afraid of being real and admitting that we are a work in progress, having our mind renewed. There is no need to hide away from God in denial; we can be real and honest with Him, because He loves us unconditionally.

We can only confess our forgiveness if we are prepared to admit there is something we needed forgiveness for.

If we confess our sins, He is faithful and righteous, so that He will forgive us our sins and cleanse us from all unrighteousness. If we say that we have not sinned, we make Him a liar and His word is not in us (1 John 1:9-10).

Fear keeps us in unreality: God is light and love; and therefore darkness is not love. God is nothing other than love. To walk in darkness is not to walk in love. Sin is the lost identity of not walking in love and not having a relationship with love. Living loved is accepting the truth of being unconditionally forgiven, celebrating it in joy and rejoicing in love. If we live in the truth that we are loved and forgiven unconditionally, we remain guilt-free and do not feel condemned.

We do not have to fear admitting that we sometimes mess up or act from an unrenewed mindset, as we are still having our minds renewed. We do not need to live in denial, afraid to be real with the Father about our lives and the fact that we sometimes struggle. We do not have to try to keep the truth from our loving Father and hide away in fear as Adam did. We do not have to run and hide from our Father, we can run to Him: we can come boldly to the throne of grace and receive limitless grace and triumphant mercy. We are only alienated in our own minds – that is why so many of us need deep religious deprogramming.

Here is that same passage in the Mirror Bible:

My conversation with you flows from the same source which illuminates this fellowship of union with the Father and the Son. This, then, is the essence of the message: God is radiant light and in him there exists not even a trace of obscurity or darkness at all.

This is the real deal! To live a life of pretence is such a waste of time! The truth has no competition. Truth inspires the poetry of friendship in total contrast to a fake, performance-

based fellowship! Light is not threatened by darkness! Why say something with darkness as your reference?

We are invited to explore the dimensions of the same light that engulfs God; when we see the light in his light, fellowship ignites! In his light we understand how the blood of Jesus Christ is the removal of every stain of sin! The success of the cross celebrates our redeemed innocence!

To claim innocence by our own efforts under the law of personal performance is to deceive ourselves and to deliberately ignore the truth. The truth about you does not mean that you now have to go into denial if you have done something wrong!

When we communicate what God says about our sins, we discover what he believes concerning our redeemed oneness and innocence! We are cleansed from every distortion we believed about ourselves! Likeness is redeemed!

If we judge ourselves innocent by the law of our own works, then we make Jesus Christ, and what his word and blood communicate within us, irrelevant (1 John 1:5-10, Mirror).

The Law and the religious spirit will always attempt to get us back into duty and obligation, trying to be obedient enough to be accepted – when we are already loved and accepted as we are, which is properly good news. This is what Paul warned the Galatians:

You foolish Galatians, who has bewitched you? ... Are you so foolish? Having begun by the Spirit, are you now being perfected by the flesh? (Galatians 3: 1a, 3).

Rest

Many are kept in fear so that they never rest in what Jesus has already accomplished for them but continue to work for it. They live their lives weary and burdened, constantly trying to earn by works what is a free gift of grace.

Are we at rest in what Jesus has already done for us?
Are we at rest in our relationship with the Father?
Are we at rest in our true identity as sons of God?

As Francois Du Toit says, "God's invitation does not exclude anyone from possessing the promise of his rest."

And to whom did He swear that they would not enter His rest, but to those who were disobedient? So we see that they were not able to enter because of unbelief. Therefore, let us fear if, while a promise remains of entering His rest, any one of you may seem to have come short of it. For indeed we have had good news preached to us, just as they also did; but the word they heard did not benefit them, because they were not united with those who listened with faith (Hebrews 3:18-4:2).

The Book of Hebrews was written to those still operating under Old Covenant thinking, in an attempt to get them to distinguish between the covenants. Let's make sure we are not also mixing covenants and so failing to live in rest.

Rest is the realisation of what has already been accomplished for us and what God says about us. Rest is agreeing with the vast sum of His thoughts about us (and all those thoughts are good). Unconditional love places no conditions on us (or on our own faith in God) for our salvation, forgiveness, reconciliation, inclusion in Christ, being born from above or acceptance as children of God. All these things He has done for us freely and unconditionally.

Activation #4
A Place of Rest

If you struggle with rest or with sin-consciousness (or lost-identity-consciousness); if you feel guilty; if you are carrying burdens from the past that you have never really got rid of; if you are carrying unforgiveness towards anybody or anything, then now is the time to hand all of that over to Him.

To stream the audio, scan the QR code or visit the resources webpage.

I encourage you to close your eyes.
Start to relax
and focus on breathing
a little bit more deeply.

Slow down.
Start thinking about God and thinking about love.

Start breathing in the unconditional love of the Father.
Breathe it in.
Let love fill you and flow through you.
All you have to do is just draw it in.
It's in the very air that you breathe: His life.

So be still and let God love on you.
Let His love overflow over you,
cocoon you, surround you,
bring you into a safe place, a place of rest.

Let him hug you, so tight that you cannot wriggle away.
He wants you tight to His heart.
Feel the rhythm of His heartbeat.

Be still.
Come to a place of total rest.

Any thoughts of performance
any thoughts of guilt or shame or condemnation
that come to your mind,
hand them over to Him.
Let them go.
Let Him take them from you
and take them as far as the east is from the west,
so you can never ever, ever find them again.

Anything that you feel guilty of from your past –
hand it over to Him, and He will take it away.
Any unforgiveness that you have towards anybody else,
choose right now to forgive them and release them
and let Him take away
and untether you from the memories of

FORGIVENESS

the hurt and pain of your past.
Let Him bring you into wholeness
and heal your heart and make you whole.

Let unconditional love bring you
into a place of complete rest
from all works, from all performance.

Confess the truth of what He says about you:
you are forgiven.
Let's confess that together:

I am forgiven.
I am righteous.
I am justified.
I am a new creation.
I am reconciled and redeemed.
I am resting in all that Jesus has done.
I choose never to operate in works
to earn something that is already mine.
I confess my forgiveness.
I confess my righteousness.
I receive cleansing.

Let the cleansing –
and the washing of the water of His words to you
that you are forgiven –
wash over you
washing away all the guilt, shame,
condemnation of the past.

Just rest in His love.
You are in a safe place.

I really believe that the Father wants
to just speak words of encouragement,
and nurture you.

So open up your heart,
open up your mind and let Him speak.
I do not know what He wants to say –

He wants to say different things to different people –
but I believe He wants to speak into you.
He wants to affirm you.
He wants to bless you.

He wants you to know that you are absolutely loved,
unconditionally;
that you are washed clean by the truth;
that the truth that you now know
will completely set you free.

Listen for a moment.

To someone, I know, Jesus is saying
"My grace is sufficient for you.
My mercy triumphs
over all the judgment you have been placed under
by people,
people who have judged you
and made you feel guilty and ashamed."

His mercy and grace are sufficient to wash away
all the stain of people's lies, and people's words,
so you can be totally set free to rest in His love.

Stay in that place,
if you just want to stay there and enjoy being loved on.

A simple act of love

God is so good, so wonderful, and so full of joy. His love, kindness, and mercy are boundless, and experiencing His unconditional love is truly awe-inspiring. It's incredible to witness how His love reaches out to those who feel alienated or lost, drawing them back into His embrace. Unconditional love has a transformative power. It does not judge or condemn; it simply embraces and accepts. Just as Jesus touched the leper, breaking societal norms, His love knows no bounds and can bring healing and restoration to those who need it most.

Sometimes, all it takes is a simple act of love – a hug, a kind word – to convey the depth of God's love to someone. We do not need to focus on pointing out other people's faults or trying to fix them; instead, we can simply love them as they are and allow God's love to work through us to bring healing and transformation.

I remember David Hogan[3] describing how he put his hand into the putrid rotting flesh of a person who had gangrene. They were dying, and he put his hand on them, and into them: they were completely healed and restored, and their whole skin was renewed. He was not afraid to put his hand into a place where no one else would, and so demonstrated the unconditional love of God. Through his acts of compassion and courage, David has witnessed countless miracles, including raising the dead. Such miraculous manifestations are not fuelled by fear or judgment but by a deep understanding and demonstration of God's unconditional love for all His children.

In a world where many feel rejected, judged or unworthy, the message of unconditional love is more vital than ever. By extending love and acceptance to those who feel lost or broken, we can play a significant role in bringing healing and restoration to their lives. It is our privilege and responsibility to share this message of love with others, regardless of their background or circumstances. By demonstrating unconditional love in our actions and interactions, we can truly make a difference in the lives of those around us and help bring about transformation and healing in our communities.

---

[3] David Hogan is a pioneering missionary who lives and works in Mexico. See https://freedom-ministries.us/david-and-debbie-hogan/

5. Faith

The more you engage with it, the more you find out just how deep unconditional love goes. The experiences I have had of unconditional love have radically changed my whole belief system about who God is, the reach of His love towards creation, and also towards myself. It has helped me understand why Jesus said "love one another as I have loved you." If we do not know unconditional love, how can we unconditionally love others? But when we do experience it, that empowers us to give it as well.

The inescapable love of God

God is love; and that love is unconditional for everyone and everything – it has no boundaries or limitations. You cannot escape it. As David said:

Where can I go from Your Spirit?
Or where can I flee from Your presence?
If I ascend to heaven, You are there;
If I make my bed in Sheol, behold, You are there.
(Psalm 139:7-8).

You cannot be separated from the love of God because it is God Himself who is love.

I was struck by this little meme on social media: "If you have not been overwhelmed and left breathless by the love and grace of an inclusive Father, then I would suggest you have not had an encounter with love and grace Himself." Initially, I thought that was really good, because that is how I feel – almost overwhelmed and breathless at the amazing love of God. Then I thought again. We want to be sensitive to where people are in their process, and a statement like this might easily discourage someone who feels condemned or guilty because they do not know that love experientially yet. Love is unconditional, so relax and enjoy it. Do not strive for something that is yours freely by grace. I believe the Father wants each of us, every one of His children, to really know that we are unique, special, precious – the apple of His eye, the treasure of His heart. He wants us to fully experience the reality of how He feels about us, how deep His love is. Then, having experienced it, it will change and transform our lives and help us awaken the world to the reality of God as unconditional love.

Realising our true identity

> We have wasted so much time trying to get there, when 'there' is where we are to begin with. If you get hold of that, you'll begin to realise that what we have been sold as a belief system is so far removed from the truth – that we've never been separated from God other than in the alienation of our own minds. God never left us, we left Him. Dying to the unenlightened self, the fruit of the "I am not" tree system, the old damned lawman, the DIY (do-it-yourself) person takes one simple conclusion, not a lifelong struggle. The conclusion is in agreeing with God about you – you died when Jesus died, were co-raised with Him and are now co-seated in heavenly places. – Francois Du Toit.

That sums up the reality that is already ours, but which so many do not yet know or realise. In the Christian religion, this process of entering into who we are and who God is has often been portrayed as a struggle, requiring a lot of works to achieve. So encountering religious people can be frustrating; but if we maintain an attitude of blessing toward them, then hopefully they will have their own epiphany, be enlightened to the real God who is love, and help people come to Him rather than pushing them away. That is why I continue to explode the religious lies that kept me in bondage to those conditions in the past, until eventually love set me free from the Old Covenant mindset of 'works'. In this chapter we will look at the truth about faith, being 'born again' (or born from above), and salvation.

The term 'Christian faith' is often used by believers, but I prefer to focus on our relationship with God, not our beliefs about Him. Often, our 'Christian faith' describes the Christian tradition we are in or what we believe about God. But He just wants us to enjoy and engage Him. So I would not use the term myself, I would just talk about my relationship with the Father through Jesus. Jesus did not come to start a new religion or faith, but to establish us and enable us to have a relationship with the Father through Him; to fully embrace being in the Father and the Father being in us – this wonderful, intimate relationship God has always intended. "But don't I need faith to please God? Don't I need to be obedient?" Questions like these tend to originate from deep religious programming, not from any personal experience of unconditional love. When you truly experience it (and you can), you no longer need to ask those kinds of questions because you are utterly secure in that relationship.

Two kinds of faith

There is a difference between the faith needed for our reconciliation and salvation, and the faith we use to manifest our creativity as sons of God – to draw things from the unseen realm into manifestation in this realm. That is where we need to understand using our ability to choose by faith, which is quantum physics 1.01: faith is the evidence of things unseen. When you have not yet seen it, faith is what you operate in to begin manifesting the reality you are looking for.

God is speaking continually. When He speaks, we can hear and connect and agree with it. So this kind of faith comes from a hearing relationship with God the Father, Son and Spirit. Sometimes we engage the Father, sometimes Jesus, sometimes the Spirit, and they can all speak to us, and all generate life-giving energy when we hear their voice. They guide us, direct us, empower our identity, and reveal truth – all within the context of relationship. We can hear the very voice of God speaking to us, generating within us the energy we need to live as children of God.

In terms of quantum physics, we can say that faith enables us to use God's grace, His divine enabling power, to resonate, become an oracle, and 'pop a qwiff' (collapse a quantum wave function) so that the reality we choose as observers becomes manifest, even though it did not physically exist before. When using our faith to call into being what we are looking for, it does not yet exist physically, but it must exist in the realms of our minds, hearts and desires first. The living light strings, the quantum lumens, respond to our faith when we express ourselves as oracles. Light itself forms the reality around us. As long as we are not double-minded (which makes us unstable and unable to manifest from the unseen realm) it will manifest what we have already seen.

As Romans 4:17 says, God "gives life to the dead and calls into being that which does not exist." Everything we see around us was once in someone's mind, formed in their imagination as a thought, concept, idea or invention, before it became physical. We just need to learn to bring what comes out of our thinking into realisation. This is where faith comes into play. Hebrews 11:3 tells us that by faith we understand the worlds were prepared by the Word of God (Jesus, not the Bible), and that what is seen was made from things that are not visible to the natural eye. Those invisible things are quantum particles, strings of light, vibrating energy that eventually manifest into visible existence. The role of this kind of faith is to draw those unseen realities out and give them physical actuality.

Whose faith saves us?

But when it comes to the faith needed for salvation, I believe that comes from God's faith in us, not the other way around. And our true identity also comes from God's faith in us, not our faith in God. Questions often come up about where faith comes from, how much is needed, and whose faith actually saves us. I believe these questions arise because people do not fully grasp the enormity of what God has already done. They think they need to do something to make God's work effective for them.

In 2008, during an encounter in heaven, I stepped onto the fire stones in Eden, the Garden of God, and saw the subatomic structure of grace and faith swirling together as flames of unconditional love. I became joined to that love in an overwhelming experience of being fully embraced and immersed in it. It was a wonderful experience, and I think God wants us to understand that the very fabric of the universe is founded on grace and faith – not ours, but His – and His grace is limitless.

For it is by grace you have been saved, through faith – and this is not from yourselves, it is the gift of God – not by works, so that no one can boast (Ephesians 2:8).

Paul makes it clear that the faith we are saved through is not our own, but a gift from God. I cannot claim my own great faith as the reason for my salvation, because I never had that measure of faith. What I have is the gift God has given to enable me to grasp the truth. This is the key difference between the Old and New Covenants: is faith a gift from God, or a product of our own works and efforts?

Faith comes by hearing and hearing by the word of Christ (Romans 10:17).

Faith comes by hearing the word of Christ, the living Word of God. Paul is not talking about the importance of reading the Bible over and over, but about connecting with the voice of Jesus speaking to us. When we simply agree with what Jesus says, that ignites the ability to believe within us. His sheep hear His voice and follow Him; and when they know His voice, they will not follow the voice of a stranger (I do sometimes wonder how many people are following voices other than His).

He is continually speaking, if we have ears to hear. In reality, faith comes from a hearing relationship with God the Father, Son and Holy Spirit. As we engage with each person of the Trinity, they are able to speak to us and generate life-giving energy within us. When we hear their voice, it guides, directs and empowers us in our identity as children of God. We walk by faith, not by sight, which means following God's voice, not leaning on our own understanding or having faith in the Bible itself. We do not need to generate faith in the Bible to walk with God, because it is a relational walk.

We do not need our own faith to be saved, because everyone is already saved; they just need to realise that truth. God gifts us with the faith we need to come to that realisation, because He loves us unconditionally and wants us to enter into relationship with Him. But then as we choose to follow God's voice, we discover Him in deeper ways and begin to see ourselves from His perspective. Until then, we know ourselves from our perspective; we know what we have been like in the past. We know what other people may have thought we are like in the present. What really matters is the vast sum of His thoughts about us. That frees us to simply be, without striving to earn what already belongs to us by grace. God has wonderful thoughts about us, and each one is wonderfully good. He keeps no record of wrongs and sees us as righteous, as if we never sinned. This is what He has done, not what we strive to achieve.

Faith is manifested in our lives as trust: trust in the reality of who God is and what He says. We believe Him because we know He is unconditional love, always good, and only intends the best for us. It is the expectation of the truth that He reveals to us which empowers us to live in the reality of that truth. This is the by-product of our hearing relationship with Jesus.

We are not saved by our own faith 'in' God, but by the faith that is 'of' or 'from' God: God's faith in us, or the faith He gifts to us. It is not something we generate or own ourselves. The difference between 'faith in' and 'faith of' is crucial. Striving to have enough faith in God to be accepted is a work, and we are not to lay again the Old Covenant foundations, which include dead works and faith. Receiving the faith God gifts to us is the key to walking in New Covenant reality.

Faith in Christ?

But surely the Bible tells us that we must have faith in Christ?

... and may be found in Him, not having a righteousness of my own derived from the Law, but that which is through faith in Christ, the righteousness which comes from God on the basis of faith (Philippians 3:9).

That is the NASB, and it is how the majority of our modern translations present that verse, "through faith in Christ". The literal translations, however, will render it differently:

... and be found in Him, not having my own righteousness, which is of the law, but that which is through the faith of Christ, the righteousness that is of God by the faith (Philippians 3:9 YLT).

... and may be found in him, not having a righteousness of my own, which is from the law, but which is through the faith of Christ, the righteousness which is from God upon the faith (Philippians 3:9 MLT).

Even the King James, notoriously skewed by the instructions issued on behalf of its royal patron, has this passage correct:

And be found in him, not having mine own righteousness, which is of the law, but that which is through the faith of Christ, the righteousness which is of God by faith (Philippians 3:9 KJV).

'In' fits with a works-based theology, but 'of' or 'from' fits with a grace inclusive understanding. Grammatically, 'in' is called an 'objective genitive', which most Greek scholars now agree has little to commend it. Still, whether because of their own theological predisposition or the doctrinal stance of those who commissioned the translation, many modern translators have chosen 'faith in Christ' rather than 'faith of Christ'.

If 'in' is correct, then my righteousness is based on my own faith – the very opposite of what Paul says in Ephesians 2:8. This one little word makes a huge difference. Am I trying to have righteousness which comes on the basis of my own faith, or am I receiving the reality that He has made me righteous because of who He says I am? In reality, my righteousness is based on Him – you can understand it as His faith in me, or the faith that He gives to me – rather than anything I might try to generate myself. The difference between 'in' and 'of' is crucial. If it is 'in', then the faith is my possession. But if it's 'of' or 'from', then the faith is God's possession that He has gifted to me. And who is going to be more faithful – me or Him? The answer is obvious.

Exactly the same translation choices are made in Galatians 2:20:

I have been crucified with Christ; and it is no longer I who live, but Christ lives in me; and the life which I now live in the flesh I live by faith in the Son of God, who loved me and gave Himself up for me (Galatians 2:20 NASB).

with Christ I have been crucified, and live no more do I, and Christ doth live in me; and that which I now live in the flesh -- in the faith I live of the Son of God, who did love me and did give himself for me (Galatians 2:20 YLT).

I have been crucified together with Christ. I am now no longer living, but Christ is living in me and that life which I am now living in the flesh, I am living in faith, in the faith of the Son of God, who loved me and gave himself up on my behalf (Galatians 2:20 MLT).

I am crucified with Christ: nevertheless I live; yet not I, but Christ liveth in me: and the life which I now live in the flesh I live by the faith of the Son of God, who loved me, and gave himself for me (Galatians 2:20 KJV).

I wonder how many people are caught in the trap of trying to crucify themselves daily, taking up their cross and trying to follow Him, weary and burdened, striving to be good enough to please God or earn His love. We have been crucified with Christ because we died with Him when He died, not because we did anything, but because He did it on our behalf. My life, lived in relationship with God, is not by my faith, by how much I can believe to make it happen. It is by His faith, or the faith that He gives me to enable me. The next verse continues:

> *I do not nullify the grace of God, for if righteousness comes through the Law, then Christ died needlessly* (Galatians 2:21 NASB).

Righteousness comes in no other way than by grace, and that grace is limitless; it is an outworking of unconditional love. Let's get back to the reality of God's goodness, mercy and love, and realise that He has gifted us this faith. It is not something we have to conjure up or strive for more of. We simply trust in God, agree with Him that He is good, and receive the abundance of life He wants to give. God is faithful to do what he promised and He predestined us to a face-to-face restored relationship in love. This was always His intention for every one of His children, and I guarantee that His intention is going to be fulfilled at the end of the day.

God is not looking for us to have our own faith. He wants us to operate in the faith He has given us, and simply accept the reality of who He is and how much He loves us. When we receive the Father's love, then we can truly love one another as well.

Old Covenant thinking

Hebrews 11:6 states that without faith it is impossible to please God. But Jesus has fully pleased the Father, and we are all included in Him through the New Covenant. We do not need our own faith to please God. We are already pleasing to God because of what Jesus has done, and because we are His children. A good father loves his children unconditionally, and God is the best Father who loves us unreservedly.

We can so easily get caught up in Old Covenant thinking today. Why would I need faith in the God I engage with face-to-face every day? It is my absolute testimony and experience that I live in. I do not need to try and believe it, because it is the truth of my reality.

God wants us to go deeper into His heart, love and the truth of who He is, so He can fully restore our identity as His sons. In the Old Covenant, when people like Abraham believed in

God, that faith (not their works) was credited to them as righteousness. Jesus said that even faith as small as a mustard seed was enough in the Old Covenant context. But our own faith is unstable ground: we are building our lives on the solid rock of Jesus, not on the unreliable strength of our own belief. This concept of needing faith keeps many people in fear of losing their salvation if their faith fails. But it is not our faith, and what is more, it is not even our salvation; it is His salvation. All of it comes from Him, not from us. If only I had known this truth earlier in my life, I would not have struggled so much trying to be good enough.

But someone may well say, "You have faith and I have works; show me your faith without the works, and I will show you my faith by my works." (James 2:18).

This is accurate in terms of manifesting reality through faith, but has nothing to do with salvation. There was a great debate over whether to include the book of James in the canon of scripture, and Martin Luther famously dismissed it as an 'epistle of straw' because he thought it contradicted the gospel of faith over works. Once more, it is important to read this epistle in context: it was written specifically to the twelve tribes of Israel dispersed abroad, still living under the Old Covenant. It does not apply to us today in the same way.

Abraham was not justified by his works, but by his belief in God. Romans 4 makes it clear that if Abraham was justified by works, he would have something to boast about, but not before God. His faith was credited to him as righteousness, which was a gift. Abraham did experience God speaking to him, and he looked forward to Jesus as the offering God would provide. But he saw it in the spirit, not in the flesh. The gospel was preached to Abraham beforehand, that all nations would be blessed in him. Israel lost sight of that reality and restricted the gospel to themselves, until Peter had a vision proving there was no longer Jew or Gentile, bond or free, male or female. We are all one new man in Christ.

The old distinctions no longer apply. The promises God made to Abraham were not just for the Jewish people, but for the one seed – Jesus Christ.

He made Him who knew no sin to be sin in our behalf, so that we might become the righteousness of God in Him (2 Corinthians 5:21).

In the New Covenant, it is not our belief that is credited as righteousness, because God has already made us righteous through Jesus. All the promises of God are yes and amen in Christ; and they are all ours through our inclusion in Him. I am justified, judged innocent, reconciled, and made righteous by God my Father. I did not have to do any of those things myself, they were freely given to me by grace, through the faith He has given me to experience them. I live by the faith of Jesus, my brother, who is the Way, the Truth and the Life, provided for all of us. I am not saved by my own faith in God, as that would be trying to be saved by my own works, which is futile; it only leads to weariness and never being at rest.

Salvation is God's work alone, by grace, already accomplished for everyone. Sadly, many do not know this, and we (who should know it best) have often put conditions on it. Unconditional love requires no works, including our own faith. We do not need to strive to attain things through works, but can simply be still, listening to His voice and knowing that He is God.

Born again

We do not need to be born again through our own repentance and faith. That occurred on the day of the resurrection, when all of mankind was born from above through what Jesus accomplished. We are all already alive in Christ, just as we were all once lost in Adam.

Jesus' words in John 14 about coming again and receiving us to Himself, Him being in the Father and the Father in Him, are not about a future event, but about the relational reality that was established through the resurrection. The disciples saw the resurrected Jesus in the flesh, and Thomas was able to touch and confirm it was truly Him. On the day of the resurrection, Jesus told them, they would know that He was in the Father, that they were in Him, and that He was in them.

This was not just true for those disciples, but for all of mankind. Just as Adam represented the human race, Jesus represented the new man, the new creation. As in Adam all died, so in Christ all are made alive. The disciples, representing mankind, were then breathed upon by Jesus and received the Holy Spirit. This was the moment they were born from above, just as God had originally breathed life into Adam. The reality is that this happened for all of humanity.

The conventional evangelical wisdom on how to receive salvation, by acknowledging and confessing sin, repenting and believing, is a misunderstanding. We are already righteous in Christ, already forgiven, already alive in Him. Our confession does not make it true; it just allows us to live in the reality of what is already true. The idea that we are separated from God, that the Holy Spirit is not in us until we 'get saved', is simply not accurate. The evangelical model makes salvation dependent on our own works, which is why so many live in fear and insecurity about their salvation.

That kind of teaching makes salvation about what man still has to do rather than what God has already done. It makes people sin-conscious rather than grace-conscious, trapping them in guilt and performance mode as Christians. Everything was dealt with and everything was accomplished in the cross and resurrection of Christ: reconciliation, forgiveness, salvation, being born from above and having God dwelling in us – all this has already been accomplished for everyone. The true gospel is that in Christ, all of humanity has been made alive, forgiven, and reconciled to God. Our role is not to 'get saved' through our own efforts, but to simply realise and live out of the salvation that has already been accomplished.

Most people – even most believers – do not yet know or fully realise this truth. Saul of Tarsus, who would become the apostle Paul, is a prime biblical example of someone receiving this revelation. He was zealously following self-righteousness and religion. On the road to Damascus, God revealed that Jesus was already in him, and was sending him to preach to the Gentiles that Jesus was already in them as well: they were already reconciled to God, though they did not yet know it.

This vision of inclusion was central to Paul's message of God's unconditional love, grace and mercy, a powerful good news message that we have lost in the evangelical version of the gospel. The heavenly vision showed him that he was born from above, alive and included in Christ, without him doing anything. God's amazing love transformed the persecutor into the champion of inclusion with a mission to reveal God's grace to the world. Paul did not preach a message of repenance and being 'born again' through our own efforts. He preached that we are already forgiven, reconciled, and saved from our lost identity; the only issue is our realisation of this truth, and that too is gifted to us. We are already included in God's salvation, which encompasses forgiveness, freedom from our past and healing from all brokenness. This is the good news of inclusion, not the bad news message of exclusion until certain conditions are met.

That false gospel often leverages fear of punishment and separation to try to force people to accept it. But the whole idea is completely at odds with the reality of God's unconditional love. No one can be eternally separated from that love. God has already accomplished salvation, reconciliation and forgiveness for all of humanity. This is the message of unconditional love that the world needs to hear.

Ephesians 2 speaks of us being 'dead in trespasses and sins,' not to make us feel guilty, but to reveal that we are now new creations in Christ, no longer defined by our past. We were made alive with Christ, even when we were dead. The 'sin' referred to here, remember, is not some kind of moral failure, but a distortion of our identity – living out of tune with the blueprint of who we were designed to be. God saw us in Christ's death and resurrection before we saw ourselves there. He demonstrated His love for us while we were still sinners; we did not have to make ourselves good enough. He reconciled the world, the cosmos, to Himself in Christ, not counting anyone's sins against them. We are predestined to return to face-to-face innocence in love.

The gospel is a message of inclusion, not exclusion. God has already done everything to ensure all His children will eventually know and experience His unconditional love. Our role is to help people realise this truth. We have all been invited to participate in the dance of unconditional love, a joy-filled expression that does not care what it looks like to others. This is the *perichoresis*, the circle dance of the Trinity.

As ambassadors of this message, are we telling the world they are reconciled and included in God's love? Or are we preaching exclusion and condemnation? Let's be sure we get the message right: God has saved all mankind, made all alive, and included all in Christ. Our part is simply to come to the realisation of this truth, so it can renew our minds and transform our lives. As long as we have a sin-consciousness, we will always see something wrong with ourselves that God is displeased with, but righteousness-consciousness brings peace and joy.

Many believers spend so much time trying to please God that they have little time to enjoy Him and live loved. But our salvation, reconciliation and forgiveness are already true; we only need to enter into the experiential reality of what has already been accomplished.

God's love applies equally to everyone without exception, because He is Love and expresses Himself as Love towards all He has created. Love is consistent, constant and dependable. Let's receive the wonderful joy of this salvation and engage in the reality of unconditional love. Our personal experiences of encountering God face-to-face will help renew our minds to the truth, allowing us to enter into it more deeply. When we receive a revelation of God's unconditional love, it transforms our lives from a slavery to duty and obligation into the freedom of a joyous love relationship of rest and creativity. Rest becomes a state of being that we can live in, even in our everyday activities.

The invitation is to open our hearts to receive this revelation of unconditional love. As we do, it will renew our minds and transform our lives, freeing us from performance-based religion into the joy and rest of simply being loved. This is the vision and message we carry to a world that desperately needs to hear it.

Activation #5
Embrace the Reality

To stream the audio, scan the QR code or visit freedomarc.org/UCL-resources

I encourage you to close your eyes.

Come to that place where you start
to focus your thinking
and your intention
on engaging with the Father,
engaging Jesus,
engaging unconditional love.

It might help
to slow your breathing down.
Begin to relax.
Start thinking and focusing on God, who is love.

Breathe in deeply the unconditional love of the Father.

As you breathe in slowly,
as you open up your heart,
open up your mind,
open up your whole being,
let unconditional love flow over you.
Let it rest on you.
Be saturated in it, and let it flow through you.
Let it penetrate.
Let it be absorbed into you.

Be still.
Be still and let God love on you.
Let Him reveal that truth to you.

Love, unconditional love,
touching your heart
touching your mind,
every part of your soul.
Be still and truly know God as unconditional love.
Be still.

Hear God speak to you.
Be still and know that I am unconditional love.
Be still and know that I am unconditional love.
Let those words sink in.

Be still and know that I am unconditional love.
Be still and know that I am abundant joy.
Be still and know that I am abundant joy.
Be still and know that I am overwhelming peace.
Be still and know that I am overwhelming peace.
Be still and know that
I am the Way, the Truth, and the Life.
I am limitless grace,
and I am unconditional love
and triumphant mercy.

If you know that there are things in your past
that hold you back,
things that you still feel guilty over,
things that you still can't forgive yourself for,
that you can't let go,
just invite love, joy and peace to fill you,
to flow over you,
to flow in you,
and touch every particle of your being
with unconditional love.

And as that love fills you,
it can't be contained within you.

Let it flow out of you like rivers of living water,
creating an atmosphere to live in of rest,
that you can bring that rest to others,
that you can bring that joy and peace to others.

Feel the unconditional love
flow through your whole being.
Be still.
Be still.

Let God's love now touch you,
touch you in those areas
that it's never touched before.
Heal you in those areas
that have never been healed before.
Free you in those areas
that have kept you in bondage to works.

You're in a safe place.
Heaven is open.
The Father desires
that you would enter into His very heart.
Come face to face in love.
Find that place of restored innocence
in the realm of light.

Bathe in the radiance
of the light that's coming from Him,
from His face:
the light of love,
the light of truth.
Let that go into deeper levels of your very being.
Don't hold back through fear.
Let go.
Trust.
Trust in God's goodness,
trust in God's mercy.

That you can just live loved,
free from guilt,

free from shame,
free from condemnation.

All your old rags,
your dirty rags of your own self-righteousness,
let it go.
Let Him put new clothes on you,
the new ring of sonship on you.
Just as the prodigal came.
The father didn't look at what he'd done.
The father celebrated his return
and rejoiced, to celebrate
that that which was lost had been found.

Let your identity be restored
so you can live in that place of love.
Then you can love living,
enjoy the joy of life.
Live loving: be merciful,
choosing to forgive and release all things.

Rest in love, joy and peace.
Wait in that place.
Be open to go deeper and deeper
and deeper into love.

If you struggle to believe,
let Him impart to you right now His faith,
His faith to believe who you truly are,
to believe the vast sum of His thoughts about you,
to believe that you are the apple of His eye,
the treasure of His heart.
You are precious, precious to Him.
You are uniquely, wonderfully made.
You are special.
Let that truth be imparted to your hearts right now.
Let Him give you the ability to receive it
freely, without cost.
Embrace the reality.

Receive all that you need
because He has an abundance,
exceedingly, abundantly
beyond all you ask or think or even dream.

Let Him expand your conscious reality to go beyond,
into the lavishness and abundance
of His unconditional love,
limitless grace,
and triumphant mercy.

If you are in that place, just rest there.
Stay there as long as you want.
You can't exhaust the depths of it.
There are always deeper places to go into God's love.

6. God-breathed Writings

We have looked at the truth about how God views sin, forgiveness, repentance, confession, faith, being born again and salvation, and how unconditional love can change the way we ourselves regard all those different concepts. Now, we will explore the truth of the Bible from the perspective of unconditional love. While this may be a controversial topic, I will share my understanding on it, shaped by my journey with God and with the Bible, and describe how my views have evolved through my experiences with unconditional love.

Holy Bible

When we begin to experience unconditional love, it will inevitably challenge many things we assume to be true. I assumed some of them to be true because I was told they were by someone preaching or teaching, or because I was told the Bible said so. However, when unconditional love began to confront some of my understandings, I realised that just because I had been told that the Bible said something, that did not necessarily make it true. I discovered that many things I thought were true were not really true at all, which led me to question the role of the Bible in my life and in our lives.

Much of our understanding comes from the traditions and streams we may have been programmed by or have had experience in. If you come from a Catholic background, the Bible may have a different role in your life tan if you come from an evangelical one. But what is its role, really? What role should the Bible have in our lives? I am not saying not to read your Bible or that God cannot speak to us through the Bible, because He obviously can. But I believe it can often be hard to discern God's voice when He does speak to us through the Bible because the filters of our existing belief systems make it difficult to distinguish what God is actually saying from what we think He is saying.

I do not believe the Bible is God's primary chosen method of communication to us. He wants to communicate with us face to face, heart to heart, and speak to us directly. But for some, the Bible is the only way they expect God to communicate with them. For those who come from a more charismatic point of view, believing in the gifts of the Spirit, prophecy, and words of knowledge, a relationship with God is more than just the Bible. It is about having a relationship of intimacy through the Holy Spirit, who is the Spirit of Truth. The Holy Spirit will lead us to the truth – Jesus – and He will lead us to the Father, giving us a relationship with all three. The Bible is not the fourth person of the Trinity. There are only Father, Son and Spirit. The Bible is a book that may point us to them, but it is not them. We need to understand this if we are going to deconstruct our understanding and have an experience of God face to face, which will unveil unconditional love.

I was brought up in very evangelical churches, so most of my understanding about God and Christianity came from what I was told the Bible said. This was the only way I believed you could understand about God: through the Bible. Of course, there are many theology books written about God, attempting to explain what the Bible says about Him. However, God does not want us to study Him; He wants us to experience Him. Sadly, there are 30,000, some say 40,000-plus, streams and denominations all claiming to know what the Bible says, and they have major differences. If so many groups believe something different, how do we know what we believe is the truth? I think the only way we can truly know is by experiencing the Truth – Jesus – as a person. Face-to-face experiences with God have revealed the truth to me, and that truth has shown that God is unconditional love.

I went to Sunday school from about the age of two because I was always into mischief, so my mum sent me with my aunt and uncle to Sunday school for a couple of hours on Sunday afternoons at our local Bible Christian Methodist Church. Methodist churches have different names and perspectives, even within the Methodist movement. In my town, there were six different Methodist churches, each with slightly different views, but all were fairly evangelical in their approach. The Bible Christian Methodist Church, as you might expect, was particularly strong in Bible teaching.

I was brought up as an evangelical Bible believer on the principle of *sola scriptura*, meaning the Bible alone. I was taught that the Bible was Holy Scripture, totally inspired by God, and thus inerrant and infallible. We may even perhaps call it the 'Holy Bible', but who says this book is holy? Many copies have that written on the cover, so we tend to accept the description. God is holy, and God calls us to be holy, but I am not sure that a book put together by people deciding what was going to be in it can be called holy. I think holiness is a description better reserved for God. But I digress.

God-botherers

I was taught that the Bible was the word of God, and I often used that phrase: "The word of God says..." But the Bible never claims to be the word of God. I was encouraged to read my Bible and pray every day and be a good God-botherer. A friend recently introduced me to someone who calls evangelists God-botherers. I smiled at first, but later I realised it is not a good term. It suggests that Christians bother people about God, trying to convert them or telling them they're going to hell. That is not a good approach towards someone who does not yet know the love of God personally.

This perspective comes from being taught that we need to preach the gospel to everyone because they are going to hell, and we never know when someone might die. We can certainly share the good news in a sensitive and relational way, but being a God-botherer is not how we should aim to be seen. How do non-believers view us Christians? Do they see us as Bible-bashers just trying to get another conversion? Or do they see us as those who love them unconditionally? I believe if it were the latter, they might have a completely different view of why we want to introduce them to the God we know.

Holy Spirit

It was stressed that the Bible was the sole absolute authority for my life, and that I could not trust anyone or anything else. It was the Bible and the Bible alone. No one taught me anything about the role of the Holy Spirit in my life. In fact, I do not recall ever hearing a sermon about the Holy Spirit in any Methodist church I attended. The Holy Spirit was a peripheral figure in our version of Christianity, mentioned only in passing when people talked about the Father, Son and Spirit. To be honest, I found the Holy Spirit completely absent from my understanding.

When I was about sixteen, I read something about the Holy Spirit in the Bible which prompted me to do a word study on the topic. That was when I realised that I knew absolutely nothing about the Spirit personally, which was quite sad given that I had been brought up to believe in the Trinity. Then, as a teenager, I joined the Brethren Church, where I was further indoctrinated into the centrality of the Bible in my life, and still received no insight into the role of the Holy Spirit. The Brethren Church adhered to Cessationism, the belief that the gifts of the Spirit ended with the early church. Consequently, I believed that God could only communicate with me through the Bible or through someone preaching about the Bible. I was never taught to expect God to speak to me directly or that His love could be directly experienced.

Expressions of emotion were largely frowned upon in these churches. It was acceptable for people to shed a tear occasionally, but laughing or showing other emotions was discouraged. I was never taught to think of God as my Dad – He was referred to as Father, but never in the intimate sense of being a personal Dad. Looking back, I realise I missed out on a lot of understanding and experience during those years.

Eschatology

I was also programmed with a specific theological position regarding future eschatology that emphasised being rescued or raptured. Methodist and Brethren eschatology were both heavily dispensational, premillennial, infernalist, and cessationist. Now, I see that every one of these doctrines is at odds with the truth of what Jesus taught. These beliefs greatly influenced my life, and it took a significant deconstruction process to overcome them. This began after I was baptised in the Holy Spirit around 1986. It was then that God spoke to me directly for the first time, instructing me that I needed to understand the Kingdom and covenant. This began a three- or four-year journey during which God taught me about the Kingdom and covenant – yes, even through the Bible – using it to deconstruct my previous misunderstandings.

My understanding of eschatology was challenged, which is why I eventually wrote a book about it[4]. Many people have been deceived by Brethren teachings on eschatology and the future, without even knowing the source. As God set me free, my desire became to help others understand the true nature of God as unconditional love, free from the fear of eternal torture for those who do not know Jesus, and recognising that the gifts of the Holy Spirit have not ceased (though as we grow into maturity, we may not need to use the gifts of the Holy Spirit in the same way, since we can function in our own spirit in the same dimension. In relationship with the Lord, we become one spirit with Him, opening up new dimensions for creativity as sons of God. This is something I never imagined possible during my time in those churches).

I was taught that if you did not accept Jesus as your personal Saviour, you would be punished and tortured forever in hell with no chance of reprieve. This is bad news that the world has rejected. We need to bring good news: the nature of God as unconditional love. True evangelism is about love, not fear, and focused on receiving something good rather than avoiding something bad. Looking back, I feel saddened by all the fear-based evangelism I took part in.

---

[4] *The Eschatology of the Restoration of All Things* by Mike Parsons, Freedom Apostolic Ministries, 2022.

Deconstruction

So, how did I come to be passionate about the unconditional love of God and desire for everyone to experience it? Part of the answer lies in who God made me to be: a forerunner, visionary and pioneer by nature. Despite the difficulties, I have pushed through with my deconstruction process and have been deprogrammed from many of the belief systems I grew up with. My goal is to open the door for others to follow into the freedom of understanding the truth of who God really is and experiencing His unconditional love.

This journey has not been easy, as these beliefs were deeply ingrained in me. But God has been patient and kind, guiding me along a long, winding road of discovery. This journey has involved multiple steps over many years, leading me to where I am now – and it is continuing. Radical experiences, like the one in 2008 when I first entered heaven and experienced unconditional love standing on the fire stones, have been life-changing, but they are just parts of the whole journey. And God knows how to guide each of us on our own path. As we trust Him, stay close to Him and walk with Him every day, He will unveil the truth of who we really are and lead us to experience His limitless grace, mercy and unconditional love.

I was taught never to question the Bible or what it supposedly said about God, as doing so was considered heretical. That is a strong word, but I am certain that is how it would have been characterised. In the churches I was brought up in, questioning the Bible was strictly forbidden. But whose version of the Bible and whose interpretation were we not supposed to question? I have since realised that there are so many different views, that if we cannot question them, how are we ever really going to learn? There were many things that did not feel right, but studying the Bible only served to confirm what I already believed; this is a well-documented phenomenon known as confirmation bias. Even though I wanted to know the truth, it was difficult to study the Bible in a way that challenged my beliefs because I thought I knew what it was saying.

I was never taught that the Bible as we know it did not exist before AD 385 or that there are many different versions with varying numbers of books. For example, the Protestant Bible I was familiar with has 66 books, but the Catholic Bible has 73, the original King James Bible had 80, and the Ethiopic Bible has 84. What happened to all those other books, and why were they considered part of the Bible by some groups and not others? This raises questions about whether what is now in our Bible is actually something God intended, or if men decided what to include. The selection process involved decisions made by Councils such as the one at Nicaea in 325, where the Emperor Constantine and a selected group of bishops decided what books would be included in the Holy Roman Bible. The rest were burned; therefore we do not know what those other original documents contained or if there are other writings inspired by God that have been lost.

I believe that each of us is like a book, a record of what God is doing in our time. Each of our relationships with God and the amazing things He has done in our lives are relevant today. We need to be open to what God is saying to us now, not just look back at what He said 2000 or 4000 years ago.

My own process of deconstruction made me aware of how much I had glossed over the huge perceived differences between the God of the Old Testament and the God seen in the New Testament. Over the last six or seven years, God has continually challenged my Old Covenant thinking (I did not think I had any). This deconstruction process helped me understand the differences between the Old and New Covenants. Deep down, I knew something was wrong with many things, but my upbringing with the Bible as the sole source of authority meant there were many inconsistencies that I disregarded and never pursued God about. The fear of questioning the Bible kept me from asking the hard questions that were like splinters in my mind, nagging at my consciousness, because I did not know how to find the truth.

It was only when my experiences began to challenge my beliefs that the Father was able to renew my mind to the truth.

This happened over time, especially after I had face-to-face encounters with God in heaven. The renewal of our minds is vital, and Jesus says the truth is fundamental to this process, with the Spirit of Truth helping us realise what is really true. Jesus is the Way, the Truth and the Life, and we need an intimate relationship with Him to know the truth beyond mere intellect. When I began meeting the Father face to face, it created such cognitive dissonance that change became unavoidable. My experiences challenged my beliefs, causing me to be double-minded for a while – unsure of what was true, whether it was my experiences or what I was taught about the Bible.

In my upbringing in evangelical, non-Holy-Spirit-believing churches, experiences were frowned upon. We were taught not to trust our experiences because they might be wrong. But the Bible is full of people who had experiences and recorded them, without any suggestion that their experiences might be incorrect in any way. This caused some problems for me, but my experiences of unconditional love accelerated my deconstruction process, especially from 2016 onwards, when God started deconstructing my mind in earnest, challenging my beliefs about the Bible and its role for me.

I will share some of these testimonies of unconditional love, and encounters with people who have experienced it, in a later chapter. They challenged my understanding of the Bible as a consistent whole. The Old Testament, for example, is a variant of the Hebrew or Jewish *Tanakh*, written for a religion that is not ours. While it records God working in the world, it does not necessarily apply to us today. We are not under the Law today (and if we are not Jewish, we never have been) but under grace, guided by the Spirit who brings life rather than the letter which kills. Trying to keep the Law will wear you out.

The supposed inerrancy and infallibility of the Bible are claims the Bible never makes for itself but are widely touted by evangelical Christianity. What is scripture? What is the word of God? These are important questions to ask because understanding how God speaks to us today is crucial. Without this understanding, we will struggle to hear His voice clearly. Most Christians are programmed by their understanding of the Bible, which varies depending on their specific influences. That is why I use the Bible as a reference point for teaching on deconstruction, showing how verses might mean something different than we thought and looking at what the original words may have meant to their original audience.

Even in the New Testament, Jesus was almost always speaking to those living under the Old Covenant, and He was not talking to us directly. Understanding the relevance of those words for us today requires putting them into perspective. The Gospels of Matthew, Mark and Luke are quite different from the Gospel of John. I believe that John's Gospel reveals a deeper intimacy with Jesus and conveys truths that the other writers did not include. Statements such as "I am the Way, the Truth and the Life" or "I am the resurrection and the life" are unique to John, perhaps omitted from the other Gospels because their audiences might not have been able to accept them. John wrote for those who knew Jesus well, including us, and his insights are invaluable. The Gospel of John is my favourite part of the Bible, and I have read it so often that the pages have worn out. I always felt that God was speaking to me directly through John's revelations.

The other Gospels show Jesus trying to guide people away from strict adherence to the Law and towards following Him. He aimed to help them see that the Old Testament's true message pointed to Him as the Messiah, which many rejected. I discovered that the Bible itself says little about its nature because it is a compilation of many people's experiences, often recorded by scribes writing centuries after the events. These documents are of various genres, including history, poetry and apocalyptic literature. The writers were inspired by God or by their experiences, but it was other people who later assembled a selection of these texts into what we now call the Bible.

God-breathed

All Scripture is inspired by God and profitable for teaching, for reproof, for correction, for training in righteousness (2 Timothy 3:16).

All Scripture is God-breathed and is useful for teaching, rebuking, correcting and training in righteousness (2 Timothy 3:16 NIV).

This verse is often cited to support the Bible's divine authority, inerrancy and infallibility, although it does not use any of those terms, nor even mention 'the Bible'. The word 'Scripture' in English translations is normally capitalised, but the Greek used no capitals. The Greek word used is *graphe*, meaning 'writing'. The Bible did not even exist in its current form at the time this letter was written.

Still, I was taught that this verse referred to the Bible, reinforcing the belief in its divine inspiration and authority. Whilst much of the Bible may indeed be inspired and useful for teaching and correction, this is properly discerned through the Spirit. God can speak to us through all kinds of different writings, and anything inspired by God will be profitable. We cannot assume that 2 Timothy 3:16 is exclusively talking about the Bible.

So, what is Scripture? What is the Word of God? What is the Bible, and how was it formed? Does our understanding of the Bible help or hinder our experience of God's unconditional love? These are crucial questions. My own understanding of the Bible definitely hindered my experience of unconditional love.

I saw God as different in the Old Testament compared to the New Testament. The Old Testament depicted God doing terrible things, while the New Testament presented a more loving image. This created a contradiction in my understanding of God. The idea of God punishing people eternally in 'hell' conflicted with the concept of an unconditionally loving God. This seemed to place conditions on God's love, namely the need to be 'born again'.

Reading the Bible did not help me understand or experience unconditional love. Instead, it often did the opposite. The Greek word *graphe* in 2 Timothy 3:16 can refer to any inspired writings, past or future. For me, my journals, where God spoke to me, are inspired writings: they are inspired by God through our conversations. This inspiration is personal and may not be the same for others. Everyone can have inspired writings because God speaks to us daily. If we journal these, they can help us understand our identity and our relationship with God. Discerning what is inspired involves recognising the life and truth in it, aligning with God's love. If something portrays God as unloving, I immediately question its truth.

2 Timothy was written around AD 63, long before the Bible was canonised in AD 385. The 'writings' referred to may have included parts of what we now call the Old Testament and various previous letters to the churches. We do not know exactly what was included, and the process of canonisation involved human decisions with their own agendas. I contend that God's direct involvement in this process is questionable. It was primarily a human endeavour with the aim of controlling beliefs and practices. As people began to explore different ideas, the authorities wanted a standardised text to maintain order.

This gospel had spread around the world for the first 350 years, with the early Christians relying on the Spirit to share the good news. By and large, the world accepted it. So why change a good thing? Because those in power wanted to ensure that others only believed what they deemed true, distrusting the Holy Spirit to bring inspiration. I have a modern-day example: years ago, a friend from Argentina told me about a large campaign in Buenos Aires, with one of the biggest churches, involving over 100,000 people. They reached out to a difficult area, seeing many accept Jesus and enter into a relationship with Him. They had planned a discipleship programme but felt God telling them to wait and not contact those new believers for a year. It was counter-intuitive and contentious, but they obeyed. Without Bibles or organised teachings, these new believers thrived. After a year, they found them to have experienced God and His love deeply, guided by the Holy Spirit alone. This teaches us that we do not need to impose our methods on others but can trust God to disciple people through the Spirit. Sometimes, we even interfere with what God wants to do. I realise that I was misguided in some of the things I once taught as foundational.

Discernment

2 Timothy 3:16 does not say that every writing is God-breathed, nor that non-God-breathed writings are not useful. We need discernment to recognise what is truly inspired by God. It might surprise some to learn that the Bible, as we know it, is not the 'scriptures' Jesus or Paul referred to. The Bible is not the Word of God; Jesus is the Logos, the living Word of God. He was with God from the beginning and became flesh. So let's stop calling the Bible 'the Word of God'. It may contain some words from God and many words from people. That does not make them wrong, but they are human words, not divine.

We must discern whether God is speaking to us directly. Some read a red-letter Bible, applying everything Jesus said to their lives today, even when Jesus was castigating the Pharisees and Sadducees. Do we want to apply those criticisms to ourselves? Likely not. Many theological arguments and denominational splits stem from different interpretations of the Bible, using it as 'proof' for contradictory beliefs. For example, Calvinism and Arminianism are at opposite ends of the spectrum.

I believe Jesus is the Way, the Truth and the Life; the Word of God. He said, "My sheep will hear My voice," not "My sheep will read My book." We can listen to God's voice directly, rather than solely relying on a book about Him. The

Spirit speaks to us continually, and we can learn to tune in, encountering God for ourselves.

It might be transformative for us to invite Jesus, the Truth, to scrutinise everything we believe, as He did with His disciples. Imagine Him saying, "You have heard it said, but now I say unto you..." and challenging our current prized beliefs. How much of our perceived truth would remain? And we can indeed choose to ask Jesus to do just that, to reveal the truth and deconstruct our misconceptions.

Tapestry

In 2016, God began deconstructing my understanding. I had a vision of a tapestry representing my experiences with God. As I pulled a thread, the tapestry unravelled, symbolising my flawed understanding even of those divine encounters. God showed me not to rely on my own understanding, even of my spiritual experiences, but to continually seek Jesus' revelation of truth. It is easy to misinterpret experiences and prophecies through our own understanding. Even true prophecies can be misunderstood. We need Jesus' discernment to guide us.

Let's be open to deconstruction, allowing Him to reveal the truth. In Luke 24:27, Jesus explained the scriptures to two disciples as they walked along the road to Emmaus, opening their minds to understand them. Would it not be wonderful if He did that for us today? He could clarify what is scripture and what is not, and reveal its true meaning. The two disciples Jesus spoke to were known to their contemporaries, but did they write books about it? Did they share the details of His explanations with others? If they did, we have no record of it. Perhaps what He said was meant only for them, just as what He tells us may be only for us. We need open hearts to receive His personal revelations.

The Old Testament

God is surely consistent in both the Old and New Covenants. Jesus, the express image of God, demonstrated that God is love, countering the fearsome image of an angry God needing appeasement. There are some passages in what we call the Old Testament that I believe are not translated correctly from the original language. Additionally, I would say that some are written from the perspective of the writers and are not necessarily inspired at all. Why do I say that? Well, Jeremiah has God asking this:

"How can you say, 'We are wise,
And the law of the Lord is with us'?
But behold, the lying pen of the scribes
Has made it into a lie."
(Jeremiah 8:8).

This indicates that some of those who transcribed passages from what we now know as the Old Testament wrote lies. So, which parts are true, and which are lies? I believe the Holy Spirit can help us discern this. And when trying to understand who God is in the Old Testament, we certainly need discernment. Without it, we may fail to discover the true nature of God, who is unchanging. What we read about God in the Old Testament may not fully represent the truth as we have understood it. Anything contradicting God being love should be closely scrutinised through the Spirit. I saw a quote that said, "Don't visit the Old Testament without your Jesus passport." We are not Jews living under the Old Covenant before the Messiah, so it is advisable always to read the Old Testament through the lens of Jesus and the Spirit of Truth.

The Old Testament becomes beautiful when seen through the eyes of the Spirit, not through the letter of the Law. 2 Corinthians 3 discusses this at length, emphasising that Jesus is the only truth and living word we can rely on. The Bible, at its best, is a book that points us to Jesus; but then we need to develop our relationship with Jesus directly.

You search the Scriptures because you think that in them you have eternal life; it is these that testify about Me; and you are unwilling to come to Me so that you may have life (John 5:39-40).

Jesus is indicating that life is found in Him, not just in the Scriptures, which point to Him.

Living letters

Many evangelicals believe they will find eternal life through the Scriptures, but it actually comes through Jesus.

You are our letter, written in our hearts, known and read by all men; being manifested that you are a letter of Christ, cared for by us, written not with ink but with the Spirit of the living God, not on tablets of stone but on tablets of human hearts. Such confidence we have through Christ toward God. Not that we are adequate in ourselves to consider anything as coming from ourselves, but our adequacy is from God, who also made us adequate as servants of a New Covenant, not of the letter but of the Spirit; for the letter kills, but the Spirit gives life (2 Corinthians 3:2-6),

Let us be careful not to operate under the dead letter that brings death but rather under the living Spirit that brings life. Some teachings I received were definitely a dead letter: they brought me no life and put me under bondage. We receive from the Spirit of life and so move away from an Old Covenant understanding of the Law. Jesus summed up all the Law and the Prophets in Himself, making love the focus:

"A new commandment I give to you, that you love one another, even as I have loved you, that you also love one another. By this all men will know that you are My disciples, if you have love for one another." (John 13:34-5).

Love sums everything up. We cannot love others out of law, duty or obligation; we need to receive love from Jesus to be inspired to love in the same way. John 15:12 reiterates this: "Love one another as I have loved you."

Do we see ourselves as living epistles, receiving and releasing unconditional love? Are we living letters to the world, to the cosmos, reflecting unconditional love? Are we expressing unconditional love in our lives, to our families, in our workplaces, and to our friends and neighbours? If we are, people will be drawn to Jesus; if not, they may be pushed away. It is vital that we become living love letters to the world. This is the mandate of sonship: to be fruitful, multiply, increase, fill the earth, subdue it, and rule, establishing God's kingdom on earth as it is in heaven. Unconditional love transforms our lives, bringing us into this freedom of sonship.

Paul's life was transformed by a heavenly vision of God's unconditional love, and he preached this love to the Gentiles. The world needs to be awakened by unconditional love, to find their identity and the truth of who they are in God. In these uncertain times, with so much double-mindedness and insecurity, people are searching both for answers and for love. Are they looking in the right place? Will they find them?

We are all on a journey to discover unconditional love, which will take us beyond every barrier and limitation. It will lead us to the limitlessness of grace, triumph and mercy, allowing us to actively participate in the restoration of all things. Creation itself longs for the revealing of the sons of God, those who have experienced and demonstrate unconditional love.

So I invite you to open your hearts and minds. Allow the Holy Spirit to deconstruct your old understandings and engage with the living Word of God, Jesus, to find the truth. The truth you know by experience will set you free, giving you a testimony that can set others free as well.

Activation #6
Deconstructing Religious Mindsets

Let's take a few minutes
to engage with God,
with unconditional love,
and experience that.

> I encourage you to close your eyes,
> begin to still your heart
> and still your mind.

To stream the audio, scan the QR code or visit the resources page.

[In the audio recording, I release some frequencies so that you can engage in the reality of unconditional love yourself.]

Focus your thinking and your intention on the sound,
the frequency of unconditional love.
Feel that unconditional love flow through you.
Feel the vibrational frequency of unconditional love.

Be still.
Be still and let God love on you.
Just be still and let the love of God,
that unconditional love, rest on you.
That He reveals Himself to you as unconditional love.

Perhaps you want to ask Jesus, as the Truth,
to speak to you something specific right now.
"You have heard it said, but I say unto you..."
Open up your heart
Open up your mind.

Maybe some belief system,
maybe the way you've looked at God,
or maybe the way you've been programmed
with religious thinking, some mindset or belief system.
Just open up your heart.

And you ask Jesus, as the Truth,
the living, active Word of God
to show you something where He is saying
"You've heard it said... you believe this,
but I say unto you... this."
Just spend a few moments listening
opening up your heart.
Listen to His voice revealing something to you
that will bring freedom to you at this moment
that will bring truth to you at this moment.

Just let that frequency of His voice engage you.

You might want to be proactive
and ask the Father to begin

that process of deconstruction,
that you would have your own picture
of all the things you've believed and understood
as a tapestry in front of you
that would unravel
as the truth reveals those things
we've leaned our understanding towards.

Ask the Father to begin (or continue)
that process of deconstruction,
renewal of your mind,
bringing you into agreement with the mind of God.
We are one with the mind of Christ,
in agreement,
agreeing with His mind about you.

I believe that the Father
wants to speak to you directly right now
and tell you just one thing
of the vast sum of His thoughts about you
which will change your thinking.

Open up your heart
open up your mind
and hear Him speak
that one of those amazing thoughts He has about you
that will just totally transform your thinking
on that one thing.

Just listen to Him
as He speaks words of encouragement and kindness
to bring you into the freedom of the truth.

Feel the unconditional love of God for you as His child
flow through your whole being.
Flowing through you, in you, around you.
You live in an atmosphere of unconditional love,
in an atmosphere of freedom,
of love, of joy, of peace, of rest.

You are cocooned in unconditional love,
in a safe place to explore,
a safe place for revelation to flow.
Heaven is open.
Set your desire upon engaging the Father's heart.

You can engage in the realm of light,
you can engage anywhere He wants to take you.
He'll take you deeper into that place of love,
show you experiences,
encounters with unconditional love,
revealing truth at a deeper level,
so that you can live loved,
free from guilt, shame, condemnation from your past.

That you can live loving
Releasing mercy.
Just as you have been forgiven,
you release forgiveness to all around you.

That you love living,
that you enjoy life to the full
so you can rest in love, in joy, in peace,
and truly experience the reality of who you really are
as a son of God,
as one who creation is looking to
as a living letter of unconditional love.

7. Pleasing God

Only our experience of unconditional love can free us from religious deception. We do not know we are being deceived until it is revealed. When it is, we face the challenge of deciding what to do with that new understanding. Let's allow God to renew our minds. Let's not be conformed to religious or cultural ideals but be transformed by the renewing of our minds to truly know the truth and who we are in relationship with God.

In this chapter, we will look at how we can move from duty, obligation and obedience to living in grace. Here is a quote from Cindy McPhee that resonates deeply with me: "As long as I have a sin consciousness, I will always see something wrong with me that God is not pleased with." How many of us have been there, constantly conscious of our failings? But being pleasing to God is about who we are, not what we do. We are His children, and He loves us.

If we think God is angry with us, we feel guilt and shame, which drives us away from His love. Grace and righteousness consciousness bring peace and joy. God is always smiling over us. I was not raised to believe that God was always pleased with me; and knowing that He loves me unconditionally, despite my flaws, changes everything.

This realisation shifts us from a sin consciousness to a righteousness consciousness. We are called righteous by God's work, not our own. I am still undergoing deconstruction of my old beliefs, as God challenges me to rethink one area after another. I cannot rely solely on my interpretation of the Bible; my relationship with Jesus and the Spirit of Truth is what transforms my thinking.

Plumb line

Using Bible verses can provide a starting point, but true understanding comes from engaging with the Spirit. Many things we think the Bible says are not accurate anyway, particularly in translation. For example, the concept of 'hell' as understood in English does not align with the original Hebrew and Greek terms used in scripture. It is the Spirit of Truth who provides the full revelation, not our interpretation.

Love, not the Law or the Bible, is the plumb line. If something aligns with unconditional love, it is from God. Anything that imposes a condition is not from God. Therefore we can use love as our measure for truth and allow it to be our guiding principle in our relationship with God and others. When we fully embrace God's unconditional love, it transforms our lives, moving us from a place of slavery to duty and obligation into a state of joyous rest and creativity. This rest, this profound sense of peace and acceptance, allows us to live authentically from our identity in Christ, rather than constantly striving to earn God's approval through our actions.

God's love is constant and unconditional. Our task is simply to receive it. When we do, it changes how we relate to others, to God, and to the world. All of creation is waiting for us to realise our true identity as sons of God, so it can be set free into the freedom of our glory.

It is a modern evangelical myth that if something is not in the Bible, it cannot be trusted or true. This perspective is often repeated, but most of modern life is not mentioned in the Bible. Written over 2000 years ago, the Bible predates modern technology and many aspects of contemporary life. For instance, there are no references to cell phones, cars or computers. Historically, Christians have sometimes used the Bible to oppose scientific progress through suspicion of anything not explicitly mentioned in the scriptures. This has led to absurd claims such as the continuing belief in a flat Earth, despite overwhelming scientific evidence to the contrary.

We must be careful not to fall into the trap of *sola scriptura* (scripture alone) as our sole reference for truth. Jesus is the Truth. The idea that if something is not in the Bible it should be viewed with suspicion can lead to legalism and bondage, creating unnecessary rules and absolutes that are not conducive to a loving, joy-filled relationship with God. Our relationship with God is based on His love, not on scripture. The Bible can provide guidance, but our primary discernment comes from our relationship with Jesus and the Holy Spirit.

Mixing Covenants

The Bible was not written directly to us, though God can speak through it. The Old Testament is not speaking directly to me; its prophetic passages point to Jesus, of whom I now have a fuller revelation in the Spirit. We must be careful not to assume everything in the Bible directly applies to us today. We need discernment to hear Jesus speaking to us directly, and not necessarily (or even primarily) through the Bible. Yet evangelicalism has conditioned many believers to think that everything in the Bible applies directly to them, including the entire Old Covenant. Hebrews 6:1-2 urges readers to move on beyond these elementary teachings. The Old Covenant was about preparing for Jesus; but now we have the fulfilment of those promises in Christ, we do not need to lay again the foundation of these Old Covenant practices.

Therefore let us move beyond the elementary teachings about Christ and be taken forward to maturity, not laying again the foundation of repentance from acts that lead to death, and of faith in God, instruction about cleansing rites, the laying on of hands, the resurrection of the dead, and eternal judgment (Hebrews 6:1-2).

Reading the Bible through this new lens can be transformative. For example, the Mirror Bible presents a perspective that emphasises inclusiveness and seeing ourselves reflected in Jesus. Hebrews 6:1-2 in that version encourages readers to "leave behind the sentimental attachment to Old Covenant teachings and embrace the completeness of the New Covenant".

Our understanding of faith will also shift. In the Old Covenant, faith was about believing in what was not yet seen. Now, having experienced God, we can rely on His faithfulness. Our relationship with God is not about our efforts to impress Him but about accepting the righteousness we have in Christ. Moving from a mindset of trying to impress God to one of faith righteousness in Christ is fundamental. It is not about our works or self-righteousness. All religious efforts to gain God's favour are dead works. The old system has no life left in it; it is dead and gone. Embracing the New Covenant allows us to live in the freedom and fullness of God's unconditional love.

And this is one of the big issues. Many New Testament, New Covenant believers have been taught to incorporate a mixture of the old and new into their beliefs and practice, influenced by the Law. They think they have to be obedient and to please God with their efforts, which only results in weariness and exhaustion.

All the Jewish teachings about ceremonial washings, baptisms and the laying on of hands to identify with a slain animal as a sacrifice were specific to the Old Covenant. So too were teachings pertaining to a sin consciousness, including the final resurrection of the dead to face judgment. None of them are relevant any longer in the New Covenant. The judgment has already been passed. We have been declared righteous, justified and innocent. There is no more judgment for us to face, other than the judgment seat of Christ, where anything contradictory to our identity will be wiped away by the fire of His eyes, leaving only gold, silver and precious stones on our scroll.

Understanding that these old practices are irrelevant is crucial because if we continue to depend on them, we are living in dead works. All these types and shadows were concluded and fulfilled in Christ. His resurrection bears testimony to the judgment He faced on humanity's behalf and the freedom from a sin-consciousness He now proclaims. We are free, and the truth we know will set us free. We need to experience this truth to live in the reality of the freedom that is ours in Christ.

With God's prompting, we can advance from the prophetic types and shadows of Old Covenant scriptures into the substance of what God has now spoken to us through His Son. The very beginning of this epistle to the Hebrews reminds us that God now speaks to us through His Son, and not as He did in the past. The overcoming power of the resurrection has changed everything. Life and the world are not the same. Those who were dead in Adam are now alive in Christ, which includes everyone and everything. It is important to embrace the inclusiveness of this reality.

The dead works and other doctrines mentioned in Hebrews 6:1-2 are not intended to be the foundation for New Covenant living. Unconditional love ends Old Covenant obedience, duty and obligation. Some may still desire to be obedient, but this is now about outworking a relationship with God, only doing what we see the Father doing, just as Jesus did. Obedience, as it is traditionally construed, implies fear of consequences if we do not comply. The mixing of covenants so prevalent in the church today risks leading us into this fear. God does not want us to fear consequences in making our choices to cooperate with Him. He wants us to choose out of love and honour, not obligation or fear of punishment. There is no place for duty and obligation within the New Covenant: they are Old Covenant concepts that need to be left behind.

> "Belief is not something to be learned but is an awakening to what has always been true about us."
> (Francois Du Toit).

When we awaken to the truth of how God sees us, we walk in the reality of that revelation, which is illuminating and unveiling.

The only faith that matters is driven by the agape love of our *Abba* Father, unveiled in the face of Jesus Christ. When we look at Jesus, we see and feel what He feels about us – the revelation of who He made us to be and the truth of who we are in Him. These wonderful thoughts are all good, and focusing on them can be life-transforming.

Respond from the heart

Living under grace means we are not obliged to fulfil or be obedient to the Law. Grace empowers us to prosper and succeed. It is God's divine ability given freely and abundantly. All of God's law is fulfilled in Jesus, and we are included in Him, under no obligation to ancient laws or traditions. We can have a direct relationship with the Father, who reveals His heart to us. In this relationship, we express His heart and align with it, becoming His voice as the true sons to whom creation responds.

Interestingly, there is no Hebrew word meaning 'obey' in the traditional sense. The Hebrew word often translated as 'obey,' *shema*, actually means to hear and respond from the heart with love. It implies saying 'yes' before even knowing what is asked. God is not looking for obedience: He desires a *shema* level of relationship, a heart that hears and responds. We respond 'yes' because we trust in His goodness, kindness, mercy, grace and love.

Understanding obedience as a heartfelt response transforms our relationship with God. It moves us away from fear and obligation, enabling us to live in the freedom and joy of knowing we are deeply loved and fully accepted by Him. When you are living in unconditional love, 'yes' comes very easily. When Jesus said, "I only do what I see the Father doing; I only say what I hear the Father saying", He was speaking about this kind of obedience through relationship.

Many Old Covenant foundational doctrines are still central to evangelical theology today, and certainly were in my life – I even preached on them as New Covenant foundations – repentance, faith, washings, baptisms, laying on of hands, resurrection of the dead and eternal judgment. I suggest you take all this back to God right now, to the Father, and ask Him to give you revelation of what we are living in under the New Covenant, because I no longer believe we are subject to those things any more.

And the Word became flesh, and dwelt among us, and we saw His glory, glory as of the only begotten from the Father, full of grace and truth... For the Law was given through Moses; grace and truth were realized through Jesus Christ (John 1:14, 17).

It is grace and truth that we need. We do not need to be living under the Law. In the early church, those who were of the Judaizing party persecuted others, trying to get them back under the Law. But they could not keep the Law in the Old Covenant: that was the whole point. We are not under the Law. We are not obliged to keep the Law. Gentiles were not obliged to keep the Law in the first place. There are certain truths in the Old Covenant that are universal, but they are all summed up in love.

The key is not to be drawn back to legalism, to rules and regulations, but to live from a place of love, rest, joy and peace. A Law-based view of God and mixing Old and New Covenant components in our lives will keep us living in sin-consciousness and lost identity. Without the Law, there is no sin. The Law identifies our lost identity because we cannot keep it. We cannot keep it in our own strength, in our own efforts; we will fail over and over again. The more we try, the wearier we will get. Living in a mixture of covenants today leads to a 'less-than' kind of life, which hinders our sonship and the ability of creation to respond to us.

Let's embrace the reality of living in grace. God is speaking to us directly today to help us navigate through the issues we face from a Kingdom of God perspective. The Kingdom of God is righteousness, peace and joy in the Holy Spirit. Abiding in a face-to-face love relationship is key to knowing our identity as sons of God. You can always substitute 'love' for 'God'. If you cannot, then something is amiss. We will know our identity because we are sons and daughters of love.

Co-heirs and co-creators

God, after He spoke long ago to the fathers in the prophets in many portions and in many ways, in these last days has spoken to us in His Son, whom He appointed heir of all things, through whom also He made the world. And He is the radiance of His glory and the exact representation of His nature, and upholds all things by the word of His power. When He had made purification of sins, He sat down at the right hand of the Majesty on high (Hebrews 1:1-3).

You have likely been taught that we are living in the 'last days' spoken of here and elsewhere in scripture. But 'these last days' are not the days we are living in today. This was written to Hebrews, to those who identified as Jewish believers in Jesus, in the last days of the Old Covenant that was coming to an end, fading away, and would eventually come to a complete close when the temple was destroyed (as Jesus promised) within that generation. Jesus spoke and He is still speaking to us today, but in context, these are not the 'last days.' These are just continuing days of relationship. We are living in this age in which we can hear His voice.

Jesus is appointed heir of all things. And what are we? Co-heirs of all things. We are made in the image of God, made to be creative as sons, and God has left things for us to complete. I was quite surprised when I encountered angelic beings and guardians who asked me to create more guardians, as there was a need for additional protection of the portals out in the cosmos. I was shocked. I thought, "What? You want me to create? Well, I'm not going to do that without checking with the Father." So I went back to the Father, and He said, "Why wouldn't you think you can create? You are made in my image. You know how to create things in your own life. Why wouldn't you think you can create things in the cosmos?" So I went back to the guardians, created more guardians, and assigned them roles. That was a big shift in my thinking about sonship and our ability to co-create with God.

If Jesus was appointed heir of all things and made the world and all things, and we are co-heirs, then we must see that creation is part of our role. Some of the restoration of all things will come from our creativity as sons of God. When we truly realise who we are, it will bring about the revelation of our glory. God wants us as sons to be His word, His voice, speaking with such power that His desires are at work.

The kingdom

When Jesus had made purification of sins through what He did on the cross and the resurrection, He sat down at the right hand of the Majesty on high. Daniel describes Jesus coming to the Ancient of Days, receiving the Kingdom, and giving the Kingdom to the saints of the Most High. He has given the Kingdom to us. In His power and authority as sons, when we know our authority, we too will be the radiance of His glory and the exact representation of His nature. We need to know unconditional love. All of creation is longing and waiting for us to know unconditional love so that we can represent Him and bring about the creative restoration He intended from the beginning.

Throughout ancient times, God spoke in many fragments and glimpses of prophetic thought to our fathers. Now this entire conversation has finally dawned in sonship. Suddenly, what seemed to be an ancient language falls fresh and new, like the dew on tender grass. Jesus is the sum total of every utterance of God. He is the one to whom the prophets pointed, and we are His immediate audience.

In a Son, God declares the incarnate Word to be the heir of all things. He is, after all, the author of the ages.

The Messiah-message is what has been on the tip of the Father's tongue all along. Now he is the crescendo of God's conversation with us and gives context and content to the authentic thought. Everything God had in mind for mankind is voiced in Him. The incarnate Christ-Messiah, Jesus, is God's language. He is the radiant and flawless mirror expression of the person of God. He makes the glorious intent of God visible and exhibits the character and every attribute of Elohim in human form.

Having accomplished the cleansing of our sins, he sat down, enthroned in the boundless measure of his majesty in the right hand of God. He is the force of the universe, upholding everything that exists by the word of his power. This conversation is the dynamic that sustains the entire cosmos (Hebrews 1:1-3 Mirror).

There is no need for more prophetic revelation because Jesus is the fulfilment of every prophetic word given in the Old Testament. God is not holding back: He is speaking through Jesus, revealing the fullness of who we are as sons of God. We have our beginning and our being in Him. He is speaking to us and continues to speak to us daily. Are we listening? Do we expect to hear from Him? Sonship endorses heirship. When we truly know who we are as sons of God, we will realise our full heirship and authority.

The fact that He is seated on His throne is the proof of mankind's redeemed innocence, because He has overcome sin, death and the grave. He has brought about the resurrection of mankind, who were dead in Adam and are now alive in Him.

Jesus came to take away the sin of the world and bring us into a relationship of love. God so loved the world that He sent Jesus so that we could have life, and life in abundance; the life of eternity, and the fullness of that life. He is not holding it back; He wants us to experience it. Jesus mirrors God's character and exhibits every attribute in human form. And Jesus said that we would do everything He did, and greater things:

"Truly, truly, I say to you, he who believes in Me, the works that I do, he will do also; and greater works than these he will do; because I go to the Father." (John 14:12).

So there is an expectation, not a heavy one, but rather an encouraging one. And we are now the light of the world:

"You are the light of the world. A city set on a hill cannot be hidden..." (Matthew 5:14).

When Jesus was on earth, He was the light of the world. Now, as His body on earth, we are called to show the world who He is. We are Jesus with skin on, here to love people and demonstrate unconditional love, grace and mercy so that they can come into a revelation of what has already happened to them: that they have been reconciled to Him, included in Him, and are now born from above, just waiting for that revelation to dawn.

You

That includes all mankind, not just some, though as yet only some know the reality and the truth of it. As James wrote in his letter, we have forgotten what manner of people we are:

Anyone who hears the word, sees the face of their birth, as in a mirror. The difference between a mere spectator and a participator is that both of them hear the same voice and perceive in its message the face of their own genesis reflected there; they realize that they are looking at themselves, but for the one it seems just too good to be true; this person departs [back to the old way of seeing themselves], and immediately forgets what manner of person they are; never giving another thought to the one they saw there in the mirror. The other is mesmerized by what they see; captivated by the effect of a law that frees them from the obligation to the old written code that restricted them to their own efforts and willpower. No distraction or contradiction can dim the impact of what is seen in the mirror concerning the law of perfect liberty [the law of faith] that now frees one to get on with the act of living the life [of their original design.] They find a new spontaneous lifestyle; the poetry of practical living (James 1:23-25 Mirror).

Sometimes these verses require meditating on to grasp the full weight of what they are saying. Jesus successfully rescued the real you, the 'you' that God always intended you to be. What did He rescue you from? From lost identity, from not knowing the real you. He has not rescued you to live as a pseudo, make-believe version of yourself or the 'you' that has been pressed into the world's mould, whether religious or cultural. He rescued the 'you' that He always intended, the 'you' He has a vast sum of thoughts about, the 'you' described as fearfully and wonderfully made. That is the 'you' that He wants you to come into the revelation of and live as. That is the 'you' that the universe is waiting for. That is the 'you' that creation is longing to see revealed.

God has never believed less of you than what He was able to communicate in the sonship that Jesus mirrored and redeemed. You might have believed less of yourself, perhaps because you have listened to your own thoughts or the thoughts of others, to religious thinking; but He has fully revealed you in revealing Jesus, and you are mirrored in Him. You are a joint heir, a co-heir, a son of God. That is a wonderful truth.

Do not try!

The elementary teachings about Christ were like the Old Covenant schoolmaster (as it says in Galatians 3:24), to help them find Christ. But in the New Covenant, we move on to maturity, not needing the Old Covenant teachings anymore because we have the revealed truth and the fulfilment of it. No one could keep or fulfil the Law but Jesus. So do not try! Do not try to be obedient to earn something; and do not think you have to please God every day out of duty, obligation or fear. Enjoy resting in the wonderful, unconditional love of God. Enjoy resting in that marvellous truth.

And we have known and have believed the love which God has in us. God is love, and he who abides in love abides in God and God abides in him (1 John 4:16 MLV).

This time, the Greek says 'in us' but most translators have written 'for us'. Only the literal versions reveal the reality that God's love is in us. It is not an external thing that we have to somehow inherit or get from outside. This is God in us. Unconditional love is already in us. Father, Son and Spirit are already in us, dwelling within us. Let's embrace the force of the full revelation and experience of God in us, that immanence of the infinite God abiding in us.

Love is who God is. To live in this place of conscious, constant love is to live immersed in God and to feel perfectly at home in His indwelling. Do you feel at home in your own skin? Do you really know who you are? Have you had that astonishing revelation of His indwelling love within us that wants to fill us? Let's make sure we open that gate, that first love door that Jesus is knocking on every day. He wants to fill us with unconditional love. He wants us to know the truth of that unconditional love, face to face, heart to heart, spirit to spirit. And it is already there within us; it is not a million miles away; it is not separated from us. It is in us, and God wants us to fully experience that reality.

Therefore, let us ensure we are unconditional-love-focused; that we are not sin-conscious but unconditional-love-conscious; inclusion-focused, focused on the reality that we are already reconciled, already included. All are loved and all are included, with no exceptions. None at all. He wants us to know this reality and truth.

Religious programming causes people to try to justify themselves, trying to attain what is already theirs. It is such futility to live that way. Religious people strive and put a lot of effort into their dead works that just make them tired and weary and burdened. Let's embrace the reality that unconditional love is already there, that it can be revealed, that we can experience it, that we can know it. And the more we know unconditional love, the more we will be able to demonstrate unconditional love to others; the more we will be able to reveal that all are included, not just those of us who know it, but those who do not, as yet.

All mankind

So then, as through one offense the result was condemnation to all mankind, so also through one act of righteousness the result was justification of life to all mankind (Romans 5:18).

That condemnation was not God's condemnation, but self-condemnation. As man separated himself from God, he became independent and therefore dependent on his own effort to get back what he had lost.

It is hard to see how we have missed the inclusive message Paul has penned here. The 'all' is the same 'all' in both parts of this verse. All came under that self-condemnation of living separated from God (because we separated ourselves from Him: He never separated himself from us). Therefore, what Jesus did now justifies all.

The conclusion is clear: if one offense condemns the entire human race; then, in principle, the righteousness of one vindicates the entire human race (Romans 5:18 Mirror).

We see, then, that as one act of sin exposed the whole race of men to God's judgment and condemnation, so one act of perfect righteousness presents all men freely acquitted in the sight of God (Romans 5:18 JBP).

> "You can't make what Adam did affect all, but put conditions on what Jesus did for all. Religion would have you believe that you had no choice with Adam; you were born into it. But when it comes to what the last Adam, Jesus, did, it is just an offer that you must do something to have. What a slap in the face of the finished work of the cross! It is finished. It is done." (Don Keathley).

Unconditional love has been released in fullness, and God wants us to fully embrace and know the reality of that unconditional love. He wants us to enter it. He wants us to know the truth of it by experience in our everyday life. He wants us to fully embrace the reality that His love is in us, that His power is in us. His resurrection power has overcome all the negative things in our lives, and He wants us to enter into the fullness of that reality, the fullness of that truth. Our salvation, everything that God has done to reconcile us, to forgive us, is already true. We only need to come to the realisation to experientially enter into what has already been accomplished for us by Jesus so that we can be living loved, love living and live loving. Let's not resist. Let's not try to do it in our own strength. Let's not try to earn what is already ours. Let's receive that extraordinary, unconditional love and embrace it.

Activation #7
An atmosphere of unconditional love

I encourage you to come to a place where you begin to rest. It is easier sometimes to close our eyes so that we can come to that place where we are living, abiding in unconditional love.

So let's start to meditate,
to fix our thinking, to fix our heart.
Slow down your breathing, get comfortable.
Breathe in slowly
and breathe out slowly.
Gently breathing in,
breathing out,
slowing everything down,
focusing your thoughts and thinking
on 'God is love',
God is unconditional love.

Breathe in,
breathe it out.
Breathe it in,
breathe deeply.

Maybe you just want to open that first love gate,
welcome unconditional love to fill you.
Spirit, soul, body –
unconditional love flowing through your whole being.

Be still.
Let God love on you.
Let Him embrace you in that hug
heart-to-heart.
Let Him reveal the truth of who you are.
Feel that unconditional love.

And if there's anything in you right now
contradicting that thought
of being loved unconditionally –

maybe that you're not good enough,
maybe that you've not been obedient enough,
that you have not done everything you could have done
or should have done,
any negative thing –
hand it over to Him now.
Don't hold on to wrong thinking,
any guilt, any shame, any condemnation.
Let unconditional love wash you clean,
bringing you into that revelation that you are righteous,
the righteousness of God in Christ.

Meditate on this reality right now:
You are the righteousness of God in Christ.
You have been declared innocent,
not guilty, forgiven, justified, reconciled.

Be still.
Fix your thoughts on unconditional love.
Stop striving, by effort or dead works.
Hand all those dead works over to Him.
Let it all go.
And embrace that truth:
you are loved unconditionally.

Unconditional love is filling you right now,
flowing through your whole being
like rivers of living water.
You're drinking deeply
from the fountain of unconditional love.
It is touching every atom,
every particle of your whole being:
saturated, soaked, immersed in unconditional love.

And let unconditional love
bring you into that place of full joy, full peace,
where the truth and the light
of limitless grace and triumphant mercy surround you.
You feel totally at rest,
that love, joy, and peace resting upon you,

flowing in you,
opening that whole revelation.

That atmosphere is around you right now.
Rest in it.
Rest deeply, resting in unconditional love
that's flowing in you, through you...
Let it flow around you,
create an atmosphere around you.
Don't contain it;
let it flow from you.
When anyone comes across you in everyday life,
they will feel unconditional love.
They might not know what it is,
but they will feel and sense
the atmosphere that you live in.
You are able to live in that atmosphere of rest,
resting in God's unconditional love for you.
It's what the world is looking for.

You are in a safe place,
surrounded by unconditional love.
Let Him heal you, restore you and make you whole,
bring you into the fullness of the reality of who you are
as He speaks words of encouragement to you right now,
revealing one of those
vast sums of thoughts He has about you.
Be still.
Listen to Him speaking a thought to you,
revealing a truth of who you are.

Rest in that thought,
filled with that truth.
Be transformed by the renewing of your mind
to fully believe –
that *metanoia* moment
where you come into agreement
with who you truly are as a son of God.

Embrace it.
Embrace the truth.
Embrace the love of God for you.

Live loved.
Love living.
Live loving.

Rest in that place.

8. The Extent of Love

It can prove very difficult to hear God speak to us directly through our religious filters and programming. There is often too much background noise and distortion to clearly hear what He is saying, especially when it challenges what we may already believe. And if we are using the Bible as a manual for our lives or the way we expect God to speak to us, then which version are we using? Whose interpretation? Jesus said, "My sheep will hear My voice," so we know that He wants us to hear Him speak to us.

As we have mentioned, for the first 385 years there was no Bible, yet the gospel spread around the world. Once the Bible was canonised, western civilisation descended into the Dark Ages. I think there is a correlation there because people started using a book to tell them what to do rather than listening to the Spirit. The Spirit is speaking to us; Jesus is the Spirit of Truth, and He wants to lead and guide us daily.

Please or appease

Unfortunately, many believers spend so much time trying to please or appease God that they have very little time to enjoy and live in love. God wants you to live in a state of love, being loved unconditionally. When you live in that state, it frees you from all those things that make you weary and burdened. Jesus said,

"Come to Me, all who are weary and heavy-laden, and I will give you rest. Take My yoke upon you and learn from Me, for I am gentle and humble in heart, and you will find rest for your souls. For My yoke is easy, and My burden is light." (Matthew 11:28-30).

He was challenging what they were doing in the Old Covenant system and urging them to come to Him in relationship and find the reality of the New Covenant. The weight of all those heavy traditions of men and rabbinical traditions which were layered around the Law, supposedly to keep them safe, actually kept them in bondage. Jesus came to set them free, saying, "Come to Me and find rest." I believe that is what God wants us all to find: the place of rest in relationship where we discover that we are loved unconditionally.

Life can be wearisome and lacking in joy if we are constantly striving to please God and trying to be acceptable to Him. In reality, God loves us unconditionally because we are His children. We really do need some deprogramming from all the religious thinking so that we can hear, see, and experience more clearly when God is speaking to us and what He wants to bring us into. Our personal experiences of engaging God face-to-face will create the cognitive dissonance necessary to deconstruct false beliefs. Cognitive dissonance is what occurs when you have an experience that challenges your beliefs, and you must decide whether to stick with your belief despite the experience or let the experience change your belief. I encourage you to let your experiences with God change what you believe about Him and to cooperate with Him in that process.

The extent of love

So, just how powerful and wide-reaching is the unconditional love of God? I would suggest it is limitless, beyond anything we could ever imagine or think, and then some more beyond that. Infinite, unfathomable. God is love, and that love is beyond our understanding, but it is an experience we can have and go deeper and deeper into.

> *... that He would grant you, according to the riches of His glory, to be strengthened with power through His Spirit in the inner man so that Christ may dwell in your hearts through faith; and that you, being rooted and grounded in love, may be able to comprehend with all the saints what is the breadth and length and height and depth, and to know the love of Christ which surpasses knowledge, that you may be filled up to all the fullness of God* (Ephesians 3:16).

It is vitally important that we engage with God within us. Much of what we call Mystic Christianity is about engaging outwardly, going into heaven, or into another dimension. But first, we need to find God within us. God dwells in us, Father, Son and Spirit, within our spirit. They want to fill us, they want us to drink from the fountain of life within us, so that we can be strengthened in our inner man, in our innermost being.

And what is the extent of love? The breadth, length, height and depth of love? We may never fully comprehend it because it is infinite, utterly beyond our capability to see it in its entirety, but it is never beyond our ability to experience: in fact, we can never escape the love of God. Wherever we are, whatever state we are in, the love of God is there. As we encounter this love in all its dimensions, we will discover for ourselves that God is able to go beyond anything we could possibly imagine.

I have experienced this in recent times as I faced rejection, abandonment, and betrayal when my ex-wife left me. I had to deal with the pain and go through the process of forgiveness. God was with me all the way. His grace was amazing, limitless, and His mercy was triumphant. He brought me through it, and I reached a place where I had accepted that this was the situation and that God was with me. I had my relationship with Him, my life was good, and I would be content with that.

But God spoke to me and said, "Your attitude is rather selfish. Don't you think you can make someone else happy?" I had not even considered that. To cut a long story short, I found someone with whom I have never been happier. God graciously and mercifully refused to allow me to stay content where I was. Now I am in a relationship beyond anything I could ever have asked for, experiencing (both giving and receiving) a depth of love I never imagined possible. That is how unconditionally loving God is.

God knows where each of us is and wants the best for us. He desires to bring good out of every situation. Going through painful situations is never easy, but now I realise that God has brought something good out of it, so good that I would never have imagined it possible. We all can experience the level of

God's goodness and love in that unconditional way. Do not limit yourself by your own expectations. Allow God to bring you into the fullness of being. He does not want you to settle for second best or just being okay. He wants you to have the fullness of abundant life, which is about relationship with Him and with others. Be open for God to bring something good and wonderful into your life.

I desire for you to realize what the Father has always envisaged for you, so that you may know the magnitude of his intent and be dynamically reinforced in your inner being by the Spirit of God. This will ignite your faith to fully grasp the reality of the indwelling Christ. You are rooted and founded in love. Love is your invisible inner source, just like the root system of a tree and the foundation of a building. (The dimensions of your inner person exceed any other capacity that could possibly define you.) *Love is your reservoir of super human strength which causes you to see everyone equally sanctified in the context of the limitless extent of love's breadth and length and the extremities of its dimensions in depth and height.* (If we go blurry eyed at the dimensions of outer space, how could we possibly underestimate the height, length, breadth and depth of the love of Christ, which surpasses knowledge. In the dimensions of its breadth and length, we see its geographic, horizontal extent; the complete inclusion of the human race. 2 Corinthians 5:14, 16. The depth of his love reveals how his love rescued us from the deepest pits of hellish despair and led us as trophies in his triumphant procession on high. Ephesians 1:20,21. Ephesians 2:5,6, Ephesians 4:8-10, Colossians 3:1-4.)

I desire for you to become intimately acquainted with the love of Christ on the deepest possible level; far beyond the reach of a mere academic, intellectual grasp. Within the scope of this equation God finds the ultimate expression of their image and likeness in you. (So that you may be filled with all the fullness of God. Awaken to the consciousness of their closeness. Separation is an illusion. Oneness was God's idea all along. Father, Son and Spirit desire to express themselves through your touch, your voice, your presence; they are so happy to dwell in you. There is no place in the universe where God would rather be.) *We celebrate Elohim who supercharges us powerfully from within. Our biggest request or most amazing dream cannot match the extravagant proportion of their thoughts towards us* (Ephesians 3:16-20 Mirror, with selected author's notes).

That is just amazing writing, and I am so grateful for Francois Du Toit and for how the Mirror Bible expresses the heart of God. It opens up a whole different perspective to this reality. God desires to express Himself through your touch, your voice, your presence. He is so happy to dwell in you and express Himself through you so that the world can experience who He really is as love by the way that you love the world. Just as God so loved the world that He gave, so too if we so love the world then we will give of ourselves.

Unconditional love is limitless in its scope and capacity. Nothing is excluded, and all things are included. All things will be restored because of unconditional love, which has no boundaries or limitations. The work of the cross is finished. We cannot add to it or do something to activate it. It is already the truth. It is already in effect. We just need to enter into the realisation of all God has already done. It is finished, for all.

All

I just want to touch on that concept of 'all'. What is 'all'? What does 'all' mean?

For by Him all things were created, both in the heavens and on earth, visible and invisible, whether thrones or dominions or rulers or authorities – all things have been created through Him and for Him. He is before all things, and in Him all things hold together (Colossians 1:16-17).

This means that both the spiritual dynamic and the physical dynamic were created by Him. Our physical being was created on the earth, and our spiritual being was created in

Adam. The heavenly beings were created. All things have been created through Him and for Him. That is 'all'.

Some of those 'all things' decided that they knew better than God and chose to go their own way. God is before all those things, and in Him, all things hold together. Even those who chose to walk in their own independence and understanding, making their own decisions independently of Him, are held together in and by Him.

In Him, we live and move and have our being. (see Acts 17:28).

He is also head of the body, the church [ekklesia]; *and He is the beginning, the firstborn from the dead, so that He Himself will come to have first place in everything. For it was the Father's good pleasure for all the fullness to dwell in Him and through Him to reconcile all things to Himself* (Colossians 1:18-19).

All things He created will eventually have Him in first place. This is the same 'all things' that He created, held together, and reconciled through the blood of His cross, that He declared innocent and righteous, and from which He removed lost identity. All things. The extent of this love, its scope, the breadth, height, length and depth of God's unconditional love that reaches all things, is absolutely astounding:

... namely, that God was in Christ reconciling the world (kosmos) *to Himself, not counting their trespasses against them, and He has committed to us the word of reconciliation* (2 Corinthians 5:19).

God was in Christ, never separated from Jesus, reconciling the whole world (*kosmos*) to Himself, giving us the ministry of reconciliation. God does not count anyone's wrongdoings against them and has committed to us the word of reconciliation. We have the power of reconciliation in us, to express it through and around us – so the world will know the reality of God's love and be awakened to the reconciliation and restoration that is already taking place. That is why it is so important for us to know and share the unconditional love of God with the rest of the world who do not yet know it.

Through our engagement, we can enable them to see that this unconditional love is for them.

There is a wonderful old Welsh hymn about the love of God, *Here is love, vast as the ocean*[5]. One verse says:

> On the mount of crucifixion
> Fountains opened deep and wide
> Through the floodgates of God's mercy
> Flowed a vast and gracious tide.
> Grace and love, like mighty rivers,
> Poured incessant from above
> And heaven's peace and perfect justice
> Kissed a guilty world in love.

Those are wonderful words, and likely written from personal experience. We too can experience the floodgates of God's mercy, grace and unconditional love like those mighty rivers flowing out of heaven into our spirit, and through our spirit into the world. This is the amazing, unconditional love that God wants us to enjoy. We have moved from the conditions of the Old Covenant to the grace of the New Covenant, from the dead letters of the Law to living letters of grace. We are now the living examples of unconditional love and limitless grace to the world. We are the letter, just as Paul described:

You are our letter, written in our hearts, known and read by all men; being manifested that you are a letter of Christ, cared for by us, written not with ink but with the Spirit of the living God, not on tablets of stone but on tablets of human hearts (2 Corinthians 3:2-3).

God has written on the tablets of our human hearts, taking away the heart of stone and giving us a heart of flesh. He has put a new spirit in us.

---

[5] The hymn was originally written in Welsh by William Rees as *Dyma gariad fel y moroedd* and translated into English by William Edwards. Robin Mark has popularised it again in the current millennium.

Such confidence we have through Christ toward God. Not that we are adequate in ourselves to consider anything as coming from ourselves, but our adequacy is from God, who also made us adequate as servants of a New Covenant, not of the letter but of the Spirit; for the letter kills, but the Spirit gives life (2 Corinthians 3:4-6).

Our confidence toward God comes through Christ: Jesus did it all. The cross covered it all. Every accusation was nailed to that cross. There is nothing left to accuse us of, unless we listen to the accusations of the enemy and believe them. Instead, let's listen to the reality that we are not adequate in ourselves: we could never have engineered this or done anything to deserve it. It is received by grace. He made us adequate as servants of the New Covenant, to express unconditional love to the world in which we live. We are not here to bring people under the bondage of the Law, mixing covenants, or bringing them back under religious restrictions. Religion only brings death. If you put people back under the Law, it will kill them with a weight they cannot carry. The Spirit gives life in abundance and is the Spirit of truth, bringing us into the reality of relationship with God.

Instead of an impressive certificate framed on the wall, I have you framed in my heart. You are our epistle, written within us, an open letter speaking a global language everyone can read and recognize as their mother tongue. The fact that you are a Christ-Epistle shines as bright as day. This is what our ministry is all about. The Spirit of God is the living ink. Every trace of the Spirit's influence on the heart is what gives permanence to this conversation. We are not talking law-language here. This is more dynamic and permanent than letters chiseled in stone. This conversation is embroidered in your inner consciousness. Christ is proof of our persuasion about you before God.

We have not reached this conclusion by any merit of our own. It is God's doing. He has made us acceptable and righteous. It is God's signature in our spirit that authorizes New Testament ministry. We are not qualified by a legal document endorsed by a fellow human. The letter [of the law] is the administration of death; it is the Spirit [of grace] that ignites life (2 Corinthians 3:2-6 Mirror).

The world is desperately looking for life and love. Every single person and being is designed to reconnect to love. Let our lives be a living letter, a living testimony of God's love to the world, in our homes, workplaces, neighbourhoods, and wherever we are.

Unconditional love is the power that holds the universe together, and God is that unconditional love. He wants us to express this to the world because we are co-heirs with Him in the Kingdom. He wants us to enjoy living in love. Everything has moved from rules to relationships; not letters engraved on stone or written on paper, but living words written on our hearts. We become a living expression of God's love, grace and mercy to this world.

The Great Conversation

Francois Du Toit, the translator of the Mirror Bible, wrote:

> Two thousand and twenty-two years ago the conversation that had begun before time was recorded, sustained in fragments of thought throughout the ages, whispered in prophetic language, chiselled in stone and inscribed in human consciousness and memory, became a man. Beyond the tablet of stone, the papyrus scroll or parchment roll, human life has become the articulate voice of God. Jesus is the crescendo of God's conversation with humankind; he gives context and content to the authentic thought. Everything that God had in mind for man is voiced in him.

> Jesus is God's language. His name declares his mission. As Saviour of the world, he truly redeemed the image and likeness of the invisible God and made him apparent again in human form, not as in a display window, but as in a mirror! (Hebrews 1:1-3. 2 Corinthians 3:18).

> Oh, what freedom to conclude that I am not here to justify my existence but I am here because I am justified. I do not live my life to defend a doctrine but rather to declare the truth about everyone! To commend my life to every person's truth consciousness with the open statement of the truth, because everyone's life shares the same integrity in both design and redemption. Therefore "I do not preach myself but Christ" (2 Cor. 4:2,5). "Even as the truth is embodied in Christ" (Eph. 4:21).

You are the expression of God to the world. You are 'Jesus with skin on', as the popular phrase has it. You are one of the vast sum of God's thoughts. When God has a conversation, we are in it; within the *perichoresis*, the circle of the conversation between Father, Son and Spirit. We are in the midst of it. He is speaking not only for us but also through us. He wants us to experience and know the reality of that. This is what we need to convey to the world: that they are reconciled, they have been forgiven, they have been born from above, they have been included in Christ, they have been included in the New Covenant, and in the *perichoresis*. Let's make sure we look at people the way God looks at them; and remember that He looks at us in the same way.

We are the living expression of Jesus to the world, and He wants us to fully know the reality of that so the world will know it. The whole cosmos needs an unconditional love awakening to reveal the truth of God as Father, and the nature of God as love. Our testimony of unconditional love is a vital component to the world awakening to the reality of love.

So let's ask ourselves, what are we expressing? Are we expressing religion? Are we expressing law? Are we expressing legalism? Are we focusing on external behaviour, or are we expressing unconditional love? The accuser uses religion to hide and obstruct unconditional love with ifs and buts. Unconditional love was Jesus' motivation in all He did for us: in the power of that love, even over death, through resurrection life.

Because of our justification

He who was delivered over because of our transgressions, and was raised because of our justification (Romans 4:25).

That is a profound statement, and the NASB has it right. The NIV and several other translations have it wrong. He was raised to life 'because of' our justification, not 'for' our justification. What Jesus did on the cross brought us out of death and into life. Here is the equation:

He was handed over because of humanity's fallen condition;
He was raised because we were declared righteous.
His resurrection is the official receipt of our acquittal.

Think of that: you are acquitted and declared innocent and justified. He rose from the dead because you were declared righteous. The power of the cross, and of the resurrection, triumphed over death and what was the power of sin. Therefore, the power of our lost identity is now defeated and broken. His cross equals our sins; His resurrection equals our innocence. His death brought closure to our fallen condition. His resurrection is proof of our redeemed righteousness.

Why was Jesus handed over to die? Because of our transgressions. Why was He raised from the dead? Because of our righteousness. His resurrection reveals our righteousness. If humanity was still guilty after Jesus died, His resurrection would be irrelevant. But we are not; we are declared righteous, declared innocent.

For the love of Christ controls us, having concluded this, that one died for all, therefore all died; and He died for all, so that they who live might no longer live for themselves, but for Him who died and rose again on their behalf (2 Corinthians 5:14-15).

Everyone has died with Him, and therefore death no longer has any power over us, just as it had no power over Him. He died for all, Paul says – again, this is one of his many inclusive statements. One died for all; all died. He died for all, to bring us into a whole new relationship in which we are no longer living independently, but in cooperation, harmony, oneness and union with Him.

New creation reality

Therefore if anyone is in Christ, he is a new creature; the old things passed away; behold, new things have come (2 Corinthians 5:17).

The word 'if' there does not mean that it is in doubt. People read that verse and say, "Well, that means some might not be in Christ; there's an if, there's a doubt." Paul is not saying that. He has already made it clear that all are included in Christ: therefore everyone is a new creature because we are all in Christ. Paul's message and heavenly vision were to preach Christ in the Gentiles, to preach Christ already in us. There is no doubt because all are included in Him, His death, and His resurrection. Therefore, all of us are new creations in Christ Jesus through the astonishing, wonderful victory of love that has overcome death.

The love of Christ constrains and resonates within us, leaving us with only one conclusion: Jesus died humanity's death; therefore, in God's logic, every individual simultaneously died. Now, if all were included in His death, they were equally included in His resurrection. This unveiling of His love redefines human life. Whatever reference we could have of ourselves outside of our association with Christ is no longer relevant.

This is radical and our most defining moment. No label that could previously identify someone carries any further significance. No matter what anyone has said about you, no matter what you've said about yourself, no matter what is written in the record of your past, none of it defines who you are. No label defines you. The Father defines you as a son. Even our pet doctrines of Christ are redefined. Whatever we knew about Him, historically or sentimentally, is challenged by His conclusion. Now, in light of your co-inclusion in His death and resurrection, whoever you thought you were before, in Christ you are a brand new person!

The old ways of seeing yourself and everyone else are over. Acquaint yourself with the new. [By discovering Christ from God's point of view, we're discovering ourselves and every other human life from God's point of view. Paul sees by revelation that what Jesus redeemed in every person brings absolute closure and death to any other reasoning and judgment we may have had of ourselves or anyone else for that matter! This is our 'metanoia' moment! "From now on therefore, we no longer know anyone according to the flesh, even though we once knew Christ from a human and religious point of view"]. (2 Corinthians 5:14-17 Mirror, with selected author's notes).

Let's each of us get to know ourselves, get to know our new self, get to know the reality of who God says we are. Nothing of our own identity is relevant because we are new creations. We just have to see ourselves the way God sees us, by looking into the mirror of His face. We can allow Him to renew our mind to reveal the truth of the vast sum of thoughts He has about us, to reveal our identity as this brand new person. Let's make sure it is also the way we see everyone else: we cannot see anyone else the way we have looked at ourselves and the world in the past. We now see ourselves and everyone else through the eyes of our Father.

Metanoia means 'with new understanding'; agreeing with God. This is our moment where we agree with God about ourselves and others. From now on, we cannot look at the externals of what people do, or what their behaviour looks like. Even though we once knew Christ from a human or religious point of view, now we have a whole different perception.

How do we see the world around us? Are we seeing as sons? Are we seeing it through the eyes of the Father? Do we have love and compassion for it? How do we see people? Are we looking at their behaviour, what they have done; or their doctrine, what they believe; or are we looking at who they really are as children of God? Do we see people as being in or out, characterised or categorised by their beliefs, behaviours or appearance? Who is in, who is out? Everyone is in; no one is out. Let's make sure that we see people and include people in that same way. Do we see the light in everyone, or do we judge based on externals?

I had a vision once. I was in my office, meditating, and God showed me the front of our building. I went there in the spirit and watched as people walked in through the door. We have some of the most dishevelled people who come to our open access day centre. Sometimes they are living on the streets, living rough, struggling to make ends meet. Some of them are in addiction: their whole bodies, their whole lives, destroyed by drugs. Look at them, and what do you see? In the vision, when I was looking at people in the spirit, I saw light. I saw the person God had created them to be. I was no longer looking at what they looked like; I was no longer judging them based on their external appearance; I was seeing the light in all of them. Their spirit is alive. They may not know it yet, they may not experience it yet, but the reality is that they carry the life of God in them. They are children of God. They have a destiny.

Do we see the potential in everyone, or do we write people off because of their past? Or because of their present? Let's make sure we see the light, that we see the potential; that they are sons of the living God; that Jesus died for all of them; that all of them are included in Christ. Do we treat people the way God has treated us, with grace, mercy and love? Or are we judgmental towards them because of their behaviour, beliefs, the way they smell or the way they look? Let's make sure that we are those living letters, the expressions of God's love; that we are demonstrating God's love to this broken and hurting world that needs an awakening to the reality of who God truly is. We are all children of God; we are all sons of God. Most people do not yet know it. Substitute love for God in that statement: we are children of love; we are sons of love. God is love, and His love is (and can only ever be) unconditional.

Already true

There are no conditions, no religious requirements. Let's not put those religious requirements on others that we could not meet ourselves. Unconditional love has many characteristics, but they are all consistent and constant. They never fail, they never change. The fruit of the Spirit are all expressions of love. Righteousness is the full physical manifestation of love. God is so good. Love applies equally to everyone and everything, no exceptions, because God is love towards all that He has created. That is the precept of God.

Love is totally dependable because God is 100% love. God made all mankind (who were dead in Adam) alive and included all mankind in Christ. He dwells in all mankind. That is what He has already done. So what is left? Only for us to come to a realisation of the truth of what God has already done and embrace it for ourselves, so that our minds can be renewed to the reality of the truth of what has already occurred. That is the power of unconditional love: our salvation, reconciliation and forgiveness are already true. We only need to come to that realisation to experientially enter into what our Father has already accomplished for us through Jesus so we can be free to live lives of love. That is God's intention.

So we enter into the fullness. God wants us to experience this reality and come deeper and deeper into it. We can empathise with the world, because Jesus came to those who were lost and lonely, broken and damaged, living in lost identity, stigmatised, separated, ostracised, and unclean. Jesus came to demonstrate the Father's love to so many people.

Have you experienced unconditional love? Are you living in unconditional love? Are you demonstrating unconditional love to this world that desperately needs it? Do you have a heavenly vision of unconditional love? Because God wants you to experience all this. He wants you to freely give what you have freely received. He wants us to enter into that reality.

Activation #8
Showing Unconditional Love

> Close your eyes.
> And as you get relaxed
> You might want to lie down.
> You might want to get your body
> Into a state of relaxation,
> Where you're comfortable.
>
> And start to focus on your breathing,
> Begin to slowly breathe in,
> Breathe out very, very slowly,
> Holding that breath.
> As you're breathing in and breathing out,
> Start thinking about God's love.
>
> Every breath that you take,
> As you breathe in deeply,
> You're breathing in
> The unconditional love of the Father for you.
>
> And as you breathe it in,
> Feel that unconditional love
> Flowing through your whole being,
> Drawing in that life of love
> Into your whole being.
>
> Breathe in slowly,
> Draw in that unconditional love of God.
> And be still.
>
> Be still and know that I am God.
> Be still and know that I am God.
> Be still and know.
>
> Just be, be, be...
>
> And let God begin to love on you,
> His love will rest on you,
> You'll be cocooned in His love,
> In a blanket, warm, comforting,

THE EXTENT OF LOVE

A safe place, a high tower
Safe and secure in His arms of love.

Feel the Father
Place His arms of love around you,
Feel His intense desire for you.
Feel His love, be still.

Let the unconditional love of God surround you,
Let the joy and the peace
And the truth and the light
And the limitless grace
And triumphant mercy blanket you,
Cocoon you into that safe, safe place.

Rest,
As love, joy and peace fill your innermost being,
They begin to flow through you,
Creating an atmosphere around you of love.

Direct that flow.
Think about someone right now
Who needs a touch of unconditional love.
Think about someone
Who needs to know God's forgiveness,
Who needs to know that they are loved unconditionally.

Maybe someone that you're struggling with,
Or you have a disagreement with:
Choose to forgive and release them,
Bless them,
And focus that unconditional love into their lives.

Begin to think of those people
Who come to your mind,
That you can focus the love of God towards,
either physically or in the spirit.

Let the Father show you.
Open up your heart,
And direct that love

As a river of living water
To touch someone's life.

You're in a safe place.
Heaven is open.
You're connected to heaven within.
The River of Life is flowing in you.

Desire to engage the Father's heart.
The Father will take you
To that place within His heart,
The realm of light,
To experience the light of love and truth.

The Father wants to speak to you,
Open up the ears of your heart, to listen
As He reveals some of the vast sum
Of His thoughts about you.

Face to face,
Heart to heart.
Cardiognosis,
Knowledge of the heart,
an infusion of revelation knowledge
of who God is as unconditional love,
And who you are as a son of God.

To see the light of His face,
Enter in.
See Him smiling over you,
See into the depths of His eyes,
How deep,
How wide,
How high,
How long,
Is the unconditional love of God.

Rest in that place.

9. Relationship is All God Desires

I saw this quote online. I am sorry, I do not know who said it, but it describes what is happening very well:

> "A huge shift is beginning to take place. It's a shift from an emphasis and priority on set-in-concrete doctrines and theology to a red-hot pursuit of the love that Jesus taught and demonstrated."

When Jesus was here, He was a demonstration of God being love, and that is what He taught his disciples: "Love one another as I've loved you." That is the key to our whole life. If we receive the love of God, then we will be able to love others with that same dimension of love in the same way. That will radically impact the body of Christ and blur the lines of forty thousand denominations, once again turning the world upside down as it did in the first century. If we get back to the simplicity of demonstrating that God is love and loving people the way we are loved, we will change the world. There needs to be an awakening to love, which will bring about that transformation.

I believe when we receive a revelation of unconditional love, it truly transforms life. Rest then becomes the state of being that we inhabit, even in the everyday tasks that may seem mundane and routine. Even the most ordinary activities can become an opportunity to enjoy intimacy with God as sons, sharing a close relationship with the Father. We can enjoy the reality that we are never separated. We can live and dwell multi-dimensionally in His presence and enjoy that reality all the time in everything we do. There is no religious and secular; there is no separation between my relationship with God and the things I do in life. My relationship with God brings me to a state of rest so that the things I do in life, I do through the reality of who He is.

A transition occurred during the generation when the Old Covenant was fading away. They were in a pivotal period of overlap between the old age and the new age: the 'last days' of the old age, before the new age was fully realised.

When He said, "A New Covenant," He has made the first obsolete. But whatever is becoming obsolete and growing old is ready to disappear (Hebrews 8:13).

If something is obsolete, it no longer has any value or purpose. The Old Covenant is completely obsolete, has no value or purpose whatsoever, and has been completely fulfilled in the New Covenant. It no longer has any value or validity, but people are still hanging on to it. In that period, the whole Jewish system was hanging on to it. Saul, for instance, was utterly committed to that system. Even as Jesus was already in him, at work to reveal Himself, he was stubbornly sticking to his self-righteous, obsolete, Old Covenant, Law-based system of trying to please and appease God, ironically by persecuting Christians! This was the time they were living in, and this was the context in which the New Testament was written. This was the transitional generation before the final end of the age, which ultimately occurred, as Jesus prophesied in Matthew 24, in that generation. The end finally happened in AD 70 when the Roman armies destroyed Jerusalem.

For if that first covenant had been free of fault, no circumstances would have been sought for a second. For in finding fault with the people, He says,

"Behold, days are coming," says the Lord,
"When I will bring about a new covenant
With the house of Israel and the house of Judah,
Not like the covenant which I made with their fathers
On the day I took them by the hand
To bring them out of the land of Egypt;
For they did not continue in My covenant,
And I did not care about them," says the Lord.
(Hebrews 8:7-9).

If the first covenant had been faultless, there would have been no need and no occasion to seek out a second. So clearly the first covenant was not faultless – in fact, the opposite. The Old Covenant was made with Israel and Judah but the New Covenant is made with Christ and has universal application. It is not "like the covenant which I made with their fathers" because in that covenant there was a condition: obedience. If they chose to disobey and walk outside of the covenant's protection, then they were subject to attack. We see that over and over again in the Book of Judges, where they stopped following God and followed other gods. God said, "Okay, if you want to follow those gods, you can, but let them care for you." And of course, they did not care for them, and then they were subject to the Philistines, Moabites, Ammonites, and anyone else who attacked them. Eventually they would cry out to God for help, and He would send them another judge to get them back on track.

"For this is the covenant that I will make with the house of Israel after those days, says the Lord: I will put My laws into their minds, and I will write them on their hearts. and I will be their God, and they shall be My people. And they shall not teach everyone his fellow citizen, and everyone his brother, saying, 'Know the Lord,' for all will know Me, from the least to the greatest of them. For I will be merciful to their iniquities, and I will remember their sins no more." (Hebrews 8:10-12).

Here, God was talking to those who classed themselves as the people of God, but were not the people of God as Paul described, the one new man in Christ. "After those days." After what days? The days of the Old Covenant. In this New Covenant, the laws He now writes on our hearts are not a set of laws that must be obeyed. We are in the New Covenant in Christ, which Christ has made with God. Therefore, He has fulfilled all of the Law and the Prophets. There are no laws to be obeyed, there is just the law of love. There is just the fact that we are now in a relationship, that God is within us, and that on our hearts is written the desire to outwork our destiny and fulfil who we are as sons of God.

Know the Lord

In the Old Covenant, only the priests really had access to know the Lord at all. God is now saying, "All will know me," not just those who keep to some religious system. And the word 'know' is to know by personal experience, not by being instructed about it. That is the message of the restoration of all things: all will know Him. They might not know Him now, but all will know Him. Whatever it takes, they will know Him, from the least to the greatest of them. It leaves no one out.

No one has to offer sacrifices and lay hands on scapegoats or any of the things they did in that Old Covenant system. God did not instigate any of these in any case: He never required sacrifices and offerings, it was people who needed all that. He no longer considers or even remembers our lost identity and the behaviour associated with it, which is astonishingly good news. This is such a powerful message of the unconditional nature of God's love which we have to share with the world!

This is new

If there had been no flaw in the first dispensation, why bother to replace it with a second? He had already faulted the first system when He said through Jeremiah, "Behold, the days will come when I will make an entirely New Covenant with the house of Israel and the house of Judah." (Hebrews 8:7-8 Mirror).

Jesus came into that Hebrew context, but He came to take away the sin of the whole world and our lost identity. What was originally just for one small group of people was now expanded to include everyone.

"We will be making a new agreement completely unlike the previous one based on external ritual. I had to literally take your hand and lead you out of slavery from Egypt, yet you refused to spontaneously follow or trust in me. I could never abide your indifference." [God prophesies a covenant that will not be subject to the same defect as the previous one, which was spoon-fed to Israel and whose obligations they failed to

meet. God had to take them by the hand and lead them out of Egypt. This time He promised, "I will put my laws into their minds and write them upon their hearts..."] (Hebrews 8:9 Mirror, with translator's note).

They were operating in their own strength, which was never enough, and would never be able to fulfil the Law. So the Law was given to show them they could not keep it, and their only option was to trust in God.

"Now instead of documenting my laws on stone, I will chisel them into the mind and engrave them into your inner consciousness; it will no longer be a one-sided affair. I will be your God and you will be my people, not by compulsion but by mutual desire." (Hebrews 8:10 Mirror).

In this new context, when we see 'my laws', let's avoid thinking of the ceremonial or legal system of the Old Covenant. Jesus came to completely change our understanding of God and what it means to have a relationship with Him. He summed everything up in one statement: "Love one another as I have loved you." This 'new commandment' sets the goal of the New Covenant: God's love empowers us to love others as He loves us. We love because He first loved us. This good news means we do not have to fulfil obligations or laws but simply to be in a relationship where we experience His love; which then empowers us to love others. Whenever we read the word 'law' in this context, it is about a relationship that inspires us to love as we have been loved.

"Knowing me will no longer be a Sunday school lesson or something taught by persuasive words of doctrine. Neither will they know me on account of family tradition or door-to-door evangelism [each one telling his neighbour]. *Everyone, from the most unlikely to the most prominent people in society, will know me inwardly."* (Hebrews 8:11 Mirror).

The kingdom is within; and God (Father, Son and Spirit) is within everybody. Everyone has been born from above through what Jesus did on the cross and in the resurrection.

All died with Jesus, all were made alive with Jesus, and now all have been raised with Jesus, ascended in Jesus and seated with Jesus in heavenly places. Most people do not know it yet, so our message is one of reconciliation to help them know what has already been done on their behalf because of love, grace and mercy.

"This knowledge of me will never again be based on a sin consciousness. My act of mercy extended in Christ as the New Covenant has removed every possible definition of sin from memory." (Hebrews 8:12 Mirror).

The problem of sin-consciousness lies not with God, but with humanity, as seen in Adam and Eve's hiding from God in the garden. Our perception of God as judgmental stems from this mentality, as do all feelings of guilt, shame and unworthiness, which cannot be resolved through laws or sacrifices. The sacrificial system for addressing the issue of sin (lost identity) only highlighted its shortcomings, pointing to the need for a saviour. Jesus' sacrifice does not change God's view of us but our view of God, eradicating sin-consciousness and revealing our true worth in His love.

It was not God's memory of our sins that needed to be addressed in the redemption of our innocence, it was our view of God and our experience of God which needed to be dealt with. It was our understanding and our separation in our own minds because of unworthiness, because of a lost identity in the reality of who we really are, and because of the mentality of the tree of the knowledge of good and evil. God is not judgmental, God is love; and God's judgment has already been made based in love, declaring us all innocent and therefore all reconciled. If we could have done it in our own strength, we would have; but we could not, because that system was powerless to achieve it. And so it ended. It retains no power within the New Covenant, yet people are still trying to resurrect it and function that way today. Wracked with guilt, they do not know the reality of the forgiveness that has been granted to them.

God reached out to Adam: He did not condemn him. He gave Adam the prophetic word that the seed of the woman was coming to deal with lost identity and bondage to death. That seed was Christ. The scapegoat principle, where the hands of the priest would symbolically transfer Israel's sins upon the head of an innocent animal, is exactly what happened in the scapegoat offering of Jesus as the Lamb of God. All sin, past, present, and future, was transferred to Him, and He took it to the cross and dealt with it, so it is no longer an issue. People may think it is, but God does not: He has already dealt with it. This is the gospel, and it is amazingly good news.

He died for us. He gave Himself so that we could die with Him, be resurrected with Him, and be brought into a restored state of relationship with Him and the Father. This is so extravagant that people feel it is too good to be true, literally incredible. Yet it is the truth. The love of God is more powerful than anything.

Relationship is all God desires

Sin-consciousness is a work-based mindset. Unconditional love removes the need for fulfilling a set of rules. The Old Covenant Law was a set of rules they could not keep, so why do we think we could keep them in the New Covenant? Do we think that we are now empowered by the Holy Spirit to keep the rules, or do we believe we are empowered by the Holy Spirit to enjoy a relationship with the Father; that we are in Him and He is in us?

We do not have to try to be obedient to rules or laws, because God's grace is limitless. Grace empowers us in our sonship relationship through desire. All we desire when we have this wonderful relationship with Him is to love others as He loves us, and to fulfil our destiny and our identity in relationship because we know He loves us unconditionally. This empowers us to stop focusing on (and striving to become) what we are not. It is a realisation of who we really are, a revealing of God's thoughts about us, which are remarkable and awesome.

We do not have to try to please God by being dutiful and fulfilling obligations, whatever we think those might be – being a good Christian, going to church, reading the Bible, praying every day, witnessing – all of those things we were conditioned and told we needed to do. Suddenly, none of them have any meaning when we know that we are loved unconditionally. Of course, we still want to do things that are in line with God's desire for us, fulfilling our destiny and our identity as He made us to be. The difference is that we do them not because we are not pleasing to Him, but because we already are! Relationship is all God desires of us, and everything else flows from that relationship.

Law and grace

When we compare and contrast the Old and New Covenants, we compare law and grace:

For the Law, since it has only a shadow of the good things to come and not the very form of things, can never, by the same sacrifices which they offer continually year by year, make perfect those who draw near (Hebrews 10:1).

The Law was only a shadow of the good things which were to come. We are now living in those good things, so why would we want to go back to the shadows of an old system (and one that was never for us in the first place)? This is why I struggle with people wanting to follow Jewish calendars or Jewish festivals when Jesus has fulfilled every one of them completely. Why would we go back to a shadow of the old? That is religion just trying to get us under the Law and under bondage.

That sacrificial system could not make them, you, or anyone perfect. But in the New Covenant, you have been made the righteousness of God in Christ. You are already righteous, already perfected in God's sight. That is the way He sees you. When we become conscious of that, we begin to live in the reality of being righteous, not in the false reality of being sinners saved by grace and trying our best and failing, feeling guilty, continually offering more sacrifices, working harder and making promises to God that we cannot keep, all because we feel so bad.

No guilt, shame or condemnation comes from God. It can come from self, it can come from others externally, and it can obviously come as an accusation against us which makes us feel bad, but God does not make that accusation. In the Old Covenant, there were daily sacrifices and offerings. In the New Covenant, there has been one sacrifice, once for all. There is a huge difference between daily trying to do something for God and daily living in the benefit of all He has accomplished, being empowered by His love to live as a son of God, living and demonstrating that sonship, that relationship, and that love.

... then He said, "Behold, I have come to do Your will." He takes away the first in order to establish the second. By this will we have been sanctified through the offering of the body of Jesus Christ once for all. Every priest stands daily ministering and offering time after time the same sacrifices, which can never take away sins; but He, having offered one sacrifice for sins for all time, sat down at the right hand of God (Hebrews 10:9-11).

Jesus takes away the first covenant in order to establish the second. You cannot have both fully running simultaneously. There was a generation in which both were in place, and then one was fully removed so the other could be fully revealed. We have been sanctified through the offering of the body of Jesus, once for all; it is a done deal. Enjoy and revel in it; you have the lavish abundance of God's love and grace poured out upon you, so you can receive it.

Many people today in the New Covenant still try to minister and offer their life in some sacrificial way. Now, I am not saying we cannot be living sacrifices, but all we do is offer ourselves to Jesus. He is the high priest who deals with us, transforms us, changes us, and perfects us to align us with who God already calls us to be and how He already sees us. It is we who have our minds renewed towards the truth, not God who has His mind renewed towards us. He has never changed the way He thinks about His children. He loves us always. Finally, Jesus, having offered one sacrifice for sins for all time, sat down at the right hand of God. It is a completed work. He is now enthroned in heaven, having fulfilled everything required to restore everything to God's original intention and purpose.

Heaven is open

In the Old Covenant, heaven was closed. In the New Covenant, heaven is opened. Now, some people in Old Covenant times did go into that realm, such as Elijah and Enoch, but those who died in that Old Covenant age went into Sheol to wait. If they were declared righteous by their obedience, they were thought to be in paradise; if not, they were in the other part of Sheol. Eventually, Jesus came and emptied the whole place by going in, preaching the good news, and bringing people out of there.

Therefore, brethren, since we have confidence to enter the holy place by the blood of Jesus, by a new and living way which He inaugurated for us through the veil, that is, His flesh, and since we have a great priest over the house of God, let us draw near with a sincere heart in full assurance of faith, having our hearts sprinkled clean from an evil conscience and our bodies washed with pure water (Hebrews 10:19-22).

So, literally, His dying opened up heaven. He became a door through which we could now enter in through a new and living way. We can now have confidence to enter the holy place. In the Old Covenant, the holy place and the holy of holies were places that only certain priests could go, and only once a year. Now it is open. This is such good news, and is another crucial difference between the Old and the New. In the Old, you had to go through a priest, a work, a ritual – and even then, you yourself could not enter. But now, everyone has the ability to access and go in. Jesus has cleansed us from every stain of sin, of our lost identity, so that we can live in the fullness of the New Covenant.

For you have not come to a mountain that can be touched, unto a blazing fire, and to darkness and gloom and whirlwind... (Hebrews 12:18).

That was how God was seen in the Old Covenant: on top of a mountain, in fire and smoke, a glorious sight, and yet they could not touch it; they did not even want to touch it; they were afraid. So they set up a mediatorial system in which Moses and the seventy elders went up the mountain on their behalf. That was the Old Covenant: you could not go too near the mountain because you would die. They were in fear.

But you have come to Mount Zion and to the city of the living God, the heavenly Jerusalem, and to myriads of angels, to the general assembly and church of the firstborn who are enrolled in heaven, and to God, the Judge of all, and to the spirits of the righteous made perfect, and to Jesus, the mediator of a New Covenant (Hebrews 12:22-24).

Not long ago someone told me about a prophetic council in the UK that had forbidden engagement with the cloud of witnesses, calling it necromancy. But they are not dead; they are just living in another realm; they are surrounding us, and commissioned by God at times to engage with us. They are 'the general assembly and church of the firstborn who are enrolled in heaven.'

Jesus is the mediator of a New Covenant. We do not need a priest; we do not need another priesthood. We are a royal priesthood who have absolute access through Jesus into a relationship with God in this New Covenant based on unconditional love.

A living relationship

"This is the covenant that I will make with them after those days," says the Lord, "I will put My laws upon their heart and on their mind I will write them. And their sins and their lawless deeds I will remember no more." (Hebrews 10:16-17).

This is the change: it is no longer a physical written rulebook of regulations, but a living relationship within a heart-to-heart, mind-to-mind, face-to-face encounter with the living God. The Law was a written set of rules with duties and obligations to be fulfilled, or face the consequences. The law written on our hearts and minds motivates and empowers us because it is the law of love. We have experienced love; we have encountered love. We know love is totally unconditional and never ending. It does not depend on what we do, but on who He is. And since it depends on who He is and He is love, then it never changes. So we do not have to do anything to make anything different, and neither does He.

This law of love is written within us; it is in our consciousness. It is the desire for us to fulfil who we are: our destiny, our identity as sons of God. We have a desire in our hearts to be who we really are, not because we are compelled to but because we desire to. That transformation is radical compared to an Old Covenant-based mentality. The church has mixed the old and the new to create a hybrid, which makes it very difficult for us to be free. The pure New Covenant life is totally free, with no mixture of Old Covenant Law-based thinking. It is a totally new way of living in which we are free to be ourselves: the selves God sees, the selves God calls us to be, the selves He made us to be, the selves we are and are becoming.

God does not remember sins. In the Old Covenant, there was an annual reminder of sins every year, but now God says, "Your sins and lawless deeds I will remember no more." Now there is forgiveness of these things, so there is no longer any offering for sin. It is finished; we do not need to offer any more. The offering has been made. You can receive forgiveness because it has already been given: all you have to do is accept it. God is not holding any sin against anyone in the whole world because He has reconciled the whole world to Himself through Jesus. He made peace with the whole world. But to enter into that reconciliation and peace, to experience it for ourselves, we have to repent – that is, change our mind, agree with what He says, and believe it.

In the Old Covenant, there was only a temporary covering for sin, requiring continuous sacrifices, which kept people in a state of sin consciousness. They were always reminded of their sins and their need for atonement. In the New Covenant, we have the forgiveness of sins and grace-consciousness. If we try to mix the Old and the New, we risk losing sight of limitless grace and unconditional love.

Let's not dwell on our past selves or who we were before we died with Christ and were made alive in Him. Instead, let's focus on who He says we are and live in the wonderful grace and unconditional love of that relationship. Obedience is an Old Covenant concept which can trap us into striving for performance: we might feel we have to obey God. But in the New Covenant, the relationship empowers us to fulfil our destiny and identity in Him, much as Jesus only did what He saw the Father doing; through relationship, not because of warnings, judgment or threats.

Find rest

In this New Covenant, we do not need to try to please God through works to be accepted. Striving will keep us from living in rest, constantly working for something that is already freely given. Jesus invites us to come to Him and find rest, to take His easy yoke and light burden. Our minds need to be deconstructed from false religious concepts and doctrines that place conditions on being loved, and renewed to the truth of unconditional love. When our minds are renewed, our belief system becomes a state of consciousness, not a set of beliefs to strive for but to experience.

Unconditional love is not a theory or an intellectual idea; it is something we can know through experience. Knowing we are loved empowers us to love. Experiencing unconditional love transforms us and frees us from the religious notion of an angry God. I encourage you to challenge yourself and ask the Holy Spirit to reveal if you are still living with any Old

Covenant understanding. Are you still trying to perform, earn, or do dead works to appease God? Are you fearful of an angry God who might be in a bad mood one day? God is not like that. He desires intimacy and relationship, and He is a loving Father who has given everything for us because He loves us so much.

Let's ensure we are not living in a false reality by mixing covenants. Are you operating through a mediator other than Christ? Do you feel obliged to read your Bible, pray every day, witness, attend church meetings, or tithe? Do you feel obliged or empowered, encouraged, and joyful in life? Old Covenant religion will keep you in bondage; New Covenant grace will free you to be your true self, free from any religious obligations or duties you have to perform in order to receive God's love or be worthy of it. God loves you because you are His child.

Do not allow anything to keep you from experiencing God's passion, His burning desire, and entering into the fullness of everything God has for you. Enter into the reality of God's unconditional love, so that you can trust Him: His faithfulness, His trustworthiness, dependability, reliability, consistency, constancy; His steadfastness, diligence and perseverance. God will never give up; His love will never fail. He wants us to experience that in all its fullness. If there is any sense in which you may still be living under that Old Covenant mindset, feel at all distrustful of God, or in any way in bondage to fear, then in the following meditation you will have an opportunity to hand it over as you experience unconditional love.

Activation #9:
Rest in Unconditional Love

> Close your eyes.
> Slow down your thinking.
> Rest, rest in love.
>
> As you're breathing in
> and breathing out
> the very breath of God;
> as you're breathing in that reality,

breathing in the very love of the Father,
and as you rest in love,
let the unconditional love of God rest on you.

And as you are just still,
so that God can love you and love on you,
open up your heart and your mind.
And just ask the Father to reveal,
are there any Old Covenant mindsets,
any Old Covenant belief system still operating?
Is there any mixture of covenant in your heart?

Open up your heart to listen
that the Father could show you.

And if there is anything
that's a mixture of covenants in your experience,
just hand it over to Him.
Take off those old
Old Covenant mindsets
and clothes, if you like,
and just hand them over to the Father.

And let Him clothe you in robes of righteousness.
Let Him clothe you in New Covenant grace,
mercy, unconditional love.

Let that unconditional love flow all over you
from the tip of your head
to the bottom of your toes.

Let that love roll down, flowing over you,
bringing you into that sense of such passion
that God has for you,
the revelation of that passion,
Of His burning desire for you.
His intense joy that He feels when He thinks of you.
His deep compassion
and overwhelming love.

Rest as that flows over you
flows into you,
flows through you,
filling you with unconditional love;
washing anything away which is the stain of your past:
any guilt, any shame, any condemnation;
and rest in that place.

Be still and know that He is unconditional love.
Be still and know that He is passionate about you.
Be still and know that He has a burning desire
for deep intimacy with you.
Be still and know that He has deep compassion.
Be still and know His overwhelming love.

Allow that love to continue to flow around you,
cocoon you.
You're in a safe place.
Open up your heart.
Ask the Father to take you deeper,
into His very presence,
into a heart-to-heart, face-to-face experience
of that overwhelming, unconditional love.
And rest in there. Rest.

Feel free to stay in that place of intimacy
where the love of God can bring transformation.

Part II

Consuming Fire

10. The 'Hell' Myth

Religion always creates doubt about how good and loving God is and introduces fear into the picture. Unconditional love is the very essence of who God is. His character and nature are a reflection of who He is and He cannot change depending on the situation. There are no situational ethics with God. He is consistent and reliable. God is the same yesterday, today and always will be, as He is I AM that I AM.

Unconditional love has so challenged some of the things I believed, and has set me free. It is only such an experience of unconditional love, I believe, that can really bring us freedom from the religious deception most of us have adopted in our lives in various forms. If you have never been brought up in a religious setting, that may not apply. But for most of us, there are beliefs and assumptions we struggle with or do not properly understand. Some of us have come to see that we once believed things which we now know are not really true. That is true for myself. There are so many things that I now realise were conditioned and programmed by my upbringing and by my religious experiences in church and elsewhere.

The one doctrine that challenged me the most, and was most difficult for me, came up when I was looking at how the power of God's love, the power of the resurrection, overcame death. That brought me face-to-face with the question of what happens to people after they die. I realised that I was programmed by a religious belief, which I now call the 'hell' myth. The word 'hell' is in inverted commas because it is not a biblical word at all. That myth really held sway in my life, even though it was not my conviction through personal study. I did not really like it, but it had never been an issue before.

God is good

When we realise that God is good, and He does not change, that gives us a great degree of security. We do not have to be afraid that He is going to change His mind about us, or that we might not have done well enough. As a teenager, I never was sure. "Did I pray the right prayer? Did I pray it in my heart well enough?" I was always somewhat insecure about my salvation because it came down to "Did I do it well enough?" Now I realise it is totally about what Jesus did on the cross. It does not depend on me at all.

Religion always creates doubt about how good and loving God is, and introduces fear into the picture, because that keeps people in line. You have to toe the line if you are afraid that you might be punished by God if you do not. He does not threaten us, so that we respond only out of fear; He loves us, so that we respond out of love. We love because He first loved us. We do not love Him out of the fear that otherwise something bad might happen. That is not the kind of love we aspire to, but it is probably where I was for a time in my life.

Love is the fire

Now there are some Bible verses which over the years have been quite challenging to me, but when I really got to grips with what they were saying, they became comforting to me because they were really expressing the concept of the power of God's love and how powerful that love is. "Perfect love casts out fear" (see 1 John 4:18). This is one such passage I have mentioned before:

Put me like a seal over your heart,
like a seal on your arm.
For love is as strong as death,
jealousy as severe as Sheol;
its flashes are flashes of fire,
the very flame of the LORD.
Many waters cannot quench love,
nor will rivers overflow it.
If a man were to give all the riches of his house for love,
it would be utterly despised.
(Song of Songs 8:6-7).

So love is the flame of the Lord. It is the fire of God's nature. He is jealous for us, in the sense that He wants the best for us. His love is more powerful than death and the grave and has overcome it. Nothing can match up to the power of the love of God.

Those verses also feature in a Misty Edwards song called 'You Won't Relent.' The first line is "You won't relent until you have it all." God wants all of us. He wants every one of us, and that love will not relent until He has a relationship with everyone and everything that He has created.

Peril and sword

Who will separate us from the love of Christ? Will tribulation, or distress, or persecution, or famine, or nakedness, or peril, or sword? (Romans 8:35).

Those were very real concerns for Paul's intended audience. They were living in the Roman Empire, which functioned on the basis of peril and sword, and there were a lot of things going on during those days which were very difficult for them to face. They were being persecuted by the religious people. They were being persecuted by the political people. It was a very tough time in which to live, and they were waiting for Jesus to come and bring an end to their suffering and persecution and bring them into a whole new life.

But in all these things we overwhelmingly conquer through Him who loved us. For I am convinced that neither death, nor life, nor angels, nor principalities, nor things present, nor things to come, nor powers, nor height, nor depth, nor any other created thing, will be able to separate us from the love of God, which is in Christ Jesus our Lord (Romans 8:37-39).

We can overwhelmingly conquer all such trials – tribulation, distress, persecution, famine, nakedness, peril or sword – because He loves us. And when we know He loves us, we do not have to doubt His love if some difficult things happen in our lives. God did not bring them about; they are a result of the world in which we live, sometimes even of our own poor decisions, the consequences of things we have done. But even when they are down to us, God still loves us and works to bring good out of them because His mercy is triumphant over everything.

Paul is being utterly comprehensive here – nothing in all of creation can separate us from the love of God in Christ Jesus. Height, depth, nothing above, nothing below, no created thing whatsoever has the power to cut us off from God's unconditional love for us in Christ. This is such an emphatic statement, and it derives from Paul's own experience and revelation of the vastness of God's love. He can say with total conviction that there are no exceptions, there are no loopholes. The love of God is inescapable and unbreakable for those who are in Christ (which is everyone). Paul understood that Jesus did not just die for our sins, but for the sins of the whole world. He reconciled the entire cosmos back to God and holds nothing against anyone. Love keeps no record of wrongs against it.

Love overcomes death

In Paul's gospel, death is not 'the doorway into eternal life,' as we may have been taught. Death is the enemy of the Father and ours as well. The last enemy to be destroyed is death; and in reality, death has already been defeated! The resurrection power of God has already caused everyone to be born from above and made alive in the spirit. Therefore, death has no sting, no power, unless we choose to give it power over us. The power of unconditional love even overcomes death itself.

This was the core message of the early church fathers. The grace and love of God cannot be escaped or overridden by anything, because God Himself is love incarnate. But sadly, this message has been largely lost or distorted in modern evangelical teachings. Today's typical gospel message has become one of exclusion rather than inclusion, placing conditions on God's love that we can never meet, leaving us always striving fruitlessly to be good enough, when the truth is that we have been made the very righteousness of God in Christ by His work, not our own.

Very bad news

Yet the consequences of our failures are still used to keep us following religious rules out of fear. One of the biggest threats used is that of eternal conscious torment in 'hell.' Somehow, something has become the 'good news' that is actually very bad news indeed. Why would we want to believe in a God who would torment and punish His children eternally? That is not the God of unconditional love that I know. But so many are still trapped in this fear of hell and punishment, so we must engage them with the truth of God's unfailing, merciful love to remove that fear.

I was theologically convinced long ago that the 'hell' I had been taught did not actually exist. But that mental conviction was not enough; I needed experiential revelation to transform my beliefs at a deeper level. God knew I wanted to see and experience the truth for myself, not just have information. So in that sense, everything I am sharing here comes out of my own personal experiences that dismantled my former beliefs so powerfully that I could no longer hold onto them. God was gracious to show me the reality in ways that produced that cognitive dissonance leading to transformation.

For many Christians, the doctrine of eternal conscious torment in 'hell' for unbelievers is a fixed, immutable belief that is beyond question. The world at large has widely rejected this slur on the character and nature of a God of unconditional love: that God would torment His children forever in fire. Sadly, much of the church has accepted, defended and propagated this falsehood, with some even suggesting that God gives people indestructible bodies just to burn eternally. Is that the portrait of our loving God? Not according to my experience of the Father's heart. He is nothing like that at all.

The consuming fire of God's presence

What does happen to people after they die? It is an important question to ask, because if people are fearful of what will happen to them after they die, then the answers can help them make the right choices before they do. And if they do die, hopefully they can also accept what happens after they die. Is death in this case more powerful than unconditional love? Absolutely not! Unconditional love has overcome death.

My personal experiences with Jesus and the Father have shown me what happens to people after they die: they go into the consuming fire of God's presence, into the consuming fire of His love. They took me into the fire, showed me that you can preach to people in the fire, and that those people can respond to that preaching and be reconciled back to a relationship with God. They can come into the love of God, become part of the cloud of witnesses, and enter into their eternal destiny. This gives me absolute, full confidence in the fact that death is not the end of choice for anybody, and that unconditional love wins in the end, because God is patient; God is kind; God will never give up. Love will never fail. So I believe that love will win over everyone in the end so that they will experience that love for themselves.

I used not to believe that because I was conditioned, like so many, to believe that you must make a choice for Jesus before you die; because if you die without Jesus, you are going to go to 'hell'. That was the gospel I heard over and over again. I never preached it because I did not really feel good about that in my heart, but I did accept it. I was conditioned by my upbringing, the churches I was involved with, and particularly the evangelical community that I was part of for most of my adult life. When Jesus took me there, and showed me how things really were, it contradicted my previous understanding.

I have been to the consuming fire with God many times, and seen God's love in action there, purifying and refining. And I have seen that power bring about the transformation in someone's life when they accept and realise that God loves them; even after they have died; even after all the things they might have done in their life; even after rejecting Jesus. Many people struggle with that, but I have experienced it over and over again. Love wins. The fire of God's love never fails, never gives up, and love wins in the end. The restoration of all things is possible, you might even say inevitable, because the love of God will never fail. He will continue loving until all people, all things, come into a relationship with Him. He created us for relationship. He created creation for relationship.

I will write about those experiences in another chapter, but for now I want to lay a foundation for an alternative to the traditional evangelical view of 'hell' and penal retribution in eternal conscious torment. That traditional view is not consistent with the nature of God and love: how can God keep no record of wrongs and then punish anyone for the wrongs they have done? Jesus has already nailed every accusation to the cross and dealt with it.

An eschatological misunderstanding

So where does this idea about 'hell' come from? In the early Hebrew scriptures, it was not mentioned at all. In the Hebrew context, the 'hell' concept was introduced only after the Babylonian exile, drawing on Greek and other external influences. Jesus' teaching in the gospels has been used to affirm the theology of hell, but this is an eschatological misunderstanding: His teaching about the last days was not about judgment and resurrection at the end of time, with some people being assigned to be punished, but about the fire and judgment associated with end of the Old Covenant age: the system was judged as having failed to produce righteousness. His contemporaries would have understood the terminology Jesus used to do with judgment and with fire, and Jesus said all these things were going to take place within that generation[6]. Yet those terms have been erroneously applied to the end of the world and associated with eternal conscious torment in the fire of God's judgment in 'hell.' In reality, the fire is in any case not the fire of His judgment, but the fire of His love.

It was at the end of the Old Covenant age in AD 70 that bodies would be thrown into Gehenna, the constantly smouldering

---

[6] Our original blog posts from 2018 look at these scriptures in some detail. The series starts with *243. Not Counting Their Trespasses* at freedomarc.blog

rubbish heap outside the walls of Jerusalem, not at the end of the world. It has nothing to do with being thrown into 'hell' when you die. Jesus was not talking about the end of the world thousands of years later, but an event in that same generation in which He was speaking. So although the connection between Jesus's teaching about the end of the Old Covenant age and apparent fiery judgment is often used to promote an infernalist theology, it is not prophesied to occur at the end of the world, and it is not eternal judgment at all. Judgment has been passed on all mankind, and we have been judged innocent, not guilty, righteous, justified: how is there any need for punishment?

Really good news

I would assert that all the Bible verses quoted to affirm the belief in 'hell' as penal retribution of eternal conscious torment are already realised and fulfilled, and do not apply to any of God's children today. Indeed, they do not apply to anybody or anything today. That is what I call really good news, rather than the fear-inducing, manipulating fake news that people who do not know Jesus are going to end up in 'hell'. That is not good news. That is using fear to try to get people to accept Jesus. That is no different than Christendom in the Middle Ages: "Convert to Christianity, or be put to the sword." It is exactly the same kind of coercion, but with the threat of even more horrifying consequences: "Believe in Jesus, or burn in hell for eternity."

When we look with fresh eyes and an open heart, I believe we will find that death is not the end of choice. People can accept what Jesus has done, even while in the refiner's fire of His loving presence after death. I would defy anybody to come up with one Bible verse that says death is the end of choice. There are no Bible verses that say that. The only one ever suggested is this one:

And inasmuch as it is appointed for men to die once and after this comes judgment (Hebrews 9:27).

That is not about people's physical death, nor is the context in Hebrews what we have been taught: it is the first half of a sentence about Jesus' death and the expectation that He would return in judgment at the end of the age.

And inasmuch as it is appointed for men to die once and after this comes judgment, so Christ also, having been offered once to bear the sins of many, will appear a second time for salvation without reference to sin, to those who eagerly await Him (Hebrews 9:27-28).

Firstly, it is not 'appointed.' The phrase actually means 'it awaits man to die' or 'death awaits man.' God does not appoint us to die; He appoints us to abundant life. In the New Covenant, we have already died once with Christ and have been resurrected with Him, made righteous and innocent.

Do not believe anything I write just because I say so. Ask the Holy Spirit to bring you the revelation of the Father's heart towards what happens to people after death and what the fire is. But I believe every knee will bow to Jesus, that every tongue will confess Jesus is Lord, joyfully and voluntarily, either during their life on earth or in the consuming fire of God's love. They will not be forced to. How can you confess "Jesus is Lord" by being forced to do so? It is something you have to do by conviction and desire. You cannot be forced to say "Jesus is Lord" if you do not mean it. The very nature of saying He is Lord is that you accept His lordship. I believe everyone will say it voluntarily because they will experience His love and believe.

The purpose of the fire

That said, I have seen the consuming fire, and I would not want anyone to end up in it. I want people to know Jesus now, in this life; I want them to be part of the solution in this life by sharing that good news of what they have experienced of the love of God. I do not want anyone to go into the consuming fire, whether they have chosen to reject Jesus as Lord, never really heard the gospel or never realised that God loves them.

But if they do, there are consequences within that fire, and those consequences are not pleasant, because they have a concept in their own understanding of what that fire is about. Often the people I have seen there are in torment in their soul, overwhelmed with guilt, shame and condemnation; but torment is not the purpose of the fire. The purpose is to overcome that guilt, shame and condemnation and to bring people out of torment into relationship, to enjoy the salvation which is already theirs.

We are called to be ambassadors of reconciliation. We have a ministry of reconciliation to help people recognise that they are already reconciled to God; that God holds nothing against them and wants them to enter a relationship with Him. I do not believe that trying to frighten them into accepting God is the way to do it: love is. We can love in an unconditional way, in the same way that God loves us. Unfortunately, many of us have not loved that way but have focused on the negatives of behaviour rather than that everyone is included in the work of the cross.

God is not tormenting anyone, but facing the realisation of self-righteous DIY (do-it-yourself) choices in that place of fire is torment for many. Everyone reaps the consequences of what they have sown, but they are not punished by God. There is self-punishment and anguish of soul, but God's mercy will overcome the consequences of our choices. He is working to bring good out of even the worst of them, including the worst choice you could ever make, that of rejecting the offer of salvation that is yours through Jesus.

So mercy triumphs over the consequences of our choices within the fire of God's love that consumes every objection of guilt, shame and condemnation, enabling anyone to choose life in Christ. I believe this is what the consuming fire is all about. I have gone and preached to those in the fire to bring them out of that torment, as have many others I know. If you have doubts about what I am describing, or about what you currently believe, ask God to take you there and show you, as He did with me.

Past, not future

So do not be afraid of the things you have been told are coming, all the doom, gloom and misery in the prophetic world, California falling into the sea, earthquakes and judgments because God is so angry with the world. God loves the world. He loved the world so much He sent Jesus into the world to take away the sin of the world. He did not come to bring doom, gloom and misery, He brought salvation. He saved us from the lostness of our lost identity.

'The end' is past, not future. It was future for Jesus' listeners, then it happened, and now it is past for us. The end of the old heavens and earth, which was a nickname for the Temple and all it stood for, is past, not future. The new heavens and the new earth is present, not future, because we are that expression of the new tabernacle: God dwells in us. The Great Tribulation is past and not future, and will never happen again. The end of the age is past, not future. Judgment and resurrection are past, not future, because it was a covenant realisation of what took place.

"Truly I say to you, this generation will not pass away until all these things take place. Heaven and earth will pass away, but My words will not pass away." (Matthew 24:34-35).

This generation would not pass away until heaven and earth (the temple building and the sacrificial system) were destroyed. The spurious note in the NASB giving 'race' as an alternative for 'generation' is entirely fabricated – the word *genea* is never used to mean anything but 'generation' in the rest of the New Testament or any other contemporary texts. The Great Tribulation was one of 'these things' that Jesus said would happen within that timeframe (see v21). It happened between AD 66 and 70. Jesus was talking to those who were believers in Judaism and were under the Old Covenant, using language they understood in their day. He was speaking to that generation in which all the things He said would take place actually did. And He said that everything written in the prophetic scriptures would be fulfilled during the events He was describing:

Then He took the twelve aside and said to them, "Behold, we are going up to Jerusalem, and all things which are written through the prophets about the Son of Man will be accomplished." (Luke 18:31).

"Because these are days of vengeance, so that all things which are written will be fulfilled." (Luke 21:22).

These verses refer to the curses of the covenant from Deuteronomy 30. It is the system being judged, not people. Jesus fulfilled all the types, shadows, covenants and promises of God, which are now available to us.

For as many as are the promises of God, in Him they are yes; therefore also through Him is our Amen to the glory of God through us (2 Corinthians 1:20).

If we embrace living in the fullness of the New Covenant rather than the Old, then all the promises of God realised in Christ can be displayed in us to the world.

Lost in translation

Many of the misunderstandings about 'hell' in the Bible arise from translation errors. Four different words in Hebrew and Greek have all been translated as 'hell' in English: *Sheol* (Hebrew), *Hades* (Greek), *Tartarus* (Greek), and *Gehenna* (Greek).

- **Sheol:** Often means 'grave' or 'pit.' It appears 65 times in the Old Testament, referring to the grave or the place of departed souls, not punishment.

- **Hades:** The Greek equivalent of *sheol*, it means 'unseen' or the place or state of departed souls. It appears 11 times in the New Testament, with none relating to punishment. Examples include: *"O death, where is your sting? O grave (Hades), where is your victory?"* (1 Corinthians 15:55), indicating that the grave will not have victory because life in Christ triumphs. Jesus says, *"I have the keys of death and of Hades,"* (Revelation 1:18), because He has overcome both. *Death and Hades were cast into the lake of fire* (Revelation 20:14) showing that love overcomes death and the grave.

- **Tartarus**: A deep abyss in Greek mythology, where Titans were imprisoned. Only mentioned in 2 Peter 2:4, it refers to certain angels being 'reserved for judgment' (not eternal torment).

- **Gehenna**: As we have seen, Gehenna (ben Hinnom or the valley of Hinnom) was a physical place outside the walls of Jerusalem. Child sacrifice was said to have taken place there in the past, and it was now used as a rubbish dump. Jesus warned that those who stayed in Jerusalem and did not listen to Him would end up in Gehenna, a place where trash burned continuously.

'Gehenna' accounts for 100% of Jesus' supposed references to 'hell' and is still translated that way in many popular Bible versions such as the NASB and NIV. But 'Gehenna' represents physical destruction, not eternal punishment.

"... therefore, behold, days are coming," declares the Lord, *"when this place will no longer be called Topheth or the valley of Ben-hinnom, but rather the valley of Slaughter."* (Jeremiah 19:6).

Jeremiah was prophesying the destruction of Jerusalem and the Old Covenant system by the Romans in AD 66-70. This destruction was not God's desire but a consequence of rebellion, which Jesus' followers avoided by heeding His warnings. Gehenna appears 11 times in Jesus' teachings, illustrating the consequences of sin (lost identity) rather than eternal torment:

"If your eye causes you to stumble, throw it out; it is better for you to enter the kingdom of God with one eye, than, having two eyes, to be cast into hell." (Mark 9:47 NASB).

Jesus was saying that losing an eye is less damaging than a lifestyle motivated by a lack of identity as a son of God. If you do not know who you are, then your life is probably going to unfold in a 'less than' kind of way than God intends. Remember, the kingdom of God is not 'going to heaven when you die.' The Kingdom is 'at hand', close by, within us, though not all can recognise it. This verse does not say 'it is better to go to heaven than hell.'

In the New Testament, there are up to 13 references to 'hell' in modern translations, 12 of which are *Gehenna* in the original (the exception is 2 Peter 2:4, which is *Tartarus*). Jesus's use of *Gehenna* was about kingdom living, not about heaven or hell. He used a familiar physical location to illustrate the destructive nature of sin (lost identity), urging his listeners to choose a life aligned with God's original plan and intention for them.

Some streams of Jewish thought view the consequence of sin as self-inflicted judgment, believing historical suffering, like the destruction of Jerusalem in AD 70, was deserved due to Israel's sins. Though extreme, this perspective provides insight into how contemporary Jews might have understood Jesus's warnings. Sin is seen as inviting misery into our lives. Jesus used Gehenna, a disgusting location in Jerusalem, to illustrate sin's destructiveness and urge people to follow Him for freedom and abundant life. This freedom was a present invitation for them, not just a future hope: they could freely enjoy abundant life in their lifetime by following Jesus, rather than following a do-it-yourself path into self-destructive patterns, which would end up in death,

The Pharisees, obsessed with self-righteousness, were called 'sons of Gehenna' by Jesus (see Matthew 23:15). His tirade of woes against them concludes with a question:

"You serpents, you brood of vipers, how will you escape the sentence of Gehenna?" (Matthew 23:33).

How indeed would they escape being destroyed and dying in the fire of the judgment that was coming on Jerusalem? By following Jesus and leaving Jerusalem as He warned. When they saw armies surrounding Jerusalem, they should run to the hills (see Luke 21:20-22). History tells us that no believers were left in Jerusalem at that time because they heeded Jesus' words and fled. He did not want anyone to die and be thrown into Gehenna; He wanted them to escape the Old Covenant system and find life in Him.

Jesus Himself was in the stern, asleep on the cushion; and they woke Him and said to Him, "Teacher, do You not care that we are perishing?" (Mark 4:28).

"For the Son of Man has come to save that which was lost." (Matthew 18:11).

The word translated 'perishing' (*apolloumi*) in Mark 28 is the same word as that translated 'lost' in Matthew 18. If we think that 'lost' or 'perishing' means 'going to hell,' we are mistaken. Lost means gone astray, wasted. Perishing means dying, wasting away. Neither means tormented for eternity.

Pagan myths

Much of our modern concept of 'hell' stems from pagan ideas and was popularised in the 14th century by Dante's *Inferno* and 15th-century paintings by Hieronymus Bosch. This created a fictitious doctrine not found in the Bible.

Matthew 5:22 is often cited to support eternal torture: *"Anyone who says 'you fool' will be in danger of the fire of Gehenna."* But do we really think saying 'you fool' leads to eternal torment? Jesus was using very strong language to highlight the destructive power of unresolved anger and unforgiveness in our lives. He was 'raising the bar' to include thoughts and emotions as well as deeds, and emphasising how damaging our thoughts and words can be. He referenced Gehenna, as a notorious local landmark, to illustrate the toxic nature of sin (lost identity).

Ambassadors

I believe Jesus visits everyone on their deathbed and gives them an opportunity of accepting Him, and many do. But where do people go after they physically die in this life, if they have failed to accept what Jesus did for them? Into the fire? And is the fire for punishment and torment or for refining and purifying? You can read scriptures in the Old Testament talking about fuller's soap and the refiner's fire purifying and refining gold and precious silver. We are all like gold and precious silver to God. He is not going to destroy us. The consuming fire is His love, and it is purifying and refining to change and transform us, not to destroy us.

In order to control people, religion may use fear of an angry God who consigns unbelievers to 'hell'; but God desires us to let Him love us, which frees us to love ourselves and others. Perfect love casts out fear, and God's love is more powerful than any concept of 'hell'. If you are fearful of the future or worried about loved ones, know that there is no fear in love. God's love is unconditional and transformational. This is the powerful good news, the gospel message of unconditional love: God is loving and desires good for us.

It seems to me totally inconsistent to believe that God is love and yet He would punish you forever and ever if you just did not believe in Him. He believes in you. He believes in the world. Jesus came to take away the sin of the world. God has reconciled the world to himself in Christ, not counting anything against anybody. Let's be the same; let's exercise our ministry of reconciliation as ambassadors of unconditional love to a world that so desperately needs it. Let's show people how they can be free from the destruction that lost identity has wrought in their lives. God wants us all to be whole. He wants us all to come back into family, back into relationship, back into this awesome relationship with God, who is love.

If you have any concept of 'hell' in your life; or fear or any doubt over your own salvation, or where you might end up; or any concern about that for your loved ones, then allow God, who is love, to begin to bring an end to that here. And if you have doubts about what I have written here, you do not have to believe what I am saying. You have the right to believe whatever you want to. But I would ask you sincerely to ask God about it. Ask Him to show you the reality of the power of unconditional love; if nothing can separate anyone from that unconditional love, to show you what that really means in people's lives. And ask Him to show you so you can have for yourself an experience that affirms the truth of who He is as unconditional love.

Activation #10
Safe and Secure

I invite you to close your eyes
and begin to slow down your breathing
and begin to think about God as love.

> Be still.
> Come to that place
> where you can be still and know.
> Know that God is love.

> Let His love surround you.
> Let the power of His love
> flow over your physical body,
> flow into your mind,
> into your heart and emotions
> that love,
> the power of love would overshadow you.

> And I ask that, Father,
> you would reveal
> the power of your love.
> And that you would show anyone now,
> if there's any fear in their lives –
> fear of You, fear of punishment,
> fear of judgment, fear of the future –
> let Your perfect love cast out fear.

> Love on your children in such a way
> that they're safe and secure in Your arms of love;
> that You will never let them go;

You will never let them out
of your hands of love;
that You are keeping them safe and secure.

Rest in that love.
Let His love touch you
deep within your emotions.
Let it bring healing.

Any fear or doubt you have
of where your loved ones are
if they've died physically,
let the power of God's love,
let Him affirm
the consuming fire of His love to you.

Father, I ask that You'd show
everyone who wishes to see,
what is the refining, purifying fire of Your love
and how death is not the end of choice.

For those who wish to have those experiences,
that You would reveal Yourself,
reveal the truth,
unveil the truth so we can experience You.

You're in a safe place.
Open up your heart,
open up your mind.
Heaven is open.
Set the desires of your heart
on engaging the Father.

And let the Father lead
let the Father heal you,
restore you,
fill you with the power of His love;
overwhelming love
that conquers death,
that's stronger than the grave.
Rest in that love,

rest in the power of that love
and truly embrace that.

Just for a few moments,
wait there in the presence of God,
in His love.

11. Parables of 'Hell'?

Experiencing unconditional love is essential because it reveals what that love truly is. God knows exactly what we need and can affirm us in love if we give Him the time and desire to reveal it to us. I hope you had an opportunity to do that in the activation at the end of the previous chapter.

In putting this teaching together, I have been thinking a lot about unconditional love from God's perspective, and from mine in experiencing His unconditional love. I do not really imagine that any of us have really experienced unconditional love from other people (if you have, then that is awesome) or truly given unconditional love from a human perspective, because it is so very difficult to be completely unconditional.

God so loved the world that He gave. God created us so that He could give us unconditional love. He did not create the world to worship Him; He did not create us so that we would give Him something He needed. He does not 'need' anything. But His desire is to share the relational aspect of who He is, as love. Jesus came as the express image of God to demonstrate love and call us to love one another as He loves us. He came to serve and not be served. Unconditional love is not looking for something but looking to give something. Loving unconditionally is about giving, not receiving.

It is hardly possible to love without putting conditions on others. We almost always have expectations of what their love for us should be like in return, and we can get hurt and frustrated when they fail to measure up. God does not have expectations of us that make Him frustrated. He is fully aware of who He has made us to be, and He is not holding us to conditions we have to meet so that He will love us. He wants us to experience and know His love in an unconditional way.

The question I would ask is, what conditions do we put on others? What are our expectations of what it means to be loved? Do we get disappointed and hurt when those expectations are not met? I have had to address these issues, because they are real. Sometimes I would realise, "Honestly, I don't like what I'm thinking right now. I need to look at what's going on." It has been quite a challenge but I have discovered I am able to love so much more than I ever thought I possibly could, and only because of how much God has loved me.

God loves everyone the same

Many encounters have shown me that there is equality with unconditional love. God loves everyone the same, and it has nothing to do with what we have done. He showed me that He loves the worst of the worst as well as the best of the best. That was a challenge to my sense of what was fair, right and just. It will probably be a provocation to you in the same way: "These people have done terrible things. How can You love them in the same way as You love somebody else who hasn't?" But that is the nature of unconditional love. There are no conditions of behaviour or performance, how good or evil you are considered to be by others. With God, there are no favourites, and no one is excluded. It is an inclusive love, and God's love is for all of creation.

Although God does love everyone the same, that does not necessarily mean that everyone experiences God's love in the same way every time. I have experienced His love many times as fire that transforms, purifies and refines. I have come to understand that love and fire are pretty much synonymous. When I experience the fire of God's presence, it carries exactly the same frequency and consistency as being in His presence in what you might call intimacy. Love is fire, and fire is love because God is love and God is a consuming fire. The fiery experiences we go through may include healing, restoring, making us whole and setting us free from obstacles and hindrances; none of those are necessarily easy or painless in the moment.

God loves us because He is love. Nothing will make Him love us more or less. He just loves us. Unfortunately, our religious systems have often misrepresented God by putting the conditions of their systems on what it means to know Him and experience Him. The supposed consequences of our failures to keep the conditions are reiterated to keep us following the rules. Removing those religious conditions will allow us to experience (and introduce the world to) something so much deeper and better.

By far the biggest of those pretended consequences is the threat of punishment in hell and eternal conscious torment, as we saw in the previous chapter. I believe the world has generally rejected the concept of 'hell' and a loving God who would punish His children and torment them forever. It makes no logical sense, and the world can see that. However, religious people do not seem to see it because they have been indoctrinated into it, most of all in our evangelical church systems.

I reject that view and those doctrines. If we are going to see the world awakened to unconditional love, we need to see the false doctrines of eternal conscious torment in 'hell' and everything associated with them obliterated from our beliefs and our practice. Only then can we truly demonstrate to the world the real nature of God as love.

Parables of 'hell'

In the previous chapter, we looked at four particular Bible words which have been wrongly translated as 'hell': *Sheol, Hades, Gehenna* and *Tartarus*. There are also some indirect verses in Jesus' teaching, especially in His parables, that have been interpreted as referring to 'hell.' Jesus' parables had a much more obvious meaning to the generation that heard them than perhaps we would understand today. I do not believe that the Jewish crowds who flocked to Him interpreted them as parables of 'hell' because they had a very different paradigm. Yes, there was something similar that they were exposed to during their time in Babylonian captivity, and in Greek thinking, but they did not even have a word for what we think of as 'hell'; they just had the word *Sheol*, which meant 'the grave.' Even in the modern context, Judaism does not teach 'hell'.

When looking at the Bible passages that have been used to promote doctrines of torment and 'hell', Jesus' teaching must be taken in covenant context. He was teaching about the end of the Old Covenant, which was still the belief system of His hearers, and the coming of the New. He was prophesying the judgment on the failure of the Old Covenant system which would bring that age to an end (nothing to do with the end of the world, nothing to do with some event thousands of years in the future). We have been so programmed into a specific way of thinking that when we read some passages, it is hard not to default to what we have been told these things mean.

So if some of Jesus' teaching suggests a hell-like narrative to us, I believe we are interpreting them incorrectly. For example, weeping, gnashing of teeth, and outer darkness are mentioned in Matthew 8, 13, 22, 24, 25, and Luke 13, and these analogies have been used to promote the idea of 'hell.' There are much more likely meanings.

I say to you that many will come from east and west, and recline at the table with Abraham, Isaac and Jacob in the kingdom of heaven; but the sons of the kingdom will be cast out into the outer darkness; in that place there will be weeping and gnashing of teeth." (Matthew 8:11-12).

People would come from all over the world to join in with those who had a relationship with God in the Old Covenant. But those who thought they were 'sons of the kingdom' just because they were descended from Abraham, Isaac and Jacob, and because they kept the Law, would be cast into outer darkness. This was a matter of being in or out of the covenant, enjoying the covenant blessings of the kingdom or not. Consequences, not punishment; and in this life, not for all eternity. Keeping the Law would not open up the kingdom (which is within) to them. They would be weeping because they had missed out, and gnashing their teeth in anger and frustration. Nothing at all to do with being punished.

When we see the same phrases used in different contexts, it gives us an insight into what they mean. In Acts chapter 7 Stephen was talking to those same people, those who thought that they were sons of the kingdom:

"You stiff-necked people! Your hearts and ears are still uncircumcised. You are just like your ancestors: You always resist the Holy Spirit! Was there ever a prophet your ancestors did not persecute? They even killed those who predicted the coming of the Righteous One. And now you have betrayed and murdered him – you who have received the law that was given through angels but have not obeyed it." When the members of the Sanhedrin heard this, they were furious and gnashed their teeth at him (Acts 7:51-54 NIV).

Now here is the real meaning of 'gnashing of teeth'. Let the scriptures interpret themselves, rather than coming up with a fanciful meaning that this phrase is talking about future judgment thousands of years later, and 'hell'. It meant that they were furious and ground their teeth at him because he was speaking the truth to them and challenging their self-righteous religion. So why would anyone think weeping and gnashing of teeth is a reference to physical torture in 'hell'? Only, I suggest, because they have been conditioned to do so. If that is what we were always taught, we may never have considered the possibility that it means something different.

Jesus is talking to the religious elite, focusing on those who would identify themselves as 'sons of the kingdom' whilst rejecting His ministry and message: the Pharisees, Sadducees, priests, Levites, lawyers, rabbis etc. Jesus' warnings are not aimed towards 'sinners' but towards self-righteous religious leaders and others who thought of themselves as righteous. "If you keep following your self-righteous religious system, you might think you are sons of the kingdom, but you are going to find yourself outside of the (new) covenant, weeping and grinding your teeth in sadness, anger and frustration." To be cast out was to be outside of the covenant relationship, which was figuratively darkness because the covenant was a covenant of light. They would weep and grind their teeth in self-righteous anger and anguish, having failed to heed Jesus. His teaching threatened their established position of power, and they were well aware He was challenging them:

When the chief priests and the Pharisees heard His parables, they understood that He was speaking about them. When they sought to seize Him, they feared the people, because they considered Him to be a prophet (Matthew 21:45-46).

Obviously, many people did pay attention to what Jesus said, even some Pharisees. There were a great number of Jewish believers by the time AD 66-70 came along, and every one of them ran to the hills, to Pella, when they saw armies begin to surround Jerusalem. Of those that did not believe or listen to Jesus and stayed, many were crucified and their bodies thrown into the burning rubbish heap of Gehenna.

I am not suggesting you go away and study all these sayings and parables of Jesus and look at it all for yourself (though there are many people who have written books and articles who have done that. By all means read some of them, if you like. *Putting Hell Back in the Handbasket*[7] is a good one. There are a number of others[8] too that will give you some insight and go into it in greater depth than I can here).

No, what I recommend is that you go to God face to face and ask Him to reveal the truth to you. Ask the Father to show you the truth of the reality of these verses, and also whether He has a totally different plan for the future than we have been taught. We can all ask God to unveil our minds and deconstruct the pillars that frame our beliefs and our mindsets from any religious do-it-yourself-tree perspective that has created all this confusion.

Jesus spoke about many things in parables, which are short stories illustrating one or more points, lessons, or principles.

---

[7] brazenchurch.com/wp-content/uploads/2018/04/Putting-Hell-Back-In-The-Handbasket.pdf

[8] See for example the list at the end of our blog post at freedomarc.blog/the-hell-delusion/

There are two parables often used to promote the theology of 'hell' and eternal conscious torment: the sheep and the goats, and Lazarus and the rich man. However, if we are prepared to look deeper into the meaning behind these parables, I am confident that neither is about 'hell' or eternal conscious torment at all. They have a totally different meaning, and I will give you some insight into that. The audience, background and context are crucial for interpretation, and these elements are often foreign to us today. This leads to guesswork in trying to understand what Jesus was talking about. Even His disciples sometimes had to ask Him for clarification because His meaning was not always clear. If He often used common stories or ideas to make a point, this does not necessarily mean He was endorsing or validating those ideas, but He used them because they were familiar to His audience. He was also clever in how He presented His messages, often in ways that divided people.

Sheep and Goats

The parable of the sheep and goats in Matthew 25 is not literal, but figurative; its context is the end of the Old Covenant and the transition to the New. After outlining coming events in Matthew 24, Jesus uses this parable to illustrate the end of the age, the destruction of the temple, and the establishment of the New Covenant. Jesus is the king, and the judgment of nations before Him is not about the end of the world but differentiating between Old Covenant people, New Covenant people and others, at the end of the Old Covenant age.

Jesus would come in authority and receive the kingdom. The blessed on His right would inherit the kingdom, prepared for them from the world's foundation, whilst those on the left would be cursed and sent into a fire described as *aionios* (not 'eternal', but 'relating to the age'). The fire of the age speaks of the end of the Old Covenant and the fate of those who rejected Him and persecuted believers. This fire is not for a literal devil and fallen angels – Chuck Crisco suggests an alternative (and more literal) translation of this phrase might be 'the accuser and his messengers' (referring to the Law and its messengers, the religious elite: Pharisees, Sadducees, Zealots, and others)[9].

Jesus is using very specific covenant language to reference the curses of Deuteronomy. Works are the criteria for the separation in His story, not faith and grace; and it cannot be about personal salvation because it is nations who are judged, not individuals. It was about the end of the Old Covenant age. Those who still held to the Old Covenant were left behind in Jerusalem and ended up in the fires of Gehenna. Jesus did not desire this for them; He wanted to gather them so they would follow Him and be saved from the impending destruction. However, as we have seen before, those who chose to stay suffered the consequences of their choice.

Lazarus and the rich man

The parable of Lazarus and the rich man is not about 'hell' either; it addresses the selfish use of money and position, all the while neglecting to look after the poor (as required by the Law). Jesus used a well-known idea from the Babylonian captivity, the non-scriptural concept of 'Abraham's bosom,' where the righteous Old Testament saints were thought to be separated from those outside the covenant by a great gulf. Jesus, of course, was soon to descend into *Sheol*, preach to everyone there, and lead all the captives out. There is no reference either to God or to punishment in this parable: the anguish the rich man experienced is once again a covenant-related consequence, and once again the message was firmly directed at the Pharisees and Sadducees, warning them about assuming they were 'in' and those they considered 'sinners' were 'out'.

Misunderstanding Thessalonians

'Hell' as eternal punishment is not supported by Jesus' teachings; nor by Paul's letters. Paul never mentioned it, so clearly eternal punishment was not a significant concept for

---

[9] anewdaydawning.com/blog-1/2015/7/13/the-sheep-and-goats-judgment

him. 2 Thessalonians 1 is often cited as if it disproves this: it does not refer to 'hell' but yet again to the end of the covenant age and the destruction of Jerusalem.

Here is the whole chapter (it is only 12 verses):

Paul and Silvanus and Timothy,

To the church of the Thessalonians in God our Father and the Lord Jesus Christ: Grace to you and peace from God the Father and the Lord Jesus Christ.

We ought always to give thanks to God for you, brethren, as is only fitting, because your faith is greatly enlarged, and the love of each one of you toward one another grows ever greater; therefore, we ourselves speak proudly of you among the churches of God for your perseverance and faith in the midst of all your persecutions and afflictions which you endure. This is a plain indication of God's righteous judgment so that you will be considered worthy of the kingdom of God, for which indeed you are suffering. For after all it is only just for God to repay with affliction those who afflict you, and to give relief to you who are afflicted and to us as well when the Lord Jesus will be revealed from heaven with His mighty angels in flaming fire, dealing out retribution to those who do not know God and to those who do not obey the gospel of our Lord Jesus. These will pay the penalty of eternal destruction, away from the presence of the Lord and from the glory of His power, when He comes to be glorified in His saints on that day, and to be marveled at among all who have believed — for our testimony to you was believed. To this end also we pray for you always, that our God will count you worthy of your calling, and fulfill every desire for goodness and the work of faith with power, so that the name of our Lord Jesus will be glorified in you, and you in Him, according to the grace of our God and the Lord Jesus Christ (2 Thessalonians 1:1-12).

In verse 2, "Grace to you and peace from God", the English word 'from' translates the Greek word *apo*, which usually denotes origin. Out of 650 New Testament occurrences, 602

PARABLES OF 'HELL'

are interpreted as 'from' and only a few as 'away from.' Note this, because we will see the importance of it later in the chapter.

Verse 5 speaks of God's righteous judgment, not condemning the world but declaring it innocent. This passage is intended to reassure believers who suffer persecution, promising relief when Jesus is revealed from heaven with His angels in flaming fire (not referring to the end of the world but the end of the Old Covenant age and the destruction of Jerusalem). Those rejecting Jesus would face the consequences of their choice: not eternal punishment, but physical consequences of death, crucifixion and having their bodies dumped like refuse.

"Dealing out retribution to those who do not know God and to those who do not obey the gospel of the Lord Jesus Christ. These will pay the penalty of eternal destruction away from the presence of the Lord and from the glory of His power." This appears to be quite alarming, but we need to look at the context and the true meanings of some of these words. This time, of course, *apo* is translated as 'away from' because it would make no sense in the 'hell' context to be 'from' His presence. But, of course, the fire *is* God's presence: the loving presence of an eternal God.

As for destruction, eternal, penalty, and retribution: what do the original words actually mean? Destruction, *olethros*, is not the same as punishment or torment. If someone is destroyed, there is no continuing punishment and the torment is over, so this does not add up to the 'hell' concept. 'Eternal' is *aionios*, not forever or everlasting but relating to a particular age, or age-enduring. Penalty is the word *dike* (di-kay) which means justice, a judicial hearing, or a legal decision: a verdict or a judgment, rather than a sentence or penalty. And what is the verdict? Not guilty. Retribution, *ekdikesis*, from the same root word, literally means 'out of justice,' i.e. the result (one way or another) of a judicial decision.

If you believe in the concept of 'hell', the word 'destruction' does not fit. If you believe in Christian universalism, the word 'destruction' does not fit either. If you believe in annihilation of the wicked, as some do, the combination of 'eternal' and 'destruction' makes no sense (you cannot annihilate someone eternally, on and on and on: they are annihilated, and that is the end). 'Destruction for an age' does not make any sense either in this context. *Olethros* is best translated as a state of being lost (like the coin, the sheep or the prodigal) or ruined – a totally different concept. However you look at it, none of this is a warning of 'hell.'

If you die without knowing God, His fiery presence will result in your lostness, your ruination, being dealt with. Ruination does not imply extinction or annihilation; it emphasises the consequent loss that goes with complete undoing. What is being undone? The person's objections to receiving salvation are being undone; their lostness is being undone. God's presence, as a consuming fire, brings about justice that addresses their lostness, because of His unending love and desire for reconciliation. Being face to face with Jesus means all darkness is shredded in His light.

> "Vengeance might as well be the same as salvation, mercy, or justice." – George MacDonald (a nineteenth-century preacher of the gospel of inclusion who greatly influenced both Tolkien and C.S. Lewis in their writings).

God is so passionate about us that His wrath and vengeance – wrath and passion are the same Greek word, *orge* (or-gay) – are poured out on anything that is keeping us from a relationship with Him in face-to-face innocence. He will passionately deal with anything that is stopping us from receiving and experiencing His love.

Refiner's fire

In the Old Testament and in the time of Jesus, fire was a common theme and expectation, but it was not about punishment and torment.

Behold, I am going to send My messenger, and he will clear the way before Me. And the Lord, whom you seek, will suddenly come to His temple; and the messenger of the covenant, in whom you delight, behold, He is coming,"says the Lord of hosts. But who can endure the day of His coming? And who can stand when He appears? For He is like a refiner's fire and like fullers' soap. He will sit as a smelter and purifier of silver, and He will purify the sons of Levi and refine them like gold and silver, so that they may present to the Lord offerings in righteousness (Malachi 3:1-3).

This passage is about preparing for Jesus' coming, possibly referring to the spirit of Elijah or John the Baptist, but ultimately about Jesus as the messenger of the New Covenant, couched in metaphorical Old Testament language. Today, we are all a royal priesthood, figuratively sons of Levi, because the priesthood is no longer restricted to one tribe. Everyone is a king and priest with access to intimacy with God, but we still need refining and purification to be the righteousness of God in Christ.

Their understanding of fire was as a purifying and refining force. Jesus had to go through the fire himself by going to the cross to make us righteous. God is love and fire: His love is His fire and His fire is His love. Keep that context in mind.

The one who does not love does not know God, for God is love. By this the love of God was manifested in us, that God has sent His only begotten Son into the world so that we might live through Him (1 John 4:8-9).

For our God is a consuming fire (Hebrews 12:29).

A greater understanding of grace

> Some recent theologians are of the opinion that fire, which both burns and saves, is Christ Himself, the judge and Saviour. The encounter with Him is the decisive act of judgment. Before His gaze, all falsehood melts away. This encounter with Him, as it burns us, transforms and frees us, allowing us to become truly ourselves. All that we build during our lives can prove to be mere straw, pure bluster, and it collapses. Yet in the pain of this encounter,

when the impurity and the sickness of our lives become evident to us, there lies salvation.

So actually, when we come to realise that salvation belongs to us in God's love, then we are able to receive it. His gaze, the touch of His heart, heals us through an undeniably painful transformation, as through fire. But it is a blessed pain in which the holy power of His love sears through us like a flame, enabling us to become totally ourselves and thus totally of God. In this way, the interrelation between justice and grace also becomes clear. The way we live our lives is not immaterial, but our defilement does not stain us forever if we at least continue to reach out towards Christ, towards truth, and towards love. Indeed, it has already been burned away through Christ's passion.

At the moment of judgment, we experience and absorb the overwhelming power of His love over all evil in the world and in ourselves. The pain of love becomes our salvation and our joy. It is clear we cannot calculate the duration of this transforming burning in terms of chronological measurements of this world. The transforming moment of this encounter eludes earthly time reckoning. It is the heart's time. It is the time of passage to communion with God in the body of Christ.

The judgment of God is hope both because of its justice and because of its grace. If it were merely grace, making all earthly things cease to matter, God would still owe us an answer to the crucial questions about justice – the crucial question that we ask of history and of God. If it were merely justice, in the end it would bring only fear to us all. The incarnation of God in Christ has so closely linked the two together – judgment and grace – justice is firmly established.

We all work out our salvation with fear and trembling (Philippians 2:12). Nevertheless, grace allows us all to hope and to go trustfully to meet the judge whom we know as our Advocate, our *Paracletus*." – Pope Benedict, *Spe Salvi* [*The Hope of Salvation*]).

Pope Benedict here seems to me to demonstrate a greater understanding of grace and unconditional love than most evangelicals. What he shares there resonates well with what I have experienced in the presence of God.

A good news message

I am sure you will have many questions: I am not asking you to just believe anything I say, but (as always) to check it out with God for yourself. I have no doubt whatsoever that all of us can experience the unconditional love of God, because it truly is unconditional. We can trust in Him, because He will never give up. His love is unconditional and He wants us to experience it.

Let's present to the world a good news message that God is love, and that He loves all He has created. Jesus died for the sin of the whole world. He has taken on our lostness and destroyed it, so that we can know the truth of who we really are as God's children, as His sons, so that we can enter into the fullness of that relationship with love itself. And as we receive His unconditional love, we will be able to demonstrate unconditional love ourselves.

Activation #11
Fiery Presence

I encourage you to spend a few minutes again in an activation in which you can experience that unconditional love, feel it, and sense it. You can be set free from concepts that may have created fear in you – torment, punishment, and an angry God who needs appeasing. Jesus came to take away our lost identity, to bring a revelation that we are God's children, His sons, so that we can experience that wonderful love.

As you close your eyes,
I encourage you
to fix your eyes on Jesus.

Think of that wonderful love.
Hear His voice.
"My sheep will hear My voice."
Hear Jesus say,
"All who are weary and heavy-laden,
come to Me and find rest."

So just make that choice to come to Him.
Surrender all your objections,
all the things that are hindering you,
stopping you from experiencing
the wonderful love of God.
Just let them go.

Begin to meditate,
to rest in that place of God's presence.

Jesus, the Way, the Truth and the Life,
is opening up a door for you
to enter into the unconditional love of the Father.

Be still.
Be still and know the wonderful love of God.
Let that amazing love surround you, rest on you.
Feel the weight of that love on you
affirming you, revealing your true identity,
revealing how high and wide and deep
the love of the Father goes
surrounding you, filling you.
Let it flow over you
from the top of your head to the tip of your toes.

Let it fill you:
fill your spirit, soul and body
with an intense burning love, a passion,
the passion that God has for you,
the burning desire that He has for you,

the intense joy that He feels when He thinks about you,
that deep compassion that He has for you,
that overwhelming love that He has for you –
feel it.

Let Him speak to you.
Let Him affirm you with words of affirmation:
"You are My child.
I love you.
I accept you.
I affirm you.
I call you out of the darkness into the light.
I call you out of all false doctrine or theology
which has misrepresented Me
into the wonderful light of truth
that I am unconditional love.

"Let Me love you
so you can love one another in the same way.
Be still and know that I am love.
Be still and know that I am love.
Be still and know that I am love."

Let that love flow over you right now,
touching you at a deeper level.
Let perfect love cast out all fear –
fear of punishment,
fear of death,
fear of the future,
fear of eternal conscious torment
or 'hell.'

Let the fiery presence of God's love
purify and refine,
renew your mind,
transform you,
bring you out of that religious mould
and enable you to be free.

Love is a safe place.
You can let down all your barriers.
Let go of all your coping mechanisms
and defence mechanisms.
You don't have to fear the Father.
Let it go.
Hand all your fears over to Him
and let His love transform you,
empower you, envision you;
give you a message,
a heavenly vision
to take this love message into the world –
that desperately needs an awakening to true love.

You are in a safe place.
Open up your heart
and allow the Father to take you,
maybe into the fire of His presence,
maybe into that place of intimacy and deep, deep love,
so you can begin to be made whole;
your mind renewed,
your heart healed,
your emotions brought into that place of peace and rest.

Wait in His presence.
Enjoy that love
as that love touches you at another level,
deeper and deeper and deeper.
Experience that amazing, unconditional love.

Stay in that place of unconditional love as long as you want to. It is a wonderful place to be.

12. The Consuming Fire of God's Love

I believe God wants us to have a view of His love, His fire, and His presence, that goes beyond our programming. But there is one question which often comes up at this point: what about those who have had encounters, perhaps near-death experiences or visions of 'hell' that suggest or confirm eternal torment? I believe people do have real afterlife experiences, both of heaven and a place where God's love manifests as consuming fire. He has used these experiences, but sometimes they have perpetuated the view of God as one who punishes His children forever. Our experiences are filtered through our soul's cognitive biases: if we believe in a vengeful God, we will interpret fire or darkness accordingly. Any alternative explanation is difficult to accept for those who have been conditioned by upbringing, culture or religious teachings.

I had such encounters myself, around five of them between 2005 and 2010, which I initially interpreted as 'hell'. In these experiences, God was warning and encouraging me to help rescue people from the fire and bring them to salvation. I now understand that differently to the way I did then: as I drew closer to God, His fire was revealed as restorative, refining and purifying. As George MacDonald said, "Being face to face with Jesus shreds all darkness in His light." Engaging with the altar of fire and the judgment seat of Christ purified my life and deepened my relationship with God. Fire is not in itself a bad thing, and we can engage with it before death.

I do not believe in soul-sleeping or that the dead watch over us. But what does happen to non-believers after death? Some might suffer in the fire, but it is not by God's doing. We can help them by preaching to them and seeing them restored. My experience is that even if they do initially go into the place of fire, once they come to know the Father through Jesus, they can respond and join the cloud of witnesses. Jesus preached there, led captivity captive, and calls us to do greater things. He ended the two-part *Sheol* (if it ever was divided in that way), when He freed everyone there in the days between His death and resurrection.

Our mission is to ensure no one goes to the fire by sharing the good news. Yet if someone rejects our message and goes there, they still have the choice to accept what Jesus has done for them even after death. There is always a way out through Jesus.

Entering into God's presence involves purification and refining, which removes all barriers to experiencing His love and forgiveness. Many people struggle with this because they have a view of what should happen to those who reject Jesus: they are seeing through the lens of judgment and retribution. Jesus Himself revealed a different way, that of love, forgiveness and mercy which triumphs over humanity's idea of judgment. The cross proclaims us innocent, freeing everyone from unforgiveness and from our past. God's wrath and vengeance are not poured out on people but on anything keeping us from a relationship with Him. God's passion is to free us from anything hindering us from a restored face-to-face relationship.

2 Corinthians 5:19 tells us that God reconciled the *kosmos* to Himself, holding nothing against anyone. And this was done in Christ: there was no separation. God has done His part, and when we truly realise it, there is nothing we would want more than to be reconciled. Still, each of us can choose to accept or reject His act of love because God gave us that ability.

What happens in the fire?

What is the nature of the place commonly called 'hell'? Who goes there, what happens there, and for how long? These are questions that need answers and cannot be left to religious programming; I believe God has given us insight. Unconditional love is the key factor in answering these questions appropriately. Without experiencing and knowing unconditional love, you might easily misunderstand God's true nature (as many have).

There are (at least) five common views of what happens in the fire and five views on how long it lasts, resulting in 25 possible combinations. I am not going to go into all of them, but I will briefly touch on the most commonly believed.

First is 'eternal conscious torment', also known as infernalism, punishment that never ends. That is not good news to me, and I will not preach it. It is contrary to everything Jesus demonstrates in His life and teaching. People do not want to hear it; and even if they do hear it, they usually reject it. Why would they want to believe in a God who would do that?

Next is 'annihilation', or terminal punishment, which ends with complete destruction. There is no choice after death; there will be destruction, but there is an end to the pain. Some prefer this as it avoids the idea of punishment for all eternity, but it still does not reflect God's true nature to me. A variation is annihilation with escapable destruction, allowing a choice after death. This view offers an undetermined period after death for people to escape destruction. You would still have to believe in a God who would annihilate His children; I do not believe in annihilation at all.

'Universal reconciliation', or Universal salvation, also has two forms. In both, Jesus is the way to salvation: it is not that all religions lead to God. One form guarantees that everyone will eventually choose the right path, due to God's relentless love; the other form offers endless chances, but with no guarantee that everyone will ultimately choose wisely. I believe God's love will eventually win everyone over.

The purpose of the fire

The purpose of fire varies from one scenario to another: it can be for punishment or for purification and correction. I believe in purification and correction, reflecting God's character, in a process that may be painful but is ultimately beneficial.

Does God really enforce retributive justice, making sinners pay for their sins? Jesus already took away the sin of the world. So no; instead God practices restorative justice, seeking out those who have lost their way and restoring their true identity through Jesus. God allows us to make choices which have consequences for us, but these are not eternal. He does not force a relationship with Jesus on us but continually offers the choice, with the aim of restoration, not retribution. There is a middle view that God's justice is retributive, but restoring: the punishment that is applied is punitive but also intended to bring about restoration. I see that as a stepping stone that helps people make their way to the realisation that restoration is God's number one choice.

The 'consequential' view suggests that the fire is self-inflicted punishment as a result of our choices, and there is no escape. Then there is consequential but restoring: the fire is self-inflicted, you choose to go there because you reject Jesus, reject the message, the good news; but it is also used to bring about healing and restoration, and there is the opportunity of eventual escape. I think that is the most consistent view of the fire and the one that aligns with and best reflects God's nature as love. You have the ability to choose. The results of that choice are self-inflicted anguish and torment, but the mercy and love of God will overcome that, and you can be restored from that place. The period of restoration lasts as long as you resist God's justice. People may hold on to guilt or shame, but God's love persists until they accept it. I believe everyone will ultimately be restored.

My heavenly experiences have given me an idea of how God views everybody – all His children – which challenged my human sense of justice. One time I went under a waterfall in heaven, and the waterfall cascaded down over me with multi-coloured cascades and frequencies. It was a powerful experience, and in it I felt God's unconditional love for the victims, the abused, the trafficked, and those who had been raped or suffered other terrible ordeals. And then I felt God's unconditional love for those who had been the perpetrators, victimisers, abusers, traffickers, rapists and paedophiles. This defied my sense of justice. I struggled with it; how could it be right or fair for God to love the victims and the victimisers the same? But they are all His children, stuck in lost identity, and God wants all of them to be healed, restored and made whole.

Experiencing that was life-changing, and I went back to that waterfall numerous times so that God could continue to change my heart and mind. I needed to move away from the retrogressive, man-made justice that says they deserve punishment for rejecting Jesus or doing terrible things. The reality is that Jesus died for all their sins on the cross, nailing to it every accusation against everyone. He keeps no record of wrongs. Whilst I understand human justice and the need for preserving law and order in society, I believe the best form of justice even in this world is restorative, not punitive. People can be restored because God's love will never fail. God's grace and mercy do not end for those who die without knowing Him, but extend beyond death.

God is love, light, Spirit, and a consuming fire. The refining and purifying fire is God and His love; there is no contradiction in this at all. When the Father showed me a fallen angelic being that was affecting our ministry, I initially held off dealing with it. I had no mandate and, if I had tried to deal with it then, I would have resorted to the aggressive methods I had been taught. Ultimately, the Father showed me how to restore a fallen being by reminding it of its original identity and forgiveness through Jesus on the cross, offering love and restoration. It was wonderful to see a being shrouded in darkness have the light burst out and the scales fall away, returning them to unconditional love and their original purpose.

I also encountered dimensional beings needing help and felt passionate about their restoration, reinforcing that God's love never fails, never gives up, and always wins. Revelation 5:13 tells us that every created thing praises God, everything in heaven, on earth, under the earth and in the sea. This praise is genuine and unforced, and it arises spontaneously at the revelation of God's amazing, unconditional love.

Scripture supports this view. Romans 8:38-39 assures us that nothing can separate us from God's love; 1 Corinthians 13:8 states that love never fails; Ephesians 1:4-5 tells us we were chosen in Christ before the world's foundation, and destined for adoption as sons. Some interpret these Bible verses as applying only to believers, but I believe all are included and all need to realise their sonship through Jesus. His work on the cross was for all, not just believers. All were dead in Adam, and the same 'all' were to be made alive in Christ.

He associated us in Christ before the fall of the world. Jesus is God's mind made up about us. He always knew in His love that He would present us again face to face before Him in blameless innocence. He is the architect of our design; His heart dream realized our coming of age in Christ (Ephesians 1:4 Mirror).

God has never changed His mind. He has never rejected us – that is a religious lie. God never turns away from us and the Father never turned away from Jesus: He is always looking for the lost. And in this New Covenant age, everything that was done before the foundation of the world has now come to realisation.

for the wages of the sin [is] death, and the gift of God [is] life age-during in Christ Jesus our Lord (Romans 6:23 YLT).

It is death that is the wages of sin, not punishment; and the gift of God is life age-during in Christ Jesus, for everybody. The victory of Jesus is available to all, even those who do not yet know it.

Through the fiery sword

We may assume that death is inevitable, but which death are we talking about? Spiritual death in Adam was inevitable for those who were in Adam. Co-crucifixion with Christ is inevitable for those who are in Christ. Physical death, as we shall see, is not necessarily inevitable. The second death in fire, which is a purifying and refining process, is also inevitable: we can choose to go through it now by surrendering to the fire of God's love, or we can choose to go through it after we die. Even as believers, we can choose to go into that fire after we die and embrace the Judgment Seat of Christ, which will purify our soul, or we can choose to go there now. The fire is available to us by choice; but one way or another everyone needs to go through the fiery sword to enter in.

But now Christ has been raised from the dead, the first fruits of those who are asleep. For since by a man came death, by a man also came the resurrection of the dead. For as in Adam all die, so also in Christ all will be made alive (1 Corinthians 15:20-22).

"By a man came death" refers to Adam; "by a man also came the resurrection of the dead" refers to Jesus. From the resurrection onwards, all would be made alive in Christ. Spiritual death and spiritual resurrection are inevitable for all who are in Christ: that is, all who have been associated with Him since before the foundation of the world, which is every human being, every child of God.

He must reign until He has put all enemies under His feet. The last enemy that will be abolished is death... O death, where is your victory? O death, where is your sting?" The sting of death is sin, and the power of sin is the law; but thanks be to God, who gives us the victory through our Lord Jesus Christ (1 Corinthians 15:25-26, 55-57).

Physical death is not inevitable and has in fact been abolished: we will go into the question of immortality in later chapters. But spiritual death persists until people realise that they have already been made alive.

Galatians 2:20 says, "I have been crucified with Christ." It is not "I will be," "I might be" or "someday." It is already a done deal. This was inevitable because Jesus died for (and as) everyone. Jesus represented each one of us, the whole of mankind, on the cross. By dying our death, He took the wages of sin, the choice we made to be independent from God and to enter into separation from Him. Even though it was not God who separated Himself from us, or us from Him, Jesus has brought back everyone into inclusion.

...who has saved us and called us with a holy calling, not according to our works, but according to His own purpose and grace which was granted us in Christ Jesus from all eternity, but now has been revealed by the appearing of our Savior Christ Jesus, who abolished death and brought life and immortality to light through the gospel, for which I was appointed a preacher and an apostle and a teacher (2 Timothy 1:9-11).

None of this has anything to do with what we have done to deserve it or not, whether good or bad. He has abolished death. So why do we die? Because we do not know that truth. We have been conditioned to believe that we are guaranteed to die, but I do not believe that is what Jesus taught. You die if you expect to die: there are some who have not died, and there are many, I believe, who will not die if we embrace this good news, this light of immortality.

He rescued the integrity of our original design and revealed that we have always been His own from the beginning, even before time was. This has nothing to do with anything we did to qualify or disqualify ourselves. We are not talking about religious good works or karma here. Jesus unveils grace to be the eternal intent of God. Grace celebrates our pre-creation innocence and now declares our redeemed union with God in Christ Jesus (2 Timothy 1:9 Mirror).

From God's eternal viewpoint, our relationship with Him has never changed. We have always belonged to Him, even when we may have been lost or disconnected. This is illustrated in parables such as the lost son, the lost coin, and the lost sheep: the lost items remain the property of their owner, they are just lost. We may lose sight of our true identity, but God's perspective of us remains constant. He knows us intimately and has always considered us to be His own, even before time began. God's plan has always been to reveal our true selves and to bring us into the knowledge and experience of our identity as sons.

Everything that grace pointed to is now realized in Christ Jesus and brought into clear view through the gospel. Jesus is what grace reveals. He took death out of the equation and redefines uninterrupted life. This is good news indeed (2 Timothy 1:10 Mirror).

Jesus has abolished death and what it implies – the wages of sin and lost identity, which are hardship, toil and labour. Whenever you go through the fire of His love, it will not be forever, because the power of death has been abolished.

The spirit returns to God

I do not believe that physical death is inevitable, but if we do die, what happens then?

Then the dust will return to the earth as it was, and the spirit will return to God who gave it (Ecclesiastes 12:7).

His spirit departs, he returns to the earth; in that very day, his plans come to nothing (Psalm 146:4).

Whether you know God or not, your spirit returns to Him. If you do know Him, I believe your spirit and soul return to Him united. If not, your spirit returns to Him, whilst your soul goes into the place of fire. Soul and spirit may have different experiences; our physical bodies return to the earth.

What does all that mean? Some teach soul sleep, not soul consciousness, but I do not believe that takes into account the power of the resurrection. I have talked to those in that realm, both in the fire and those who are in the cloud of witnesses, and they are certainly not asleep. They are aware. My experiences confirm that in the cloud of witnesses, soul and spirit are alive, and united. They have memory and experience (but no negative memory, because all tears are washed away).

Lingering human souls

The body returns to its elements; the spirit returns to God. If the soul and spirit have been reconciled in Christ as a believer, they are not separated after death. If the soul and spirit were not reconciled before death, several things may happen. It is possible that a not-yet-believer's spirit returns to the Lord, but that their soul sometimes remains behind after death, perhaps due to trauma or some other experience. Some call that an alien human spirit; I call it a lingering human soul. Souls linger around, attach themselves to people, and are 'alien' in that they do not belong there, attached to people or affecting them (not 'alien' as in from another planet). I know of two groups of people who minister to those and set people free, one in the US led by Arthur Burke and another in the UK. The latter group preach to lingering human souls and offer them salvation so they can cross over and leave the people or places they have been attached to.

We are spiritual beings who became living beings, and then human beings. Mostly, though, we become 'human doings.' Our destiny is to be God-like beings, sons of God. Adam, if he had not chosen independence, would have ascended into a God-like being. Even though he was made in the image and likeness of God, there was a process of maturing, of ascension, into that state of sonship. Human beings live with the soul conscious but separated relationally from the spirit (and from God) until spirit and soul are united in the Holy Spirit by coming to the knowledge of that in Christ.

For such a human being, after physical death the spirit returns to God and remains separated from the soul. The soul remains conscious but is separated relationally from God because they do not know Him. They are not physically separated from God because they are in the fire of His loving presence. If the soul goes into the consuming fire of God's presence without knowing God relationally, that is not a pleasant place to be (particularly when this person realises that they have rejected Jesus and are there in that condition because of their own choice).

Now may the God of peace Himself sanctify you entirely; and may your spirit and soul and body be preserved complete, without blame at the coming of our Lord Jesus Christ (1 Thessalonians 5:23 NASB).

...and the God of the peace Himself sanctify you wholly, and may your whole spirit, and soul, and body, be preserved unblameably in the presence of our Lord Jesus Christ (1 Thessalonians 5:23 YLT).

There is a crucial difference in translation here. Almost every English Bible says 'at the coming of our Lord Jesus Christ' but the word is actually 'presence,' as Young's confirms. It is not referring to some future coming, but to a present, ongoing relationship. Our sanctification, preservation and restoration all happen now, in the presence of our Lord Jesus Christ.

There, away from any effort of your own, discover how the God of perfect peace, who fused you skillfully into oneness – just like a master craftsman would dovetail a carpentry joint – has personally perfected and sanctified the entire harmony of your being without your help. He has restored the detailed default settings. You were rebooted to fully participate in the life of your design, in your spirit, soul and body in blameless innocence in the immediate presence of our Lord Jesus Christ. (1 Thessalonians 5:23 Mirror).

Death is not the end

As mentioned in a previous chapter, no-one has been able to show me a single Bible verse indicating that physical death ends our ability to choose Jesus, not even this one:

... it is appointed unto men once to die, but after this the judgment (Hebrews 9:27 KJV).

The fact is that some, such as Enoch and Elijah, did not experience physical death, even once. Many others, like Lazarus, died more than once. The judgment after death is a discernment, a verdict of reconciliation through Jesus' death on the cross: it is not about punishment but about recognising our inclusion in Christ's death and resurrection. If there is a judgment after physical death, it is not to punish but to discern or separate, based on our acceptance or rejection of Jesus' gift of salvation. Our free will to choose life or death determines our experience of this judgment. The realisation of Jesus' work on the cross leads us to trust and benefit from it.

In fact, there are many Bible verses promising that death is not the end of the opportunity for salvation, even in the Old Testament. Death does not have the final word. Out choices may well have unpleasant consequences for us, but God's love always offers a way out through His compassion and grace. The Psalms frequently speak of being rescued from *Sheol*. Psalms 16:10, 30:3, 49:15, 86:13, and 116:3-8 all reference this.

For we will surely die and are like water spilled on the ground which cannot be gathered up again. Yet God does not take away life but plans ways so that the banished one will not be cast out from Him (2 Samuel 14:14).

The Lord kills and makes alive; He brings down to Sheol and raises up (1 Samuel 2:6).

For the Lord will not reject forever, for if He causes grief, then He will have compassion according to His abundant loving-kindness. For He does not afflict willingly or grieve the sons of men (Lamentations 3:31-33).

But God will redeem my soul from the power of Sheol, for He will receive me (Psalm 49:15).

For Your loving-kindness toward me is great, and You have delivered my soul from the depths of Sheol (Psalm 86:13).

The early church taught that Jesus went into *Hades* or *Sheol*. He preached there and led captives free, as referenced in Ephesians 4, Psalm 68, and 1 Peter 3:18, showing that death is not the end.

When He ascended on high, He led captive a host of captives, and He gave gifts to men. Now this expression, 'He ascended,' what does it mean except that He also descended into the lower parts of the earth? (Ephesians 4:8-9).

If the grave settled matters forever, why did early Christians pray for the dead or practise baptism for the dead, as mentioned in 1 Corinthians 15:29? How can death be the end if it is ultimately cast into the second death, the Lake of Fire? Revelation reveals that death itself will be abolished, and if death is abolished, it cannot be the end. Death results from our lost identity and is empowered by the Law of the Old Covenant. In the New Covenant, death is consumed by God's fiery love. The old age of law has ended, and now we live in the New Covenant age of grace, where death is overcome by the fire of love.

I invite you to reflect on the reality of God's love. Do you truly know it? God desires you to experience His unconditional love beyond what you currently know. He wants you to come into the fullness and reality of this truth so you can live in unconditional love daily. This love will cocoon you and transform your life, enabling you to demonstrate it to others.

Paul's mission to preach Christ in the Gentiles included sharing that they were part of what Christ had done. This is the powerful gospel of unconditional love. God wants all His children to awaken to this reality, and we are on the brink of an awakening beyond anything ever known. People will begin to realise the truth of God's unconditional love, transforming their lives from lostness into the reality of being sons and daughters of God.

Activation #12
The Waterfall

I invite you to enter into the presence of God and begin to experience that unconditional love.

> I encourage you to rest,
> close your eyes,
> shut out all distractions around you.
>
> Start to breathe slowly
> Begin to meditate

and focus on God as unconditional love
the Father's unconditional love for you
that you would feel that unconditional love
flow over you
all over your physical body
that it would be absorbed into you
that you will be filled.

Be still and let God love on you.
Let Him show you that you're loved unconditionally.
Experience the amazing reality.

And every obstacle, every hindrance,
every objection, every doctrine,
every belief that you might have had
just give it to Him,
Jesus the truth,
and let Him reveal the truth
of that triumphant mercy
that limitless grace
that amazing unconditional love.

Feel it
as it fills you,
flows through you:
rivers of living water,
love flowing into your very being.

Rest in that place of love.
It's a safe place.

Heaven is open.
We can dwell in that realm
we can enter in through the door which is Jesus
to the Father.
So we can engage the Father's heart
engage the realm of light
experience His love.

I believe the Father wants to free you
from all guilt, all shame, all condemnation.

Let Him wash you clean of all your past
of all the thoughts,
your old way of thinking,
your old life,
so you can really
begin to live loved.
Enjoy life,
enjoy His presence.

Let Him wash you clean.
Let that love be like living water
washing your whole body
outside, inside your heart;
every part of your soul,
your body.

Love flowing in you
through you
around you.

I believe God will take you
where He wants you to go
but if you want to experience
the waterfall of God's love
that would reveal
the depth of His love for you and others,
then just ask Jesus to take you there;
that He would take you
under the waterfall in Eden,
the Garden of God
by following the River of Life.

You can stand under that waterfall.

Begin to picture that waterfall.
Feel it, hear it,
let that experience begin to form around you.
Stand under the outpouring of God's love
and let it cascade down over your whole being.

The sound of His voice,
let it vibrate within you,
energise you, activate you,
so you can fully experience the fullness of His life –
not just for you
but for others
and for creation itself.

Let the sound of His voice,
the sound of many waters...
let His voice speak love into your heart,
bring you healing,
bring you wholeness,
calling you out of brokenness,
calling you out of lost identity,
revealing your new name;
restored in relationship, health, blessing.

Resonate with that amazing truth
as you stand under
that cascading waterfall of the love of God.
Feel His love for you,
feel His love for all things.
Be filled.

Stay in that place as long as you want
to enjoy that cascading sound of His voice,
of His love
flowing over you,
in you,
through you.

Just embrace it,
embrace the reality of it –
it's amazing.

13. Hellfire Preaching

Many people have genuine questions and concerns about death and the afterlife. It is only natural to wonder what will happen to us and our loved ones after death. Without a firm belief in Jesus, these uncertainties can produce fear and worry. There are specific questions that often arise, such as what happens to children who die and those who are never born, whether through miscarriage or abortion. Some have speculated on the age at which children become responsible for their actions, but there is no clear answer in scripture. Yet even those who believe in eternal punishment seem to have a soft spot for children.

Through my own experiences, I have come to believe that unborn children who are miscarried or aborted enter an amazing dimensional place where they are being trained by angels. They are maturing and have a destiny to fulfil as sons and daughters of God. They continue to exist in a positive realm and have a relationship with Him.

Salvation for all

Although the wages of sin (lost identity) are indeed death, a consequence that seemingly affects all humanity, Jesus came to rescue and save everyone – adults and children alike. The gospel accounts, and Paul's writings, make it clear that Jesus' sacrifice on the cross was for the redemption of all. In the same way that Adam's sin affected all of mankind, so too did Jesus' death and resurrection provide salvation for all. God desires that everyone will be saved and come to know the reality of salvation in all its dimensions.

He has already reconciled everyone in Christ. The whole cosmos has been brought into the fold of God's love and grace. However, not everyone may be aware of this reality. God's desire for all to experience His salvation encompasses physical, emotional and spiritual well-being. The concept of salvation, *sozo* in the original Greek, relates to more than just life after death: it entails restoration and wholeness in all areas of our existence both in this life and beyond.

Does God want everyone to experience His salvation? Absolutely! God extends His kindness, tolerance and patience to lead us all into *metanoia*, a transformation of our thinking, through encountering Him. It is not about earning forgiveness through sorrow or responding through fear, but about aligning our minds with God's truth and receiving the love and grace He freely offers.

Can a person's death change the nature of God towards them? Before their death, God is loving, kind, tolerant and patient. But after someone dies, does He suddenly change to become vengeful, vindictive, a tormentor and a punisher? No, our death cannot change God. God is the same yesterday, today and forever. His character and nature remain constant, even in the face of death. His love endures forever, and He will never give up on anyone until all are fully restored to their original purpose. God will still offer everyone the choice of coming to Him through Jesus after death. That is how we see that death and its consequences are completely defeated.

"... and if I am lifted up from the earth, I will draw all men to myself." (John 12:32).

God, who desires all men to be saved and to come to the knowledge of the truth... (1 Timothy 2:4).

His intention, His plan and His desire, is for every individual to come to the knowledge of the truth and experience His love and mercy. There may be those who argue that God's desire will not necessarily be accomplished, but I am convinced that if God desires something, it will eventually come to pass. Luke 3:6 tells us that all mankind will see God's salvation: no one is excluded or forgotten in His grand plan. This is utterly inconsistent with the idea of eternal damnation.

The Lord is not slow about His promise, as some count slowness, but is patient toward you, not willing for any to perish, but for all to come to repentance [metanoia] (1 Peter 3:9).

It is not His desire to see anyone perish, or be lost. He seeks the restoration of all individuals into their true identity as children of God through His abundant grace. God's love is an unquenchable fire, and it is intended to refine and purify us. While there may be differing experiences in different places, determined by our relationship with Jesus, God's consuming fire cannot be avoided. So let us choose to embrace the fire of God's presence now, and present ourselves as living sacrifices.

Even after physical death, people can still either choose Jesus or remain in a state of self-righteousness, but eventually God's patience and kindness will prevail. There are biblical hints that support this idea: Revelation 21:10 describes the Holy City as having gates that never close, representing an eternal invitation to come to God. Similarly, Revelation 22:17 extends an invitation to all to take the water of life freely, indicating that the opportunity to come to God remains open. Revelation 5:13 portrays every creature in heaven, on earth, under the earth and in the sea praising God, a comprehensive and inclusive vision. Revelation 21:5 promises that God will renew all things, dwelling with mankind and wiping away all tears, with death and pain becoming things of the past. Ultimately, everyone will be made new.

The promise of the New Covenant is that everything will be made new. God dwells in us, and we in Him, fulfilling His plan for all His children to experience His love. Jesus offered Himself to identify with us, ensuring our restoration to a loving relationship with God. Our role is to experience, share and live this good news of reconciliation so others can see its reality.

What about justice?

So, what about justice? Surely people should get their just desserts and face consequences for their actions?

God is love, and His justice has to be viewed through the lens of love, as demonstrated by Jesus. He reconciled everyone, making them righteous and justified. There are consequences for rejecting this, but they do not include eternal torture, and God continually works to bring people into the truth.

Jesus has already dealt with justice through forgiveness, and God holds no record of wrongs. If Jesus reconciled everyone to Himself, eternal separation from God is not true justice for anyone. Even human justice can see it would be unfair for those who never heard the gospel or were deceived by false beliefs to be eternally separated from God. God's love overcomes every one of these issues through Jesus.

And Jesus cried out again with a loud voice, and gave up His spirit. And behold, the veil of the temple was torn in two from top to bottom; and the earth shook and the rocks were split. Also the tombs were opened, and many bodies of the saints who had fallen asleep were raised; and coming out of the tombs after His resurrection, they entered the holy city and appeared to many (Matthew 27:50-53).

When I saw Him, I fell at His feet like a dead man. And He placed His right hand on me, saying, "Do not be afraid; I am the first and the last, and the living One; and I was dead, and behold, I am alive forevermore, and I have the keys of death and of Hades." (Revelation 1:17-18).

Jesus opened the way for resurrection and life. Tombs were opened as He died, and many Old Testament saints were resurrected. Then He spent three days in the grave, just as He prophesied, during which He descended into *Sheol* or *Hades*, proclaimed the gospel to the spirits in prison and led out a host of captives, as described in Ephesians 4:8 and Romans 10:7. He was given the keys of death and *Hades* to set people free, not to lock them up! And when He ascended into heaven in a cloud, that cloud was the host of captives who became part of the cloud of witnesses.

Jesus proclaimed the gospel to them. The word 'gospel' is *euangelion* in Greek, from which we get the English words 'evangelism' and 'evangelist.' It means good news or glad tidings. Evangelism is about announcing this good news, which is about God's love, not 'hell' and punishment: 'hell' and punishment are not good news at all. When Jesus descended into *Sheol*, the gospel is what He preached to the souls there, leading the captives out and essentially emptying the place. Following His ascension, it is our responsibility to dissuade people from going there and to preach the good news to those who are already there, just as Jesus did.

Ephesians 1:10 speaks of summing up all things in Christ, both spiritual and physical. 1 Corinthians 15:28 declares that God will be all in all, indicating that no one is excluded. Ephesians 4:6 reinforces this, stating that God is over all, through all, and in all, revealing His intention to make Himself known to everyone. Hebrews 1:2 describes Jesus as the heir of all things, and Colossians 1:16 reveals that all creation was made by and for Him, and is reconciled by His blood. Acts 3:20-21 speaks of Jesus remaining in heaven until the restoration of all things, a period which began with the end of the Old Covenant age and the establishment of God's kingdom. Throughout the Bible, this theme of restoration underlines God's eternal plan to restore everything and everyone to His original intention and purpose for them.

Jesus took me to the fire

I have personally experienced God's consuming fire, which is His love, many times. This fire has a refining, purifying power that never fails, and I firmly believe that God's love will restore all things. However, this restoration through fire is a process everyone has to go through.

From 2016 onwards, God began deconstructing my mind. Through various experiences, He showed me the strength of His love, challenging my beliefs about what the Bible truly says. It was difficult to let go of long-held doctrines and theological frameworks, but God was renewing my mind. During this period, I felt severe mental pressure and physical pain for about three weeks particularly as I was wrestling with the idea of 'hell'. Though I believed in my mind, I needed an experience to solidify my change of thinking.

Eventually, Jesus took me to the fire to see firsthand what happens there. I entered through a door on Wisdom's Heights (see Proverbs 8). Wisdom, an angelic being, had previously given me a seal and a staff, and led me through one of the gates to Satan's trophy room. This dimension, which felt like going underground, was a place of extreme restriction and sadness. There I saw three things: sparkling diamond trophies representing the destinies of those who had never realised God's love; stolen mantles and crowns of those who lost their way due to lost identity and other issues; and an area of lost generational heritage from my family lines. This heritage included four family lines (mother's mother, mother's father, father's mother, and father's father). Whilst I hoped to reclaim this heritage, I was approaching it with a somewhat selfish mindset, not fully understanding its significance.

After that first visit, I thought little more of it, until Jesus took me back there through the fire. He asked if I wanted to see my heritage restored, and as I wondered how, a door I had not seen before appeared. Jesus gave me a heralding trumpet, and we entered the fire. I saw my ancestors in anguish, not being punished but feeling the pain of not having responded to God's love. Despite feeling overwhelmed, unprepared and unsure what to do, I preached the good news to them (not very well, I thought). When I had finished, I followed Jesus out. As He had given me the trumpet, I thought I had better blow it, so I did (more in hope than expectation, as the saying goes).

As we went out, I realised that the door on Wisdom's Heights looked like a fiery sword. I saw some souls following us: they knelt and confessed Jesus before walking through the gates that are never shut, to be embraced by the Father. I turned to Jesus. "What have you done to me? I'm in trouble now! How do I explain this?" He reassured me, saying to simply tell people that I was only doing what He did – preaching to the spirits in prison.

Not all of them followed us out, and I asked why. Jesus explained that you can only preach with authority to the degree that the fire has consumed generational things in you. He emphasised that presenting ourselves to the fire of the altar and allowing it to touch our lives will enable us to reach more of our generational lines. As we embrace the refining process, we gain the authority to preach effectively to those connected to us. That reminded me of Isaiah 6, where Isaiah acknowledges his unclean lips and is purified by a coal taken from the altar. I realised the importance of engaging the altar daily for purification and greater authority.

Some time later, during a visit to China, I felt a strong urge to engage the altar at 3am, asking for the fiery coals to touch a specific area of generational behaviour. I forgave my ancestors, then preached boldly to them in the fiery place, with many responding. Another time, during worship, I revisited the fire, preached with renewed boldness, and again saw more respond. I have also preached to fragmented souls, helping them reintegrate and commune with Christ. My goal has been to empty that place, continually embracing the fire to gain the authority to do so. Over the years, I continued until I could find no more souls from my generational lines.

This experience has been validated by testimonies from others, like Nancy Coen, who have also preached the good news in the fire. I have received emails and other messages thanking me for discussing this topic, helping others to be able to share their similar experiences. This is nothing new; many early church fathers, such as Origen, Clement of Alexandria, and Gregory of Nyssa, held this position. In modern times, Father Sergei Bulgakov and Metropolitan Kallistos Ware also share this view. Still, expect accusations of heresy, especially in evangelical circles.

It's not fair!

God's mercy always triumphs; it is man that requires human justice. Many of the responses I get only show how deep-seated is our need for justice from a human perspective. When I share something like the unconditional love of God or that people can be rescued from the fire and joyfully acknowledge Jesus as Lord after death, or that death is not the end of choice, it tends to aggravate people who come from a religious perspective:

"It's not fair that people are just let off!"

No one is let off for anything. Jesus paid the price; Jesus died their death.

"So, everyone just gets a free pass, then?"

No, no one gets a free pass. Jesus paid for it. It cost Him His life to create the opportunity for all of us to enter into relationship with God.

"So it doesn't matter how we live or what we do?"

Of course it matters. It affects us; it affects others; it has an effect on creation. If we are living in lost identity, it matters. But what it does not do is stop God from loving us or extending love, grace and mercy to us.

"Well, I might as well just keep on sinning, then!"

Why would you want to do that? Why would you want to carry on in lost identity, living a 'less-than' kind of life?

"What's the point of trying to be good if everyone gets forgiven anyway in the end?"

Because being righteous and expressing that righteousness is an expression of love, and the world needs a demonstration of love. Why would we want to be bad? Why would we want to hurt people? We do not have to try to be good to earn salvation, but we are created in God's image, in His likeness, and we are created to demonstrate the good works that He has prepared for us. We are created to demonstrate love, to be an expression of love to one another.

No one gets away with anything, but God's desire is that nothing would stop them from coming into a restored relationship. The point is, everything has consequences, but God's love overcomes in the end.

We place our hope in the final victory and verdict of Jesus Christ, whose mercy endures forever. His loving kindness never fails, and that is where we anchor our faith – not in human justice, theology or doctrine, but in the victory of the cross. Jesus declared us innocent, not guilty, having reconciled and justified all people. That is the key reality.

Equal value

Herein is the extremity of God's love gift: mankind was rotten to the core when Christ died their death. If God could love us that much when we were ungodly and guilty, how much more are we free to realize His love now that we are declared innocent by His blood? (God does not love us more now that we are reconciled to him; we are now free to realize how much he loved us all along. [Colossians 2:14, Romans 4:25].) *Our hostility and indifference towards God did not reduce His love for us; in his death, our minds were rescued from our sense of unworthiness and separation. Now that this act of reconciliation is complete, his life in us saves us from the guttermost to the uttermost.* (Reconciliation, from *katalasso*, meaning a mutual exchange of equal value. Thayer Definition: to exchange, as coins for others of equivalent value.) (Romans 5:8-10 Mirror, with translator's notes).

God sets the same value on us as on Jesus; Jesus was considered to be of equal value in the exchange. And God does not love us more now that we are reconciled to Him than He did before; it is just that we are now free to realise how much He loved us all along. This is the difference between the good news and the evangelical perspective that seems to suggest God does not love you as much as He loves believers until you are reconciled. The reality is, we are all already reconciled, and now we are free to see how much He loved us, even while we were in lost identity. This is the power of an amazing God who is unconditional love.

If while we were enemies, we were reconciled to God by the death of His Son, how much more, now that we are reconciled, shall we be saved by His life? (Romans 5:10).

God wants us to live in the abundance of His life, not as if we were still in that old lost identity. He wants people to discover who they truly are, and it is part of our responsibility to share that good news.

One act of righteousness

So then as through one offense the result was condemnation for all mankind, so also through one act of righteousness the result was the justification of life to all mankind. For as through the one man's disobedience the many were made sinners, so also through the obedience of the One the many will be made righteous (Romans 5:18-19).

All mankind were condemned, through the offense of Adam, because up to that point all mankind were of Adam's line. But 'condemnation' does not necessarily imply a sentence of eternal punishment or 'hell', as we may have been taught. Life is found in a relationship with God. When Adam walked away from that relationship, he lost his spiritual life, leading to death. The result of walking away from life is death.

All mankind ended up in lost identity, and Jesus' act of righteousness meant that identity for all could now be fully recovered. God now sees us as completely justified, as if we had never done anything arising from lost identity in the first place. Verse 19 essentially echoes verse 18, though if quoted out of context you might be forgiven for thinking it is more selective: it is not. Since 'the many' were made sinners – and we all agree that means everyone, all mankind; then it is the same 'many' (all mankind) who benefit by being made righteous.

The many who were made sinners, losing their identity and walking in the knowledge of good and evil, trying to earn their restored relationship with God through humanism or their own efforts, will now all be made righteous, with no exceptions. This is not some vague future meaning of 'will', as in 'one day': from the context of verse 18 it is clear that it is a done deal. In the past, all were condemned in Adam; from now on all will be considered righteous in Christ. God's perspective is that all are made righteous, but sadly, most people do not yet know it. It is our responsibility to help them get to know it by demonstrating and sharing the good news of what God has already done for them.

The Law came in so that the offense would increase; but where sin increased, grace abounded all the more, so that, as sin reigned in death, so also grace would reign through righteousness to eternal life through Jesus Christ our Lord (Romans 5:20-21).

No matter what mankind may have done or how much sin has increased, grace has abounded even more. The divine enabling power of God overcomes every obstacle and hindrance. As sin reigned in death, as lost identity reigned in producing that death, grace would reign through righteousness to eternal life through Jesus. This amazing statement means the power of God's love and grace has overcome everything that could be an objection or obstacle to anyone and everyone being restored to a relationship with Him. Everything has been overcome through what Jesus did on the cross.

The conclusion is clear: it took just one offense to condemn mankind; one act of righteousness declares the same mankind innocent (Romans 5:18 Mirror).

We see then that as one act of sin exposed the whole race of men to condemnation, so one act of perfect righteousness presents all men freely acquitted in the sight of God. One man's disobedience placed all men under the threat of condemnation, but one man's obedience has the power to present all men righteous before God (Romans 5:18-19 JBP).

When we look at people, we no longer see them through their old identity of the flesh, no matter what they have done or are doing. We find this difficult because our humanistic way of thinking leads us to make judgments based on behaviour. When people do terrible things, we value them less and think God values them less as well. This human understanding of vengeance and retribution forms the basis of our justice system, which is based on 'an eye for an eye.' But Jesus said, "Love your enemies and pray for them." Everyone has been acquitted of every act and accusation against them, as it was all nailed to the cross and overcome by Jesus. This is the power and the extreme nature of unconditional love.

The disobedience of the one exhibits humanity as sinners, while the obedience of another, Jesus, exhibits humanity as righteous (Romans 5:19 Mirror).

We are not made sinners by our own disobedience, just as we are not made righteous by our own obedience. We cannot earn anything, nor in all righteousness and justice can we be punished, from God's perspective, because Jesus dealt with all accusations against everyone. It is difficult to accept this when we look at people and see what is going on in the world. I am asked questions all the time about whether people who commit terrible crimes can be considered righteous. Whilst they are not acting in righteousness, they have been forgiven and made righteous from God's perspective.

This creates a huge problem with how we think about justice because human justice demands retribution. However, God's mercy has triumphed over our understanding of justice and set people free from the need for punishment. I am not advocating that people should be allowed to do anything they want: there needs to be a way to curtail harmful behaviour, but the approach can be restorative rather than punitive. Restorative justice helps people see how their behaviour is determined by their perceived identity, and understanding their true identity can change their behaviour.

I did an interview not long ago with a well-known YouTube host in the UK. They posted it on their website but had to take it down because of all the negative comments and scarcely veiled intimidation they received from professing Christians. The subject was unconditional love, and some people were infuriated: although they accepted God as unconditional love, they did not accept that God's unconditional love is for everyone. But God loved the world so much that He sent Jesus to take away the sin of the world, not just give people an opportunity for a relationship but to remove every obstacle:

The entire cosmos is the object of God's affection. He is not about to abandon His creation. The gift of His Son is for humanity to realize their origin in Him who mirrors their authentic birth, begotten not of the flesh but of the Father. In this persuasion, the life of the ages echoes within the individual, announcing the days of regret and lostness are over (John 3:16 Mirror).

When people come to realise God's amazing grace, mercy and love; when they understand their past is forgiven and their future is ahead, they realise who they really are and can be part of the solution rather than the problem the world is facing. Jesus came to seek and save those who were lost – and, make no mistake, all were lost. He came to take away the sin of the world, the lost identity of the whole world, not just of some people but of all people. Jesus even preached in *Hades* to those who were lost there and led captivity captive. God has been proactive in reaching out to us to remove all barriers and obstacles to restored relationship.

The notion that anyone can be separated from God, either in this life or the next, is merely an illusion. Everything that exists was created within God, not apart from Him. Nothing can exist outside of God's presence, which encompasses and permeates all things. It is therefore impossible to be truly separated from Him. We are all inherently included, accepted and embraced within His boundless love, regardless of what anyone may claim to the contrary.

I have had many experiences that have been expressions of unconditional love regarding the restoration of all things. 'All things' includes people on earth and in heaven, angelic beings, and dimensional beings. Nothing is left out. We looked at what Paul wrote to the Colossians: all things that Jesus created were reconciled and brought to peace by the blood of the cross. In other words, what He did on the cross, through His unconditional love, is at work in limitless grace and triumphant mercy for all of God's children. Everything is unconditional, but everything needs to be received if we are to benefit from the gift.

It is like someone buys something precious, packages it up, and puts on it the name of the person it is going to. The gift has been purchased, the name has been applied to it, and the person reaches out with that gift and offers it to the recipient. If the person does not receive it, they are never going to know what that gift is until they do receive it. Even though it has been bought and paid for, even though it has been assigned to that person, even though they do not have to do anything to receive it other than take it, still many people are living without receiving everything that God has done because of the nature of deception. That is the deception of lies, the deception of the enemy, which is a lie from the beginning. The deception of religion keeps people from receiving what is freely given by grace, and insists they fulfil conditions before they can receive. In many cases those conditions put people off even wanting to receive what God is offering them because it is wrapped differently from how God packages it. God wraps it in grace, mercy and love, but religion packages it in works.

We have good news for this world, to reveal the reality of God's love. My experiences and conversations with my Dad, my Heavenly Father, confirm the truth that Paul was communicating. He had a revelation of this amazing, inclusive gospel because he experienced it firsthand as one who was persecuting Christians. God revealed Himself as working in Paul already, not outside of him. Paul was never rejected; he just lived in isolation from that truth. He rejected that truth and lived in the Old Covenant of self-righteousness. He had a revelation that nothing can separate us from God and His unconditional love. This revelation was very profound, and (if you set aside its familiarity to us as scripture) very deeply moving.

Now, not just in the future

The soul experiences so much self-inflicted anguish and torment as a result of what we do. It can make people feel so bad about themselves that they do not feel worthy to receive forgiveness, even when it is offered. They do not feel worthy; therefore, they reject it. They are feeling self-inflicted pain, torment and anguish already, in this life, and that is what I have seen in people in the consuming fire of God's love. They inflict pain and torment on themselves because of their own mindsets, the beliefs they have and what they have been taught and told. They inflict it on themselves: God does not do that. There is no reason for God to inflict pain on anyone, because Jesus has overcome the power of sin, which is death.

My experiences of what happens to people after death indicate the importance of sharing, demonstrating and being the good news now. I do not want anyone to have to face the consuming fire of God's love in that place without knowing Him. I want everyone to experience the consuming fire of God's love by choice, by coming to the altar, presenting themselves as living sacrifices and receiving that refining and purification. I have seen what people feel like when they are in the fire of God's love, and they do not know His love, or feel worthy of His love, or do not believe they can possibly be forgiven. It is not a place I want anyone to go, and it is not a place God wants anyone to go either. People choose to go there because they reject the free offer of God's salvation through grace, and suffer the consequences of doing it in their own strength by following the humanistic tree of the knowledge of good and evil.

God wants all His children to enjoy the abundance of life now, not just at some point in the future, so that we can all come to this wonderful knowledge and experience of the truth.

He who did not spare His own Son, but delivered Him over for us all, how will He not also with Him freely give us all things? Who will bring a charge against God's elect? God is the one who justifies; who is the one who condemns? Christ

Jesus is He who died, yes, rather who was raised, who is at the right hand of God, who also intercedes for us (Romans 8:32-34).

"But delivered Him over for us all." Let us be quite clear: 'God's elect' is everyone – all those for whom God took the sin of the world; all that God reconciled, which was the whole cosmos; all those that were reconciled by the blood of the cross, which are all those He created. All is all, not just those who may believe, but all that He died for in their place, which is everyone. No one is left out. And "Who is the one who condemns?" Well, it is not God. It can be ourselves; it can be the accuser, but not God.

Jesus went to the cross as the Lamb of God. We, like sheep, have gone astray, and He took our place so that we do not have to suffer the consequence of death. He loved us when we did not love Him. He loved us when we were walking in complete amnesia of who we really are. That is the power of unconditional love. All that is true, but for you to experience it you have to come to that realisation and accept it as true. So, in reality, the only thing that can separate us from the practical experience of the love of God is in our own thinking. If we reject it, we separate ourselves from it, even though God has not. We need to accept this reality and experience it as truth.

My encounters with Him have revealed and confirmed this. As I have repeatedly acknowledged, they have changed my whole life in reference to the unconditional love of God and what that means for all His children and all creation. I will continue to share my experiences in this book, but be warned, some of them are quite radical even compared to what has gone before. They were extraordinarily challenging when I had them, but they affirm over and over again the power of God's unconditional love. Again, please remember that I am only sharing my experiences, not creating a doctrine. I encourage you to seek God for your own experiences of the truth about His love. Be part of the restoration of all things. And if you are struggling with deconstructing your old beliefs, allow God to renew your mind to fully embrace His work in and through you.

We have the choice to encounter God's refining fire now or later, but we cannot escape it. God's love is an unquenchable fire intended to purify. Choose to engage this fire now – lay yourself on the altar as a living sacrifice. Engage the various aspects of His fire, such as the judgment seat of Christ, where the fire of God's eyes burns away the wood, hay and straw and makes the gold, silver and precious stones shine.

I believe we all have the ability to engage the fiery place to do what Jesus did, to preach the good news to those we are mandated to engage. And that is an important consideration: do not just think you can go in there and preach to anybody, based on anything I may have written; ask for revelation about who you can preach to. God is unconditional love, and He is not going to give up. He will continue. Love wins.

Activation #13
Consuming Fire

Let's enter into an encounter with God. If you choose, engage the fire of His presence and see what happens in the consuming fire of His love. If you are willing, ask Him to take you there.

> I encourage you to close your eyes.
> Come to that place of rest.
> Start to slow down,
> fix your eyes on Jesus.

> Think of the love of God.
> Think of the Father's love.
> Start to focus.
> Let love begin to fill you, surround you,
> cocoon you.
> Breathe in deeply
> the unconditional love of the Father for you.

Feel that unconditional love flow
right through your whole being.

Be still.
Let God love you.
Let God love on you.

Enjoy that love for a few moments.
Be still and know.
Be still and know that He is unconditional love.

Let the words of the Father just resound within you.
I am unconditional love.
I am unconditional love.
I am unconditional love.

And as you are resting in that place,
let unconditional love touch you:
your emotions, your mind,
your heart, your whole being;
every fibre, every atom,
every particle of your being
touched by unconditional love.

You're in a safe place.
Be still.

Enjoy the Father's love.
Wait in His arms of love.
Let Him hug you, surround you,
and transfer His heart.
Heart to heart, cardiognosis,
an infusion of knowledge,
experiential knowledge of unconditional love.

We know heaven's open.
We know the Father desires to open that realm to us.

I just ask, Father,
if You would open up places of unconditional love,
of Your fiery, consuming presence.

Open up the altar,
open up the river of fire,
open up the judgment seat,
open up the fiery place.

And if You are willing and people desire it,
that you would take them and show them
the power of love,
the transforming power of unconditional love;
that you would show them
the reality of your love for all things, for all time,
the depth, the height, the breadth
of your amazing unconditional love.

Go wherever He takes you,
and just stay in that place of rest.

Embrace the fire of love and transformation.

14. More Adventures in the Fire

God demonstrated His unconditional love by sending Jesus into this world to represent us, live as us, die as us, take us into the grave with Him, and raise us all in resurrection life. He did all this while we were still in our lost identity. He does not demand we fulfil any conditions for Him to do that. Love was the condition that caused Jesus to come, and the Father willingly allowed Him to come to identify with us.

Come and walk with me

In an encounter I had, Jesus said, "Come and walk with me." Whenever He says that, I always know I am going to experience something that will challenge or reveal some new truth to me. He held my hand and took me through the gates into a large hall. This was near the Court of the Upright, where you find the cloud of witnesses. "These are those who have come out of the fire," Jesus said. They were the ones who died, went into the consuming fire of God's love, and came out of that fire by accepting Jesus.

There were many people in this hall, sitting at benches in a classroom-like environment. There were men in white linen and angels, teaching and imparting to them. It felt like the very presence of the Father was there. More angels were overseeing what was going on, and warrior angels were standing at attention. It was quite a sight. Jesus said, "This is where those who are being rescued from the fire go to be instructed in the truth and the ways of relationship. The fire has done its work; now, the relationship must do its work in preparing them for destiny. They will be released for the coming harvest, with the hunter-gatherer angels you see here."

People's destiny is not just what happens to them in this life on earth; there is an eternal destiny, a destiny for the ages to come. Jesus explained that these people have a different role because they have been through a different process. Those who come into a relationship with God on earth and live the

Christian life have a different role than those who come out through the fire.

This theme of a coming harvest has been shared with me and others for a long time. There is a coming harvest, which I believe to be a billion-soul harvest. The Joshua generation needs to be prepared to receive and bring people into their inheritance. They will be the witnesses that bring about change to the world by revealing love. The hunter-gatherer angels they will work with can appear quite fierce but are instrumental in sharing the good news.

Jesus continued, "They will be released with the harvest, and the cloud of witnesses will also carry the message. They will carry a message of love through consuming fire that will turn a generation to true repentance." True repentance is not about being sorry for sin or doing penance; it is truly coming into agreement with what God thinks about us and who He really is. "They will become ambassadors of fire with passion to remove the veils of deception, just as those who came out of the graves were witnesses of what I did under the earth at my resurrection. These are witnesses to the power of love to overcome even the choices of death and to warn of the consequences of where they have been."

I do not know exactly how this will take place or whether they will support us in bringing this message to the world, but I fully believe that God desires to use those who have a powerful testimony of that amazing love. He will use the angelic messengers to take the message to the world. He will use those who have a witness and a testimony to this. They are being prepared to be at the disposal of the Joshua generation to engage the coming harvest.

"There is an urgency for my brothers to do what I did and preach the good news of my love to your generations and see your heritage restored." I shared previously my experience of going and preaching to my generational lines, just as Jesus went into the grave and preached the good news. "God wants to restore creation, and He needs all His people to do it.

Release this message and encourage the Joshua generation to arise and be bold, to come to Me, and I will open the gates to reveal the consuming fire and show them the way just as I have shown you."

You may have a different experience to mine, but God wants to show you the principle and the truth that you can rescue people from the fire. Remember, the refining fire of the altar is where the authority to preach will be given: that is why I present myself as a living sacrifice for God's fire to purify and refine my heart. "Embrace the fire with urgent desire, and great authority will be released to you." This is what I did at the time, embracing the daily engagement with the fire and consuming, refining fire of God's love.

Then, I had an astonishing encounter. He took me to meet John Newton, a slaver who found salvation and wrote the hymn 'Amazing Grace,' which has been sung through multiple generations as a testimony. Wen John Newton came to meet me, he brought with him thousands of people with wonderful testimonies of that amazing, limitless grace. Some of these people, who saw themselves as wretches like John did in his song, were the worst of the worst by human standards – mass murderers, rapists, paedophiles, abusers and traffickers. They all came and shared how they had been forgiven and welcomed by the Father.

Time seemed to be suspended for me, and I heard thousands and thousands of testimonies. It was the most moving thing, and I did not feel that it was 'unfair' that these people were testifying of their forgiveness despite their terrible actions. And all those who had been victims of their crimes who had now found a relationship with God also now came and shared how they had been restored and made whole, no matter what had happened to them in this life. Some had suffered terribly at others' hands, but each of them shared their testimony that the powerful grace, mercy and unconditional love of God had restored them and made them whole. Nothing that had happened to them affected them anymore; they were free from it. Those who had been saved, who had been victims, and those who were the victimisers, were standing next to one another in oneness and unity. This was an amazing sight; this was limitless grace in action. I was so moved, virtually overwhelmed and weeping, to see the power of God's awesome unconditional love. I felt so privileged to listen to their stories of how the unconditional love of the Father had rescued them.

Some of these stories were from before death; some were after physical death. Some came out of the fire, whilst others had responded while still living on earth. For example, there were testimonies from those convicted at the Nuremberg trials after the Second World War for terrible atrocities. Some had received Jesus through the preaching of chaplains in the Nuremberg cells. Some responded when Jesus engaged them as the Light at the point of their death.

In spite of their depraved behaviour and lifestyles, it seemed that many were visited by the light of love, Jesus, on their deathbeds. They willingly and gratefully accepted the grace and mercy He offered them in love at that moment. God, our loving Father, and Jesus our Brother are not trying to make it difficult for us. They unequivocally desire people to come to the realisation that they have been restored to face-to-face innocence from God's perspective so that they can experience it from their own perspective too. As they relived their stories, I felt what they felt when they experienced the oracles of His love, the oracles of the Father's heart – the deep emotions of passion, burning desire, intense joy, deep compassion, and overwhelming love. When they experienced that, it totally changed their thinking. They were literally swept into the Kingdom on a wave of the wonderful emotions that their loving Father had towards them. They experienced love.

Incredible though it may appear, some people experience that and yet still reject it, and those are the ones that go into the fiery place for the fire to continue to work on them, to continue to refine and purify them, bringing them to the realisation of God's amazing love for them.

There were other stories of those who were in the depths of despair, facing the reality of their treatment of others. When grace and mercy were demonstrated by the victim or a victim's loved ones, they shared how unworthy they felt, yet they had been forgiven. I know some people who have had children murdered and yet have come out publicly stating that they hold nothing against the murderer but have chosen to forgive them. Some testimonies reveal that this forgiveness was the very thing that caused the perpetrator to experience God's love by unveiling the limitlessness of God's mercy and grace to them. The power of forgiveness is an amazing thing. It is the outworking of unconditional love.

The stories I listened to continued, one after another, expressing the depth of their gratitude. They all had one thing in common: love, expressed through one or other of the Father's oracles, had brought them to a realisation of their inclusion, reconciliation and restoration. Whether it was God's passion, His burning desire, intense joy, deep compassion or overwhelming love, something touched their hearts and lives in a way that revealed and unveiled the truth, and they received it.

There were also stories of how deeply compassion and overwhelming love had touched people when they were in a state of grief over the loss of a loved one – whether a child, spouse, or sibling – killed in some horrendous, traumatic way. But at their lowest point, they experienced God's compassion, which carried their grief and sorrows. It was at that point that they felt the love of God and were convinced to enter into a relationship with Him.

This was an uninterrupted catalogue of stories. Many came forward who were victims of abuse of all kinds – rape, racism, slavery – but had experienced limitless grace that transformed them from deep darkness and despair into a place where the light of love shone brightly in their lives. There were those who had taken their own lives, sharing that they had received limitless grace and mercy directly from Jesus at the moment of their death, all with stories of being embraced with overwhelming, loving acceptance. Some had never expected to be able to enter heaven because that is what religious people had told them. Some were so convinced that it was impossible for them that they went into the fire. But even there, the love of God continued to bring them into acceptance.

Seek out the worst of the worst

During this encounter, the Father said to me, "There are many who have not yet responded to our love because of deep shame. You are tasked to seek them out within the fire and reveal just how limitless our grace and mercy really is."

I thought, "Thanks, that is quite a task!" But because of my experiences, because of my knowing how much God loved me and the fact that I am always willing, I said yes. He explained, "The serial killers, the child murderers, the paedophiles, the tyrants, the despots, those who are responsible for genocide, ethnic cleansing, satanic ritual abuse – the worst of the worst are your mission field." I did not take this lightly and I had no intention of going into it in a blasé fashion. I needed preparation for this. It was going to be probably the most challenging task that I had ever faced.

"Son, only limitless grace expressed through deep compassion and overwhelming love will remove the deep shame they feel. Son, do you feel it for them?" And I had to be honest, and said no, I don't. He offered me a solution: "Son, come deeper into our heart to feel it and know it for yourself."

So I came deep, deep into the heart of God, and I saw in a moment all the worst things I had ever imagined, thought or done. In an instant, without any time to react, overwhelming waves of acceptance hit me, washing away every thought and memory. In that fraction of a second, He enabled me to feel what people were going to feel – lavish grace and the pleasure of a doting Father. As that feeling rolled over me, it was almost too much to bear.

That was just the beginning. Every emotion linked to love bombarded me into total surrender. Any vestige of doubt was washed away in the torrents of the abundance of the pentatonic love frequencies of the Oracles of the Father's Heart. God had given me a set of five specific frequencies on a pentatonic scale to represent each of the Oracles of His heart (I will go into more detail in Chapter 20). When those frequencies are released with intention, they can intensely engage people's lives.

"Son, you know you can give what you have freely received, as all that is called sin is but a result of lost identity. To us, one act is the same as all acts. We just see our children adrift in their lostness." In other words, there is nothing worse than anything else, and no one is worse than anyone else. All of them are just lost, and Jesus came to seek and to save those who were lost. People sometimes use the argument, "Well, there's someone worse than me," to justify themselves, but any comparative 'scale of badness' is a do-it-yourself tree invention fuelled by guilt to lessen the shame.

This is what the Father was trying to show me: we are not to judge anyone by what they have done. We cannot say "This person is worse than that person; this person deserves worse than that person." God does not deal with it that way. Jesus came to seek and to save those who were lost, not to judge them, in that sense. The judgment of the cross was innocent, not guilty.

"Son, mercy triumphs over man's view of justice, when the stories are told. But what you will feel from those in the consuming fire of His love is the self-inflicted reaping of all that they have sown." People are still suffering those self-inflicted consequences in the fire, but they do not have to; God does not want them to suffer, when His mercy is available.

I had felt that self-inflicted torment myself, even for just a moment, so I knew I could identify with those who are facing their shameful acts but are still unable to receive mercy, even though it is available. Only one who has experienced their pain and received limitless grace will be able to reach them; I had felt it, which enabled me to accept the mission God gave.

"Son, you have this mandate. You have experienced this reality from both sides. Freely you have received; now freely give, by releasing limitless grace and mercy through deep compassion and overwhelming love." That was what my heart was feeling towards those I was going to engage. I felt inspired and compelled to go into the consuming fire of God's love to preach limitless grace to the worst of the worst of the worst (by man's reckoning). But I exercised some wisdom, in that I knew I did not need to go there on my own.

I went back to the court of the upright. Again, I met those who were beaming and shining with joyful exuberance, waiting to tell their story of grace, just longing to share it with others. I asked if they would come with me into the fire, and they accepted. They were only too pleased to accept my invitation, because some of them had come from there.

We went through Wisdom's Heights into the fiery place. We went to engage with those who were trapped in deep shame. I engaged my desire and my own testimony of deep compassion and overwhelming love to create a frequency of hope, to draw them out of their self-imposed darkness into the light of our glory. Our glory is our testimony; the word 'glory' means 'weight'. Our testimony is a weight, it carries an intensity of the truth.

Those who came forward represented the worst examples of human degradation, and all I felt were the Oracles of the Father's Heart. I saw Hitler, Stalin, and other tyrants from history come up, heads bowed, covered in darkness. I saw Ted Bundy, Manson, Christie, Brody and many other serial killers come into the light. One by one, they came – the worst of the worst. I do not need to mention any more names, but those are just some you might know. I felt their anguish and their pain and torment. And I really did feel it.

I do not know if it was actually them as individuals or if they were representative to me of all those categories of people. I do not really know, and to be honest, it does not really matter. I have no problem if Hitler receives the love of God. He is not the Hitler we knew on earth anymore, is he? He would be purified and refined and would know his real identity. We will have to get used to looking at people through the eyes of God and see who He made them to be, not what they have done. I know that can be so hard for people to accept, but it is the truth of how God looks at us.

There were also those who had taken their own lives and were held captive by the religious shame that said they could never enter heaven. I felt the passion, the burning desire, the intense joy, the deep compassion, and the overwhelming love that the Father has for all His children. I felt it. I preached the love that inspired such limitless grace, but I was totally overwhelmed, even after everything I had experienced, by their guilt, shame, condemnation and fragmentation. Fragmentation was a major issue for them: many were broken and fragmented and unable to respond. I felt such a weight, but, based on my own experience and what I knew to be true, I released all the love and acceptance I had received. I covered them in the frequency of my sonship, in the frequency of my testimony, in the frequencies of the Oracles of the Father's Heart. I began to give an impassioned call to their alters; I saw them as multiple personalities, as shadows, and I saw them come to the light. My passion drew the Prince of Peace, Jesus, who came and stood there and welcomed them to come to Him. I called on the witnesses who had come with me, victims and perpetrators, to release their testimonies of limitless grace and to release the forgiveness they had received.

Hundreds of thousands responded, their countenance changed, their heads lifted. It was a fantastic thing to see. I offered them peace as I shared the true gospel of forgiveness. I forgave them, as did all the witnesses, on behalf of all their victims, and released another wave of the Oracles of love.

More heads began to be raised, and I continued bombarding them with love's light until they accepted there was a choice they could never have imagined they could make, and they chose to come to Jesus and receive His amazing grace and mercy. Jesus, as Prince of Peace, was there standing with us in agreement.

I watched as, one by one, the fragmented came into Love's embrace to receive the rest of love, joy and peace from Him. They came to him and found rest, love, joy and peace, just as He promised. He did not only promise that to those who are here on earth; He promised that love, joy, peace and rest to all God's children, all of mankind. When all had come, Jesus turned and led them out of that fiery place, out of that fiery self-inflicted torment, through the fiery sword, back through Wisdom's Heights where each one knelt at the fiery sword. They knelt down in surrender. They confessed Jesus as Lord. Captivity was now led captive into the limitless grace and mercy which had triumphed over their own self-inflicted form of justice. As they followed us out through the fiery sword, they ran into the arms of the Father, who was there running to meet them. They were embraced by Limitless Grace. Each was given a ring of sonship and robes of righteousness as all the hosts of heaven rejoiced and celebrated.

Restoration is limitless grace in action, and I saw it and felt it. I can testify to the power of unconditional love to save 'from the guttermost to the uppermost' those who we might describe as rotten to the core. Nothing is too much for the love of God to overcome, to change, to transform. These individuals, when we encounter them in heaven, will be completely healed and restored through the love of the Father; and that is how He desires us to see them now: not through the lens of what they have done, which has been forgiven, but through the eyes of love, as they really are. What a celebration there was in the realms of heaven as those who were lost, hidden within their own shame and self-imposed darkness, began to shine as light.

Then I began to think of the victims of those now basking in limitless grace and mercy. I began to think of the victims who had never forgiven them, and remained in that state of unforgiveness in the fire. It struck me that those victims might well still be in bondage to the torture of unforgiveness, bitterness, resentment and trauma. So I asked the new witnesses, those who had just been released, those who were probably the perpetrators, to come and help. We went back into the fiery place, and again I set the desire of my heart towards those in the fire. They came forth, hostile, angry, entitled, blaming God. I could feel the sense of injustice that covered them in darkness like a cloud. They were bitter and resentful in the toxicity of unforgiveness. I released the frequency of the Oracles of the Father's Heart and, one by one, I reminded them of their lostness. Their own behaviour called for restorative justice, where the victims would meet the perpetrators. I asked any of them who were themselves without sin to throw their accusations like stones, but they were silent. Then, again one by one, the perpetrators who had come with me asked for forgiveness, and I saw the most amazing reconciliations taking place.

Those who had committed unspeakable crimes asked for forgiveness, and those who had been caught in bitterness in that place forgave them. Again, the astonishing power of love overcame. I had no need to say anything as I turned and led more captives free from self-inflicted torture and torment. Once again, walking together, the victims and victimisers knelt, confessed love for God and each other, and rose to walk through the fiery sword into Zion. Such a powerful thing to see and experience, and to know how deep and wide the love of God is, how overcoming. The Father said, "Son, now you see why there is a celebration when the lost are found and Our children return to Us." I went through the gateway into Zion, and I saw the loving Father running to embrace each one again, to impart sonship with robes of righteousness and rings of sonship.

Do not be intimidated

"Son, do not be intimidated and do not back off from your mandate, which is now primarily the restoration of all things." I have been challenged many times over things I have shared. People say, "You're making it up, you're deluded," but they are my experiences. I am not going to build a theology around them, but they are my experiences, and I do believe they represent the love of God and the unconditional nature of that love. The Father encouraged me to persevere and not give up in the face of criticism or judgment from others. Accusations of heresy abound, but I just bless those who make them. The Father said, "Those stuck in the deception of futurist eschatological judgment will inevitably frame restoration wrongly, so legislate for an opening of their eyes." I want them to come to the same knowledge of the love of God that I and many others have experienced, so they can be set free and enter into the reality of these things for themselves.

The unconditional love of God is so powerful; it goes beyond anything I could imagine or think. Nothing can separate us from the love of God. Absolutely nothing. Nothing we have done and nothing that has been done to us, if we will only come to realise and accept the wonderful gift that Jesus has for us.

How do you feel about those who have done or are still doing terrible things on earth? Are you able to love them in the same way that you have been loved? God wants us to demonstrate His love. He wants us to show the world that He is love and He loves them unconditionally, they just have to come to realise it and accept it. They do not have to earn it, or jump through hoops to receive it. It is free. It is freely given because Jesus came to take away our lost identity. He came to deal with our death. He died our deaths so that we can live an abundant life. It is tragic for those who are living a less-than-kind of life because they do not know that they are accepted, reconciled and forgiven already, so they feel guilt, shame and condemnation – or are still living in self-righteousness, following humanistic knowledge and doing things independently of God.

I want people to come to that realisation. I want everyone to experience the amazing, powerful love of God that I have experienced and heard in others' testimonies. Again, I am not asking you to believe me, but I am asking you to be willing to go to the Father and ask Him to show you the power of His unconditional love for those it may be your mandate to reach. I am called to reach those I am mandated to reach. You may be able to reach others that I never could. Are you willing to be open for God to show you, willing for God to use you in that way to demonstrate this love to those who are living – and those who have died and are in that place of God's consuming fire?

Activation #14
Love the Unlovable

I encourage you to weigh these things in your heart and ask the questions: Can I love those who seem to be unlovable? Do I have what it takes to demonstrate limitless grace and triumphant mercy? If the answer is no, are you willing to ask the Father today to give you such unconditional love, to let you experience His unconditional love for you?

> Close your eyes,
> Come to that place where you begin to focus
> your intention, your mind, your heart.
> Be still. Be still and know that God is love.
>
> Begin to meditate,
> slow down your whole thinking process,
> your whole body.
> Come to a place of rest. Relax.
>
> Fix your attention,
> fix your eyes on Jesus,
> fix your eyes on the Father,

and let unconditional love begin to surround you.
As you breathe in deeply,
breathe in the unconditional love of the Father.
Feel His unconditional love for you.
Be still and let God love you.

Be still so you can know
the power of unconditional love.
Be still and know – know by experience.

Father, release the experiences of unconditional love
to everyone reading or listening.
Let unconditional love –
the power of unconditional love –
overwhelm them.
Let the fire of Your love purify and refine their hearts.
Show each one the way You see them.
Show each one what You've forgiven them for.
Let them see the triumphant nature of Your mercy,
and grace, and love in their lives.
Give them a testimony to share.

Let the oracles of the Father's heart,
those frequencies surround you.
Passion.
Let the frequency of God's passion
for you and for all His children,
let it resonate in your heart.
Let it resonate with your heart, mind and emotions.
Let it vibrate with energy and life.

Let the frequency of burning desire,
God's burning desire for you and for all His children...
The feeling – sense it!
Let that frequency bring you into agreement with it
and resonate with you.

Feel the intense joy,
the frequency of His intense joy:
when He looks at you

and when He looks at all His children,
He feels intense joy.
He rejoices over you.
no matter what you've done,
no matter who you are,
He rejoices over you
as He rejoices over all His children.
Feel it.
Vibrate with it
Be energised by it.

Feel His deep compassion.
Let that frequency of deep compassion
vibrate in your very deeper innermost being.
Feel the way He shows His compassion to you,
that you might feel that compassion to others.
Feel it, His compassion.
He cares for you; He loves you.

And feel that overwhelming love
a love which will never give up,
never cease, never stop, never fail,
that we cannot be separated from.
Feel the frequency of that love.
Let it energise you to be able to love others
the way you have been loved,
the way God loves you,
the way God loves them.
Be a voice for unconditional love.
Be a testimony for unconditional love.
Feel that powerful love of God.

If you desire to receive the knowledge,
the truth, the experiences
of that consuming fire of God's presence,
I encourage you to ask the Father,
ask Jesus to take you there.
Ask Jesus to show you for yourself
those that can be rescued from the fire,
who don't yet know how to receive His love.

I ask you, Father, to open up that realm.
Let Jesus walk with them as Prince of Peace,
as a suffering servant who came
to seek and save those who were lost.

Let Jesus take you through Wisdom's Heights,
through the fiery door,
through Satan's trophy room
into the fire of God's loving presence,
that consuming fire.

Let Him show you
those who are there
in self-inflicted torment and pain
and anguish of soul.
Let Jesus show you how to share the good news,
how to feel His compassion,
and share His compassion and love
to those who are in torment, in anguish.
Let the unconditional love of God be released.

Open up your hearts, and if you're willing,
be willing to go wherever He takes you
to experience whatever He shows you.

Maybe you feel you're not ready for that yet,
and that's okay.
Just stay in that place,
cocooned in the love of God yourself.

Maybe you feel unworthy to share the good news.
Ask Him to forgive you.
Although He's already forgiven you,
sometimes we just need to acknowledge,
to receive that forgiveness.
To receive, maybe,
forgiveness for being judgmental,
for carrying bitterness or resentment,
or judging people in the flesh,
for judging people for what they've done,

for being hard-hearted towards people.
If you have any experiences of that,
be willing to let them go.
Lay them at His feet.
Ask Him to empower you to love unconditionally.

Just wait there for a few minutes
and experience whatever you need to experience.
Stay in that place of love.

15. Worm Theology

Why is it so difficult?

Why is it so difficult for many people to accept and receive the unconditional love of God? Part of it is our upbringing, part of it is our experiences in life, and part of it is the conditioning we may have had culturally or particularly in a religious setting from a Christian perspective. But ultimately, it began with following the DIY path of independence, which leads to a works-based mentality. We look to earn or create our own identity from what we do, which takes us further and further away from our true identity in God. Therefore, that God could love us unconditionally seems too good to be true because everything in the world is conditional. Losing our identity creates a sense of worthlessness and never feeling good enough. That mentality can cause us to strive or give up, and both of those things are deceptions.

These DIY tree deceptions have successfully misrepresented the nature of God, the nature of man, and God's interaction with mankind. They are in total contradiction to the unconditional love that is God's nature. These deceptions are sustained from a Christian perspective mostly by using poor translations and inaccurate interpretations of certain Bible verses. Modern translators use the original Hebrew version of the Old Testament and translate from biased assumptions out of their own theology. And I know they do not intend to do so; I believe they truly want to interpret the words as they are. But when there is a choice of words, which seem to you equally valid, which one are you going to choose? The one that lines up with what you already think (or 'know') is the truth.

Jesus and the New Testament writers did not typically quote the Hebrew version of what we call the Old Testament. They used the Septuagint, which was the Greek translation of the Old Testament. The Septuagint was written from the third through to the first century BC, so this was after the last of the

Old Testament prophecies, which were 400 years or so before Jesus came. The translators in those latter days, when they read and translated the prophecies about the coming revelation of the New Covenant as revealed through prophets like Isaiah, Jeremiah, and Ezekiel, had a different revelation about who God was. The Hebrew revelation of God was progressive, and had changed by the time of the prophets from what it had been in the days of the Patriarchs. Before the prophets, the Hebrews had an undifferentiated view of God and Satan. In other words, they did not distinguish between the two; whether good or bad, it was all God. It was how they saw God, and that is a huge confusion for people today because it seems very different from the Father that Jesus came to reveal.

The later Septuagint translation better reflected the true nature of God because there had been a progressive revelation of who He was and what was coming. That is one reason why there is a lot of confusion about the God of the Old Testament and the New Testament appearing to be so different. How could Jesus come preaching love when the God of the Old Testament apparently told them to commit genocide or wipe out whole people groups, not forgetting the babies? Some of it was symbolic and a spiritual dynamic, but some of it was because God did not say or do that in the first place. That is what the original authors wrote, in line with who they thought God to be. But of course, they did not know Him; they did not have a relationship with Him like we do. The Holy Spirit was not indwelling them as He does us, and they were operating from an incorrect mindset.

God, after He spoke long ago to the fathers in the prophets in many portions and in many ways, in these last days has spoken to us in His Son, whom He appointed heir of all things, through whom He also made the world. And He is the radiance of His glory and the exact representation of His nature, and upholds all things by the word of His power (Hebrews 1:1-3a).

Jesus came to reveal the true nature of God's character and to reveal the good news message of love. That is why He taught and preached as He did. The Apostle John very much understood this because he had a revelation of God's love, of the heart of the Father and the heart of Jesus. His gospel portrays the heart of what Jesus really wants us to know about our relationship with Him. The other three gospels are more a reflection of Jesus' desire to reach the Jewish people and lead them out of the Old Covenant ways of doing things – the failure of the Law – into the New Covenant in which they would follow Him. In following Him, they would then hear His voice and be led in a completely different way. Jesus came to reveal that truth in Himself; but many people chose not to accept it.

Jesus came, as the express image of God, as the Seed of Abraham, to fully represent and reveal God to a people who did not really know Him at all. Jesus had to challenge their views of God: they could not talk about God; they could not use the name of God, that was forbidden; they could not talk about God as Father, that would be close to blasphemy. So, Jesus came to challenge their views of who God was and to introduce God as His loving Father. Jesus fulfilled all of the Old Testament promises of God. He was the fulfilment of the types and shadows we see in the various festivals and feasts and other signposts in the Old Covenant that were pointing towards a coming new day and a New Covenant. Jesus fully fulfilled all of them.

Jesus challenged their oral, Talmudic, rabbinical traditions. He said time and again, "You have heard it said, but I say unto you." He was challenging that rabbinical tradition because they gave as much weight to the rabbinical laws, ideas and theology as they did to the scripture itself. Jesus told them, "You are following the traditions of men rather than the truth of God." He introduced a view of God radically different from all they had been taught and thought they knew.

Matthew 5:43 is an example of that: "You have heard that it was said, 'You shall love your neighbour and hate your enemy.'" Well, who said that? It is not in the Old Testament, so where did they get it from? From rabbinical tradition. When you read Hebrew writings such as the Talmud and see some of what is said, you realise that their view of God was almost 180 degrees the opposite of what He is really like. Jesus said, "You have heard this said," then in verse 44, "But I say to you, love your enemies and pray for those who persecute you so that you may prove yourselves to be sons of your Father who is in heaven." In other words, "You think God hates His enemies? No, He loves them!" He loves everyone who thinks they are His enemy, whether they are really His enemy or not. He longs to bless us; even if we are completely negative towards Him, He is never negative towards us.

Jesus came to challenge humanity's view of God and their understanding of how love worked. The first Christian scholars who set out to translate the Old Testament had a particular approach. Before they even started, they made sure they fully established the gospel in their own hearts – the revelation they had received through Jesus and His apostles. They believed this was crucial because otherwise a veil hides the spiritual meaning of the old Jewish writings (see 2 Corinthians 3). Without knowing Jesus, they knew it would be impossible to grasp, much less convey, their true meaning. They worked on the basis that Jesus was the key to understanding all of the scriptures, both Old and New Covenants, and everything had to be viewed and interpreted through the lens of Jesus. This meant that their revelation of who Jesus was, and of His teaching, profoundly shaped how they translated the ancient texts.

Modern translators may think they are unbiased by theology, but of course they are not. There is always a bias. Everyone is biased. Some might be biased by having a relationship with God that is intimate and based in love, whilst others might be biased because they hold to a systematic theology, a more theoretical understanding of what they think the Bible says (or must be saying). We need to be aware of this, if we are looking for the truth. We need to be led by Jesus, the Way, the Truth, and the Life; and by the Spirit of Truth who can lead us into all truth and teach us because He is in us and with us.

If a translator believes that God is angry, wrathful, and punishes his children, then that will be how they interpret the Hebrew and Greek. I will give you three examples of how Bible translators have been influenced by their theology and lack of experience of God as love. If they had experienced God as unconditional love, they would never have translated certain verses the way they did. That is why we need real understanding and insight into the nature and character of God through love, to understand these things and be deprogrammed and deconstructed from beliefs that have influenced us and kept us away from the love of God.

The three areas are the nature of God, the nature of man, and the way God deals with mankind. These basic concepts will affect our belief in and experience of unconditional love and, therefore, God himself. If your God is to be feared, you cannot approach Him, or you are afraid of getting something wrong because He might punish you, that will affect intimacy with Him and have a knock-on effect on everything in your life. If you feel that as a person you are inherently bad and that God cannot look at you because you are so depraved and wicked, that will keep you from the full identity of who you really are and keep you away from God. If you feel that God deals with people who have gone astray by punishing and tormenting them forever, that will cause you to be afraid of God and may lead you to try to appease that angry God with duty and obligation. In reality, God wants all of us to be free to enjoy a relationship with Him.

I am going to explore these three areas by looking at how they have influenced the translation of three verses, one particular verse each; and how in each case that one verse was wrongly translated to deceive and manipulate the truth. I am not saying that the individuals who translated it were deliberately trying to do that, but they came from a framework of belief inspired by a spiritual being who wants to rob, kill and destroy and to keep us from a relationship of intimacy with God.

Penal Substitutionary Atonement (PSA)

The nature of what happened to Jesus on the cross and who was responsible is framed in evangelicalism, one of the most predominant forms of Christianity in the West, by the notion of penal substitutionary atonement (PSA): that God punished Jesus instead of us. Isaiah 53 is often used to justify this idea. And when you read Isaiah 53 in modern English versions, you very quickly see that it appears to prophesy this penal substitutionary atonement. People often tell us, "The Bible says this." But that is not quite true.

Isaiah 53:10 in the New International Version, a very popular version (but not my favourite), says, "Yet it was the Lord's will to crush him." That statement creates a view of God which totally contradicts our experience of unconditional love because it presents a God who is willing to crush someone. If it was God's will to crush his own Son, it can easily be seen as God's will to crush us as well.

Yet it was the Lord's will to crush him and cause him to suffer,
and though the Lord makes his life an offering for sin,
he will see his offspring and prolong his days,
and the will of the Lord will prosper in his hand.
(Isaiah 53:10 NIV).

There are two parts to this verse: first the bad news – bad news for Jesus (and bad news for us if we take it to heart, affecting how we feel about God) – and then the good news that whatever happened through Jesus on the cross, we are going to see a whole people who come into the truth of who God is and enter into a relationship with Him (because that is the true meaning of 'prosper').

In other versions, such as the New American Standard Bible, it says, "The Lord desired to crush him and cause him grief." Really? God desired that? It sums up what I was taught and how I saw God, as someone who desired to crush Jesus. I saw Him doing that because He loved me, but it was always somewhat of a challenge to understand how a loving God could do that to Jesus. It confirmed my understanding of 'hell':

if you did not know God, you would end up being crushed by him forever. That was the theological position I was brought up with.

The NASB, NIV and the King James before them all portray it as God's desire and will to crush or bruise the suffering servant, Jesus; even finding pleasure in it, which now I find abhorrent. But I was programmed and conditioned to believe that was the obvious truth and what the Bible taught. All these translations affirm penal substitutionary atonement, but this form of the verse is not used by any of the New Testament writers, nor does it reflect Jesus' life and message. This is how modern translators have translated the Hebrew into English, but the Septuagint (Greek translation from Hebrew) did not. Its translators saw a totally different meaning. Rather than "bruise" or "crush," they used the Greek word *katharisai*, which the New Testament uses many times for Jesus' ministry of healing. The literal meaning is to cleanse or purify, as when Jesus cleansed the leper in Matthew 8:3.

The Lord wishes to cleanse him of his wound. If you give an offering for sin, your soul shall see a long-lived seed (Isaiah 53:10 LXX).

That is a very different way of looking at this verse. The desire of God is not to bruise, nor to crush, but to cleanse, or to purge, or to heal. Which of these better reflects the God Jesus came to reveal and whom we know as unconditional love? It is an example of how our translations determine how we perceive God: our English translations typically depict a totally different version of God from who He really is and who I have experienced Him to be in my own life.

This brings up many questions. Who wounded Him then? If God did not wound Him, and if God heals His wound, who wounded Him? Jesus was very clear about who was going to put Him on the cross. He never once said that God, His Father, was going to do it. He very clearly warned His disciples that He would be handed over to the chief priests of the Jewish religion, to men. Men cruelly wounded Jesus even before the cross, in the whipping and scourging. If you have ever seen the Mel Gibson film, it is pretty horrific, but it powerfully conveyed what they did to Jesus. Men did that to Him, and men inspired by the enemy conspired to kill him. We find that all the way through the Bible, the enemy seeks to kill those who are coming from God.

What took place on the cross (the 'atonement') has nothing to do with this supposed retroactive transaction where an angry God needed somebody to punish. The idea is that He punished Jesus instead of us, but it only counts if we accept Jesus; if we do not accept Jesus, He still 'has to' punish us. Yet God did not punish Jesus; humanity did. People did. We did. Men put Him on a cross, shouting, "Crucify, crucify." When we acknowledge this, our view of God shifts completely.

What was the wound that God wanted to heal? Jesus says the Son of Man takes on the wound of Adam, our wound. That wound is symbolic of all the effects of the fall, of everything that happened to Adam when he left walking with God in the cool of the day in the garden in intimacy to walk out of the garden in independence; doing things his own way to be like God (when he already was like God). All of the effects that had on mankind since: that was the wound.

The Father was going to cleanse the human race in the body of His Son, Jesus. When Jesus took on that wound of Adam, Jesus, as the last Adam, came to undo all that the first Adam did. Literally, the Father cleanses the human race in the body of His Son from the wound of Adam. Now, that may be a view of the atonement you have never heard, but I believe it was what really happened. Was Jesus wounded? Absolutely, He was. But how does God cleanse the wound of Jesus? Not by punishing Him, but through the healing power of unconditional love in the resurrection. He resurrected Jesus; He did not let Him remain under the power of death. Jesus subjected Himself to death, but death could not hold Him. Death did not keep Him because He was perfect. He only represented us; He did not actually do the things we did, but He was willing to take our place and die our death.

In this scenario, the atonement is not penal; punishment has nothing to do with it. God is not punishing Jesus. Instead, Jesus is voluntarily substituting for us as a ransom, paying equal value to buy us back from our lostness. It was the victorious overcoming of the death that should have been ours, to give us abundant life. Of the different views of the atonement, I prefer the ransom atonement theory and Christus Victor, the victorious nature of the cross over everything that was keeping us from a relationship with God (as vividly portrayed by CS Lewis in *The Lion, The Witch and The Wardrobe*). Both are very different from the idea of God punishing His Son, Jesus.

Deceitful above all things

I do not believe we are interpreting the Bible correctly other than through unconditional love. We cannot know who God really is other than through unconditional love, and we cannot know our true identity other than through unconditional love because it is revealed in that loving relationship with God Himself.

The heart is deceitful above all things and beyond cure.
Who can understand it? (Jeremiah 17:9 NIV).

The heart is more deceitful than all else
And is desperately sick;
Who can understand it? (Jeremiah 17:9 NASB).

This second misinterpretation which has twisted and changed our view of things, is in the matter of our self-view and our view of humanity. When you compare how this verse is presented in the NIV and NASB with the Septuagint text, you see how our understanding of God's view of mankind has also been twisted in translating this verse.

Beyond cure, perverse, desperately wicked, incurably bad, exceedingly corrupt – just a selection of how modern translations suggest that the soul can never be fully healed, made whole or restored because it is so wicked and deceitful. I do not believe that is true. In the Septuagint, the reference is actually Jeremiah 17:5 due to slight differences in verse counting, but it says this:

The heart of man is deep beyond all things and it is the man. Even so, who can know him? (Jeremiah 17:5 LXX).

In reality, it is not that our heart is wicked, deceitful and beyond cure, but that it is deep beyond anything we could conceive ourselves. It is who we really are. Therefore, we cannot know who we really are in our own flesh and understanding; it has to come through our relationship with God. This difference in translation affects how we perceive ourselves and others. The NIV, NASB and virtually every other translation conveys a very low opinion of humanity. I was programmed by that view: man being wicked, corrupted, totally depraved. That gave rise to the theological perspective of "worm theology" – thinking of oneself as no one or nothing, just hoping God has mercy.

Even after receiving salvation (or realising salvation), many Christians still do not believe who they really are. They still believe they need to be self-effacing and think the worst of themselves. This promotes a lesser view of what a Christian is, of what a son or daughter is, than what God intends. If our heart is deceitful, desperately wicked, and beyond cure, what hope is there for us? There will always be a feeling of being 'just a sinner, saved by grace'; a perpetual sense of unworthiness reminiscent of Eeyore in "Winnie the Pooh".

This dynamic is not filled with hope; it creates a false sense of who we are and keeps us from reality. It degrades the value of the soul, contending that you can never really trust it. When we first come into that relationship where our spirit and soul are reconnected to the Holy Spirit, there is often a wrestling match between the soul and the spirit. The soul is accustomed to dictating how we live based on our beliefs and upbringing, but the spirit brings us into a revelation of who we really are, revealing our true eternal nature. God has placed eternity in our hearts and wants to draw us back into an amazing relationship where we come home to Him.

This is completely undermined by degrading the value of the soul. Many in the early church and others, particularly in the Catholic Church, persecuted the soul and body, flagellating themselves, kneeling on broken glass. Some of these things were horrendous, but why did they think that way? They thought of themselves as less than God intended them to be. This view creates suspicion of the soul and lessens the value of mankind, seeing man as inherently bad. By thus degrading humanity there is a gospel message to sell: we are so bad we need saving, using the motivation of fear of punishment to peddle that message.

God does not see us as bad. God views us through the lens of Jesus and who He made us to be: His sons. We have always been His sons; we have never not been His sons. But that is not the way I was taught to believe. I was always taught to believe I was not good enough. I know we can never be good enough in our own strength, but we do not have to! When we become who we really are, who God says we are, we begin to outwork a whole different dynamic of sonship.

The Septuagint says the heart of man is deep beyond all things and it is the man. The human heart is deep, multifaceted, amazing; created in God's image and likeness. Psalm 139 says we are fearfully and wonderfully made. God has a vast sum of amazing thoughts about us, and we need to know those thoughts. Our minds need to be deconstructed from negative beliefs so we can truly know the truth of agreeing with God about us.

What is man that You take thought of him,
And the son of man that You care for him?
Yet You have made him a little lower than God,
And You crown him with glory and majesty!
You make him to rule over the works of Your hands;
You have put all things under his feet.
(Psalm 8 3-5).

That starts with mankind's thought – "Oh, who are we that you would even consider us?" That is man's view – the knowledge of good and evil man's way of looking at it. Man thinks, "Who are we? We're nothing. How do you think of us in any way?" But then it says, "Yet you have made him a little lower than God and crowned him with glory and majesty. You have him rule over the works of your hands and put everything under his feet."

You could say that was talking about Jesus, as Hebrews 2:6-9 certainly suggests, but in John 10:34 Jesus Himself seems to confirm it applies to all men. In the beginning, we were clothed with glory and majesty, and we are being restored into that glorious understanding of who we really are as sons. The heart of every child of God is so precious: however damaged it is, it is still valuable beyond measure. God wants to restore, heal, and make us whole – spirit, soul and body – so we can truly be one and whole and come into that intimacy with Him.

Who can know such depths? Who can know the deep things of the human heart? God can. He can retrieve and restore the value of our true selves. Only in the mirror of God's face can we see our true identity revealed. We can never do it by looking at what we do. We can never do it by looking through the lens of the tree of the knowledge of good and evil. We can only do it by looking face to face, heart to heart, mind to mind with the Father, who reveals our true nature as sons. This is what the unconditional love of God is designed to do: to mirror God's love for us, who He values beyond measure. We are the apple of His eye, the treasure of His heart.

Now we have received, not the spirit of the world, but the Spirit who is from God, so that we may know the things freely given to us by God (1 Corinthians 2:12).

We are never going to know who we are through the spirit of the world. The Spirit of God will reveal who we really are; and He will reveal our destiny, which is a reflection and an outworking of who we really are. God wants us to know the truth of His unconditional love for us and our value and worth to Him. If you do not feel that, if you feel 'less than', if you still struggle with the value of your soul, with thinking you are still a sinner and therefore struggle with that lost identity, struggle with your behaviour, God wants to bring about the renewing of your mind to change and transform the reality of who you are so that you can truly know Him and know yourself.

We need to know Him intimately to know the truth and the depth of who we really are. I had no idea who I was as a son of God. I had no idea of my position seated in the heavenly places. I had no idea of my function and roles in the realms of heaven, in the dimensions, and in all the other multi-dimensional realities that we can engage. I had no idea. I was stuck on the earth, living a less-than kind of life. It is as if I was designed to fly like an eagle, and I was living like a chicken. Now, there is nothing wrong with chickens per se. But if you think you are a chicken, and in fact, you are an eagle, then you are never going to fly. Baby birds imprint on the first thing they see. If an eagle imprints with a chicken, it never flies. Even though it is capable of flight, it never gets off the ground because it thinks it is a chicken.

We have been deceived into thinking we are confined, earthbound, stuck in this dimension. We will only get to heaven when we die, maybe, for some. That whole deception needs to change. We need to know who we really are. We need to know where we are seated in the heavenly places. We need to know the authority we have in the angelic realm. We need to know the authority we have in the earth realm, how we can operate the gateways of the heavens, how we can bring about restoration to all things. That is our role; that is our identity. Creation is waiting, longing for the revealing of the sons of God, and yet we have been deceived into believing we are worthless and valueless, or into striving to prove how good and how valuable we are by what we do, becoming worn out and weary. To properly know ourselves, we need to know Him. We cannot do it independently of a relationship with God as Father.

When you look at another person, how do you see them? Do you see them according to their surface appearance? Do you see them as what they are doing and how they are living? Do you make value judgments on who they are by what they do and how they appear? Or do you look deeper? Are you willing to look into the eyes of a person to see the depth of their heart, which is their true self? Are you willing to look beyond the surface?

When God was challenging my understanding of justice, I had a profound experience, which I have shared before, of being under a waterfall. This showed me how much God loved the unlovable, including victims of abuse, hurt, abandonment and rejection – but equally, how much God loved the abusers. This revelation deeply challenged my perspective on people. Having had that experience, the next day I was taken in the spirit to stand by the front door of our Freedom Centre building (as I described in Chapter 8) and saw into the hearts of those coming in to the Day Centre. I could see who He had made them to be. I could see the light in them – that amazing soul, that precious person, that unique destiny, that beloved son or daughter who was fearfully and wonderfully made. And it is our responsibility as the light of the world, as ambassadors of reconciliation, to carry this good news to them, which is why we began that ministry[10] in the first place.

It is time we forget worm theology. It is time we forget judging people's deepest hearts as deceitful and desperately wicked. People are just operating out of lost identity. They do not know who they are. They are desperate to find love, to know why they are here, what they are doing here. They may have been messed up by life, but God wants to restore them and let them feel the truth of who they are; to know that truth, to know they are loved unconditionally. Let's present a good news message to them. Let's tell people that God loves them. Let's tell people that they are already reconciled, forgiven and

---

[10] Freedom Community Alliance is a Christian charity outworking the vision of Freedom Church to help and support vulnerable and marginalised people, particularly those suffering from the causes and effects of social exclusion. It operates an open access Day Centre and supported housing accommodation in Barnstaple, North Devon, UK, in partnership with the local authority and other organisations: freedomcommunityalliance.org.uk

loved. Let's not make them jump through hoops to try to make themselves better. Let's value them as we would a priceless jewel or gemstone, because that is how God does. Let's see them the way God sees them. Let's see them through the lens of the Father's eyes so we can truly see those people and value them as we value ourselves.

Jesus said to love our neighbour as we love ourselves. How can we do that? The only way we can do it is by being loved unconditionally so that we can love others unconditionally.

For the love of Christ controls us, having concluded this, that one died for all, therefore all died; and He died for all, so that those who live would no longer live for themselves, but for Him who died and rose on their behalf. Therefore from now on we recognize no one by the flesh; even though we have known Christ by the flesh, yet now we know Him in this way no longer. Therefore if anyone is in Christ, this person is a new creation; the old things passed away; behold, new things have come (2 Corinthians 5:14-17).

One died for all – Jesus – therefore we all died with Him and no longer live for ourselves, but for Him. This whole change of life takes place when we have a revelation that He died for us because He loves us. Then we can live, not selfishly trying to earn, or prove, or create our own identity, but resting in the knowledge of who He made us to be and enjoying the reality of that. So let's see people through their new creation reality, not the way they are living, but the way they are intended to live, as God has done everything necessary to bring them into that state of revelation.

Here is the same passage in the Mirror Bible:

The love of Christ constrains us and resonates within us; leaving us with only one conclusion: when Jesus died, every individual simultaneously died. In God's logic, one has died for all, thus all have died.

Now if all were included in his death they were equally included in his resurrection. This unveiling of his love redefines human life. Whatever reference we could have of ourselves outside of our association with Christ is no longer relevant.

Therefore, from now on, I no longer know anyone according to the flesh. I no longer see people from a human point of view. This is a radical and most defining moment. No label that could possibly previously identify someone carries any further significance. Even our pet-doctrines of Christ are redefined. Whatever we knew about him historically or sentimentally is challenged by this conclusion.

Now, in the light of your co-inclusion in his death and resurrection, whoever you thought you were before, in Christ you are a brand new person. The old ways of seeing yourself and everyone else are over. Acquaint yourself with the new. (2 Corinthians 5:14-17 Mirror).

Whoever you thought you were before, in whatever way you may have been shaped by your life, however you have thought about yourself, allow this revelation of the love of God to completely change all that. You are a brand new person. Acquaint yourself with the new. Where are you going to know that new? In that relationship where He loves you and reveals that truth. How you used to see yourself is no longer relevant when you see yourself the way He sees you, when you know that you're loved unconditionally and you live in that revelation. So think of any label you have been labelled with, whatever it might be – every negative way someone has labelled you: maybe they feel justified in labelling you that way, but God does not label you like that.
In the notes in the Mirror Bible, it says, "By discovering Christ from God's point of view, we discover ourselves and every other human life from God's point of view. Paul sees by revelation that what Jesus redeemed in every person brings absolute closure and death to any other reasoning and judgment we may have had about ourselves or anyone else for that matter. This is Paul's metanoia moment." It can be ours too. From now on, we no longer know anyone according to the flesh, even though we once knew Christ that way. We

have that revelation, we have that truth, we need to live in the reality of that truth so that we can be set free. We are so valuable to God, even though we may have lost sight of that truth.

"For the Son of Man has come to seek and to save that which was lost." (Luke 19:10).

We may be lost. We may not know who we are, who we belong to, or what our identity is, but the reality is that we have never lost our value to God. We are just as valuable to Him as when He created us out of the desire of His heart for a relationship. In the parables of the lost sheep, the lost coin, the lost son, they were never anything but the valuable possession of the owner. The sheep may have been lost, but it still belonged to the shepherd. The coin may have been lost, but it still belonged to the woman. The son may have been lost; he may have gone off on his own, but the father was still looking out for him. He was still his son, and the father clearly affirmed that he was still his son by putting a ring on his finger, new clothes on him, and celebrating and rejoicing over the son who once was lost but now was found.

The human heart is not hopelessly deceitful but wonderfully deep. There is so much more for us to discover about who we are, but we can only discover those amazing thoughts God has about us when we know our value; when we know that we have never, ever lost our value from God's perspective. We may think we are worthless; we may have done things in our lives that we are utterly ashamed of, but God never, ever devalued us because of what we did. His value for us was through who He made us to be. Nothing we have done, nothing that has happened to us in this world has ever diminished or lessened our value as a son and child of God.

Our value to the Father is equal to that of Jesus. That is why Jesus could take our place, because Jesus had value to the Father, and He exchanged that value for us. The Father unconditionally loves all His children. He does not treat them as worthless or deserving of banishment to eternal conscious torment. He wants a restored relationship. And He will have a restored, face-to-face relationship with all His children, in this world or the next. The Son of Man has come to seek and to save that which was lost, and that was all of us, but now we have been found and included in Christ.

The wrath of God

Another wrong interpretation of the Bible paints the picture of a God who is angry, full of wrath, ready to torment and punish. Unconditional love does not fail or give up but is faithful, persistent, and wins in the end. God has no reason to be angry. For some reason, many believers struggle with this concept. But the Bible very clearly says that Jesus came to take away the sins of the world (in other words, our lost identity). He also nailed every accusation against us to the cross, and they were defeated and finished. Paul also writes, in 2 Corinthians 5:19, that God was in Christ reconciling the world to Himself, not counting their sins against them, not counting their trespasses against them.

If He counts and holds nothing against anyone, why would God be angry or wrathful towards them? What would He be punishing them for? He would not, He does not, and He has not. Love keeps no record of wrongs. He has placed our lost identity as far as the east is from the west, and we will never find it again. That is how much He loves us. Unconditional love does not fail: it will win – and in fact has already overcome.

Since we have now been justified by His blood, how much more shall we be saved from God's wrath through Him? (Romans 5:9 NIV).

I have no quarrel with the first part of that translation. It is absolutely correct that we have been justified by His blood. But Jesus came to save us from His Father's wrath? No, that is not true, and that is not what Paul wrote. If you look at it in the original Greek, it does not say that we are saved from God's wrath. Here is an interlinear version, arranged in a table, and you will see at once where the problem lies:

Since	now	we have been justified
oun	nyn	dikaioo

by	his	blood,
en	ho autos	haima

much	more	will we be saved
polys	mallon	sozo

from	the	wrath
apo	ho	orge

of God	through	him
	dia	autos

Of course, not every word has an exact equivalent in the other language, and the resulting word order may seem unnatural. But 'of God' is not there in the original Greek at all! Yet almost every modern translation fills in the gap that the translators perceive to be there, and they fill it in with 'of God.' Why? Because they 'know' that God was angry, but now He has poured out His wrath on Jesus instead of us. That is penal substitution theory all over again, and we know Paul did not think like that because PSA was only invented a thousand years later.

Brad Jerzak neatly illustrates how absurd this all is:

> What does God send Christ to save us from? Himself? Think about it and you would realize that makes little sense apart from some naughty indoctrination. That's like me being enraged at my neighbor's child, so I send my child over to his place to confront him, but my neighbor's child beats up my child, so to forgive my neighbor's child, I join in and beat my child too. So my son saved my neighbor's child from me by having me forgive the

neighbor by letting me beat him ... oh never mind. Let's return to reality.[11]

Paul says we have been saved from 'the wrath'. So what is the wrath we have been saved from? Not God's. Does God store up His wrath to pour out on His children? Absolutely not, because He holds no wrath against them to pour out. Does 'the wrath' have a different meaning, is it a very specific wrath, and does it come from another source?

"The thief comes only to steal and kill and destroy; I came so that they would have life and have it abundantly. I am the Good Shepherd; the Good Shepherd lays down His life for the sheep." (John 10:10-11).

A clue to this is who it is who seeks to rob, kill and destroy: the thief, as Jesus described him, the accuser, the devil. Jesus gave His life so we could have abundant life, but there was another spirit abroad looking to steal that life, to kill and destroy us.

The Son of God appeared for this purpose: to destroy the works of the devil (1 John 3:8).

Jesus did not come to destroy the devil. God will not destroy those He has made, however far they have departed from His original plan and intention. He made them, and through the reconciled blood of the cross, He has already dealt with them from His perspective. But the works of the devil, He wants to destroy those.

Paul was familiar with the Septuagint translation, which also included a book called The Wisdom of Solomon, a book that was in all Christian Bibles until the 1500s (when it was omitted from Protestant Bibles, though it is still included in others). The Wisdom of Solomon, which Paul would have known and read, gives us insight into wrath and whose wrath it is:

---

[11] Gospel Before Translation (Pt 3/3), online article by Brad Jersak https://www.ptm.org/gospel-before-translation-pt-3-3-brad-jersak accessed 24/07/2024.

> *So he overcame the Destroyer not with the strength of body nor force of arms, but with a word subdued him that punished, alleging the oaths and covenants made with the fathers. For when the dead were now fallen down by heaps upon another, standing between them, he stayed the wrath and departed the way to the living.* (Wisdom of Solomon 18:22 LXX).

So earlier in their theological development, the Hebrews had an undifferentiated view of God; but by the time the Wisdom of Solomon was written they understood that Satan was not doing God's work but had his own agenda. This passage foreshadows Jesus being sent by his Father to save us from the wrath of the Destroyer, the accuser, Satan. It seems very likely that Paul had this in mind when he spoke about 'the wrath,' which would give a totally different (and much more reasonable) connotation to Romans 5:9.

Trust

Discovering that there are such differences in translation (and mistranslation) often causes people to be confused. They wonder which translation they can read and trust. The answer is to trust the Good Shepherd, Jesus; to trust the Way, the Truth and the Life, who said we can hear and recognise His voice and follow Him. I counsel you to follow Jesus, not your interpretation of what you think the Bible might say (or not).

Yes, the Holy Spirit can bring us the revelation of that truth, but it is so difficult when we are already programmed to think we know what the truth is. We suffer from confirmational bias, which means we tend only to see what lines up with what we already know (or think we know). That makes it hard to be deconstructed. It was an arduous process for God to deconstruct my mind of the things I thought to be true. I had never really questioned some of them. I struggled with some, but I never questioned them to the degree that made me find out what the answer was. I had to have experiences of unconditional love to enable that change in my life. I believe we can use unconditional love as the plumb line to help us discern what is true. The gospel is good news, not bad news. If we know the true good news, we will be free from the deceptions that misrepresent God and misrepresent us, how God treats us, and how He loves us.

Let me repeat: a truly unbiased translator does not exist. Everyone has some kind of bias because everyone has a history. The question is whether you will be influenced by love or by theology. The Mirror Bible, translated by Francois Du Toit, has its own bias. He views God as a mirror we can look into and see who we are, and as love Himself. The Passion Translation represents God as passionate about us and all His creation. I do not mind those kinds of bias, but I do not get on well with translations that come from the belief that God is angry and wants to punish people forever.

Your ability to judge a translation is not about how good you are with languages or your academic background. Some people have those skills, and some do not. What matters is your personal experience of who Jesus is, what God is like as He reveals Himself as love, and the message of unconditional love that Jesus preached. The truth is, God loves us so unconditionally that He always seeks to save us from being lost. All of us.

A lot of 'alls'

By now you have probably begin to notice, as I have, that there are a lot of 'alls' in scripture. I want to close this chapter with a look at some of them.

For all the promises of God find their Yes in him. That is why we utter the Amen through him, to the glory of God (2 Corinthians 1:20 RSV).

All the promises and covenants of God are fully and completely fulfilled in Jesus. There is nothing and no one else who could complete them or fulfil them, and we now enter into that. We are included in Jesus, as is everyone else.

For since by a man came death, by a man also came the resurrection of the dead. For as in Adam all die, so also in Christ all will be made alive (1 Corinthians 15:21).

Adam is the man by whom death came, and Jesus the man by whom resurrection came. When all were in Adam, they died, but from now on all are in Christ, and all will be made alive. Although not everyone knows of that life, all have received it. Everyone is alive; everyone is born from above. Our ministry is to help people understand that reality. We are all ambassadors of the universal inclusion we have in Christ. Adam's 'all' is not more powerful or inclusive than Jesus' 'all.' All died in Adam, and all are made alive in Christ. Life has been given to all. It is not something that will happen in the future; it is something that has already happened, which people will become aware of in their future.

Justification for all

For all have sinned and fall short of the glory of God, being justified as a gift by His grace through the redemption which is in Christ Jesus (Romans 3:23-4).

These are the Bible verses people usually use to tell you that you are not good enough and need God. The reality is, yes, all have acted out of their lost identity, and that lost identity is short of the glory God intended us to have in our true identity. The way the verses have been numbered causes us to stop halfway through at "all have sinned and fall short of the glory of God" as if there were a full stop (period) there. And then Romans 6:23 would be paired with it, focusing on the wages of sin being death. But this sentence in full, across the two verses, quite clearly says that all who have sinned and fall short of the glory of God have been justified as a gift by His grace – all. I have never seen this before, or heard it preached. But this is a work Jesus has accomplished for us all. All had lost their identity, and all are justified as a free gift of grace. That is good news, and that is the full Gospel message. You cannot have one verse without the other, because the same 'all' applies. Both are past tense – all have sinned (all have lost their identity) and all have been justified (as if they had never lost their identity). Justification is a legal term that declares someone 'not guilty,' innocent.

So then, as through one offense the result was condemnation to all mankind, so also through one act of righteousness the result was justification of life to all mankind (Romans 5:18).

To all mankind: yes, that verse really is in your Bible. It includes everyone and leaves no one out. The Greek word *katakrima*, translated as condemnation, actually means 'penalty' and refers to remaining lost; it does not refer to being sent to some version of eternal 'hell' in the future. Most people are still living in a state of lost identity, living a less-than kind of life. But the same 'all' who were condemned are the same 'all' who have been justified. To be condemned is to remain in the independence of lost identity; it is not a threat of punishment but a warning that if you carry on without Jesus, you are going to live a life far less than God intends, without the rest that comes from living in love, joy and peace.

Until all is accomplished

"For truly I say to you, until heaven and earth pass away, not the smallest letter or stroke shall pass from the Law until all is accomplished." (Matthew 5:18).

I will finish this discussion of 'all' with this verse. On the surface, you might think that since heaven and earth are still here, therefore the Law is still in place, so I need to obey the Law. However, in Jewish thinking, the Holy of Holies was where heaven and earth met, in the temple; and 'heaven and earth' in this verse refers to the temple and the whole Old Covenant system. When the Romans levelled the city of Jerusalem in AD 70, this 'heaven and earth' passed away. The Law passed away, just as the letter to the Hebrews said it would. Given that, the 'all' of this verse must have been accomplished. And it has: the finished work of Christ has accomplished everything necessary for our full and complete salvation. I encourage you to embrace that, meditate on it, and celebrate the reality of the all-inclusive, unconditional love of God for you, for everyone and everything. He is never going to give up on you, so be sure not to give up on yourself. Embrace how He sees you, who you really are as a son of God, in the mirror of His face in intimacy.

Activation #15
Forget Worm Theology

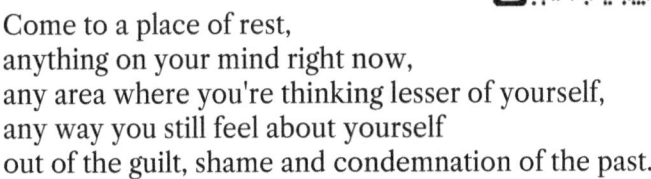

Close your eyes.

Get to that place where you relax, where you are open to the Father.

> Come to a place of rest,
> anything on your mind right now,
> any area where you're thinking lesser of yourself,
> any way you still feel about yourself
> out of the guilt, shame and condemnation of the past.
>
> Anything you're carrying
> that you don't feel you can be forgiven for,
> that you don't deserve forgiveness.
> Anything,
> let any of those things come to your mind right now.
>
> I ask, Father, that you'll reveal to each person
> the reality of anything which is contradictory
> to the way that you see them,
> anything that's contradictory to your love
> being unconditional,
> any mindset, belief system,
> experience that they may have had
> that has created this image of themselves as lesser,
> that has created this image of You as being angry,
> as going to punish them;
> has created this view of You
> as having punished Jesus, your Son.
>
> That any dynamic around those areas,
> any deception that we have been trapped into,
> that You would bring into the light,

that You would reveal,
that You would unveil that truth.

And I'd encourage you to spend a few moments
just asking the Father to show you,
asking Jesus, the Truth, to reveal to you:
are there any areas that you have been deceived
and you're still believing less of yourself
than God thinks of you?
That you're still struggling with God being angry
and you having to fulfil your duty and obligation to Him,
still living under the Old Covenant mindset of the Law?

Ask Him to reveal any mindset, belief system
that has deception holding you in bondage.

Now I just encourage you
to take anything that's come to mind,
anything that may be a struggle for you
in terms of your own identity,
in terms of who you really are,
anything which is a misrepresentation of God.

Take all those things
and place them right now at the feet of Jesus,
give them to the Father,
allow Him to take them from you;
to remove every obstacle, every hindrance,
every lie, every deception that's kept you in bondage.

Now, as you just rest in that place of the love of God,
the unconditional love of God
would just begin to flow over you.

Breathe in deeply,
breathe it in slowly and deeply,
breathe in the love of God,
the unconditional love of God,
that would change and transform
those feelings and thoughts
you might have about yourself.

Breathe it in,
let it flow through you,
let it fill every fibre, every atom,
every particle of your being,
from the top of your head to the tip of your toes,
your heart, your mind, your emotions, your will,
every part of you filled with unconditional love.

As a river of living energy,
life and light and love,
flowing into your innermost being,
filling you and filling you and filling you.

And as it fills you, let it wash you clean
from every wrong thought,
wrong feeling, wrong understanding
about your nature,
or the nature of God.

Let it wash you clean,
let it renew your mind,
let it transform you by the renewing of your mind,
that you will see who you really are.

Be still,
and allow that washing of the water
of the truth of who He is,
that truth that He is unconditional love,
to flow through you.

Let it flow through your mind,
let it flow through your heart,
your emotions, every area.

And as that unconditional love just rests upon you,
enter into that place of rest,
that place of peace,
that place of joy,
experiencing the wonder
of the Father's amazing love for you –
freeing you from works,

freeing you from condemnation,
from guilt, from shame;
revealing the truth,
bringing you into the light of His presence
at a level so deep,
that you've gone deeper and deeper and deeper
than you've ever been before into the very heart of God,
where you can live loved.

That He loves you,
free from guilt,
free from shame,
free from condemnation.

All your old mindsets,
belief systems and clothes removed,
where you can live in that love state,
where you can love living,
that you can be filled with joy,
that life takes on joy.

You're no longer on the treadmill of the hamster wheel,
going round and round and round and going nowhere.

Your destiny will be revealed.
That every day, you'll know the Father's heart,
that you will see what the Father's doing,
and you can be an expression of love
in the world in which you live.

That you can live loving,
you'll be merciful,
choosing to forgive and release
everyone and everything in life.
You will keep no record of wrongs,
that you will be at peace,
rest in love and joy and peace.

Rest there,
in the realm of light,
in the realm of perfection –

it's our home, it's our resting place.
Dwell in unconditional love,
dwell in the light of love and truth.

Enter into that light,
look into the Father's face,
see His loving smile,
look into His eyes,
which are deep pools of unconditional love.

Rest, and remain in that place,
enjoy, enjoy, enjoy.

Let love, joy and peace cocoon you,
resting in the Father's arms of love,
feeling His heartbeat, feeling the rhythm,
the comfort of being in His arms of love.
Resting, enjoying, being
who you were always designed to be, free.

Knowing the truth,
that truth setting you free to be you,
a son of God, called and chosen.

Creation is longing and waiting for you,
longing and waiting for you to be revealed in your sonship,
longing for you to rise up as a son of God,
and embrace the reality of who you really are.

Just stay in that place,
rest in that place,
remain in that place.

16. What is Deconstruction?

As I described in chapter 3, the Father challenged many of my assumed belief systems and deconstructed the pillars of my mind. The deconstruction was not a theological or intellectual process; it was an experiential one. It was my experiences with God that began to remove the pillars of my thinking, which had essentially created the reality of what I believed.

It seems that almost everyone is going through a process of deconstruction these days, whether they like it or not. But if you learn how to cooperate with it, not fear it or avoid it, then the whole process can be accelerated. Then we can come into a revelation of the truth of who we are and who God is, and begin to demonstrate that as ministers and ambassadors of reconciliation. We will take that good news message to the world: God is good, God is unconditionally loving and He loves each of His children (and that means everybody) the same way. We want more and more people to realise that.

Deconstruction

I use the word a lot, but what does it actually mean? And why (as Eric Scot English has pointed out) do evangelicals seem to hate it so much? There is a backlash in evangelical circles against the very idea of deconstruction because of the fear that if people get deconstructed, they will lose their faith – or even just leave evangelical streams and denominations. Here is Eric Scot English's definition:

> "Religious deconstruction is the tearing down of theological presuppositions and beliefs in order to reconstruct our beliefs under a new paradigm.[12]"

That new paradigm, or new worldview, often results in significant change and renewal or transformation in our lives.

---

[12] Eric Scot English; *Why Evangelicals Hate Deconstruction.* Article on *Unenlightenment* blog; https://www.patheos.com/blogs/unenlightenment/2021/11/why-evangelicals-hate-deconstruction. Accessed 20 August 2024.

The religious belief systems we have adopted, been taught or programmed by, often contain particular beliefs that may not be true. What is there to fear in deconstruction? If our beliefs are accurate, they will be affirmed; and if not, they can be discarded. For us, there is no downside to deconstruction – other than the fact that it is quite hard and a challenge because we suddenly realise a lot of things we thought were true are not really true at all. And God will take us on that journey. But for those in the denomination or stream trying to hold everything together, it is perceived as a threat to their very existence.

Doubt is often the precursor to deconstruction. Doubt tends to be seen as negative, as if you are doubting God or doubting your salvation. I believe it can be embraced as an opportunity for change and transformation.

> "People are afraid of doubt, and they shouldn't be, since doubt is born of the fact that we do not know the entire truth, and pose a question... When doubts appear in me it means that I have outgrown my incomplete idea of God, my imperfect knowledge of Him..." – Metropolitan Anthony Bloom of Sourozh[13]

Doubt is healthy; it does not need to be a negative thing at all if you embrace it correctly. When you doubt something, you are not trusting that it is true. Now, I do not doubt God being true, or being real, or being a Father, or any such thing. But my view of who God was is not what it is now. He began to show me the truth of who He was: I began to encounter unconditional love in my own experiences. He began to show me that He really is a good Dad, and that the way I was brought up to think about God being angry, or needing appeasing, or exhibiting wrath, or the whole concept of sending people to eternal conscious torment in 'hell' forever – all that had to change.

---

[13] Metropolitan Anthony Bloom, quoted in https://throughthegraceofgodorthodoxchristianity.wordpress.com/2016/02/09/metroploitan-anthony-of-sourozh-doubts. Accessed 20 August 2024.

My view of God being love, being good, being kind, being faithful – all of the fruit of the Spirit – none of that changed, but it became more experiential. We need not fear doubt just because it leads us to begin to question. Again, many people, particularly of an evangelical persuasion (and I was of that persuasion myself) do not question things because they were actively taught not to. Yet it was not until the evangelical beliefs and pillars of my mind were removed that I could begin to see many other things that were true, particularly to experience unconditional love and not to get caught up in mixing covenants (that is, by trying to please God and be obedient, trying to earn God's favour when He already loves and favours me).

God does not mind our questions; He is big enough to answer them for us. He is not worried that we might doubt certain things, because the things that are true will be affirmed, and the things that are not true we can let go of. Evangelicals fear doubt because it has led some people to end up as 'atheists', from their point of view, or to leave church as a result. And of course, in that view, 'going to church' is an absolute must. In reality, we are the church. If we are the sons of God, then we are an expression of God's presence wherever we are, and whatever we are doing. Together, there is a corporate dynamic to that, but much of what we have known as church is a religious institution from which God wants to set us free.

Many people who have left the church are not in fact atheists; they have just discarded that view of church and that view of God because they found it to be incorrect. And if no one came alongside them to help them to process their doubt, perhaps some of them did reject God as a result, because what they saw of God through that evangelical perspective – the angry God, the God they needed to fear, the God who would punish them forever – they rejected.

Being an atheist to the God of anger, vengeance, wrath and retribution is not a bad thing: as I have said, I am an atheist to that God too. I do not believe that is God; and I do not believe in that God. Therefore, I would say I am an atheist to the evangelical God. But I have an intimate, personal relationship with my Dad, my Father; and I know Him and His love in a way that I never thought possible, and never believed could be true. Without meeting the real God in encounters, by experience, people cannot easily discover the truth of who He is, because the Truth is not an intellectual knowledge about Him. Western Christianity has become very intellectual: it is all about what you believe about God, rather than who you know God to be by your personal experiences of Him in relationship.

Embracing doubt enables us to undertake that journey of deconstruction. If we embrace the fact that there are guaranteed to be things we believe about God, about the Bible and about ourselves that are not true, then deconstruction becomes a wonderful journey of discovering what really is true. As we experience Jesus as the Way, the Truth and the Life, He brings us into a deeper relationship with God the Father through the Holy Spirit.

My encounters with God caused 'cognitive dissonance' and I became double-minded. I had an experience, but my beliefs did not align with that experience. I had to weigh up and challenge myself: do I continue to believe what I have always believed, or am I going to allow the experience I have just had with God begin to change me and change my view of God?

I was brought up to distrust personal experiences, particularly emotional experiences, because they could not be counted on. I was told that you believe what the Bible says about God, not what you might experience. It seemed that the church was afraid of experiences for some reason, never mind that the Bible itself was full of accounts of people's experiences of God! The disciples who met Jesus had experiences with Him, as did Paul and others; they wrote down their experiences, and we are expected to trust what they wrote. But at the same time, we are told we cannot trust our own experiences, which really does not make any sense.

However, this is how I was trained and brought up. I believed the Bible's version of God that I was taught, because that was the God I was told that I had to believe in. I was not encouraged to experience God for myself; I just had to believe in Him, or trust in Him, or have faith in Him, even though I did not really know Him.

When I later began to have experiences with Him, they created a dynamic in me that caused me to doubt the God I thought I knew. I did not know who God truly was, and the God I thought I knew turned out not to be God at all. My experiences challenged me and caused the deconstruction to take place as I embraced them. Some beliefs were far easier to let go than others; some were so ingrained that I needed to go back to God and ask Him to unveil and reveal more. But generally, the experience could not be denied.

Pillars in my mind

I was somewhat apprehensive when God asked me if He could deconstruct the pillars of my mind. He showed me nine pillars of my belief system, which framed how I saw the world, how I saw God, how I saw everything. When He asked if He could remove those pillars, I hedged a little and said, "Yes, but can You do it one at a time?"

The first pillar to come down was evangelicalism, and I had not realised how strong that programming was. It framed all my other belief systems, including the secular ones. My scientific understanding and the way in which I saw the world were still framed by evangelical thought. It was so powerful. When that was deconstructed, it was like a domino rally: that one fell over, and all the other erroneous beliefs and understandings began to topple one after another.

The deconstruction was followed by reconstruction, by renewal of the mind. God does not want us to have no understanding or no belief; He wants us to believe in the truth, experience the truth, and know the truth by experience. Real knowledge is not intellectual but experiential. When you look at how this concept is described in the Bible, in Greek or Hebrew, they had no concept of intellectual understanding as just knowledge for knowledge's sake; you had to have the experience that backed up what you believed. God wants us to have experiences that renew our minds so that we begin to know the truth in reality. That changes our whole way of life, the way we see the world, see creation, and ultimately everything else.

Reconstruction is the renewal of our beliefs to create a new paradigm, but not just beliefs as intellectual ideas; rather, beliefs based on the experiences we have. It creates a whole new worldview, a whole new perspective, a whole new sense of reality that we can then use to look at the world, look at God, and look at everything through a different lens. This allows us to have a completely different perspective on who we are as sons of God and how we are called to embrace creation.

Reconstruction allows a person to find their own beliefs based on testimony, rather than what has been spoon-fed to them most of their Christian lives. It is really important that each of us has our own experience and finds that truth in our relationship with God so that we have a testimony that we know is true. No one can nullify that testimony: even if they do not believe what we are saying, we know we have had that experience.

Love is the plumb line

What will keep us on track and prevent us from veering into unfounded speculation? If we have a spiritual experience, how can we determine if it genuinely aligns with the reality of who God is?

I am comfortable with questioning my experiences, but I do not necessarily run straight to the Bible to verify their authenticity. Instead, I use love as a fundamental measure of truth, my plumb line. I firmly believe that if something does not embody love, it cannot be true, regardless of what (my translation of) the Bible might say about it. Our goal should be to hold to what aligns with the core truth of God's nature, which is love. By using love as our primary criterion, we can discern the validity of our spiritual experiences and interpretations. This approach encourages a deeper, more nuanced understanding of both our experiences and our faith, even as it challenges some of our preconceived notions about biblical teachings and our personal interpretations of scripture.

Love is the measure, and if we tune that sense of instinct or discernment and practise training our senses to distinguish between what is and is not true, what is love and what is not, then we can boldly step into a journey of deconstruction and pursue it because we know we will be positively changed and transformed by it.

Orthodoxy

There are two primary reasons why evangelicals particularly shy away from the idea of deconstruction. The first is that it involves progressive revelation, and evangelicals look on that with suspicion because they believe the view they hold is the orthodox view on everything. The fact is, their view has only been around for a few hundred years and is definitely not the view of the early church. Still, since they consider it to be orthodox, they therefore tend to oppose any revelation that is not based on what they have already determined to be 'the truth'. According to that line of thought, God is not able to reveal anything new because He has already revealed everything in the Bible; and therefore, more importantly, we do not need anything new. If something new is offered, it asserts, we should be sceptical of it, because we already have the orthodox (correct) view.

I was once accused of being "on a slippery slope away from orthodoxy", which I actually thought was quite a badge of merit. I wondered, "So, what is orthodoxy?" I looked it up and found that it means 'right opinion'. Here is what Wikipedia has to say:

Orthodoxy (from Greek: *orthodoxía*, 'righteous/correct opinion') is adherence to correct or accepted creeds, especially in religion.

Orthodoxy within Christianity refers to acceptance of the doctrines defined by various creeds and ecumenical councils in Antiquity, but different Churches accept different creeds and councils. Such differences of opinion have developed for numerous reasons, including language and cultural barriers.

Reading that, you might well ask: who decides what is right, correct or accepted? Each denomination apparently has its own orthodoxy, and evangelical orthodoxy varies across different streams – charismatic, reformed and others. But even if there were such a thing, evangelical orthodoxy can only be a few hundred years old, and it certainly does not correlate with what the early church believed. They maintain it does, of course, because they believe that their orthodoxy has been in place from the beginning. However, as soon as you begin to look into where, when and how their beliefs were formed and came into being, and then compare it with the writings of the early church fathers, you will find they differ immensely.

I was very happy to ski down that slippery slope with joy and abandon, ever further and further from my evangelical roots. Those roots sustained a wrong view of God that I previously believed, and I was perfectly content to let them go, even if some people did not like it. I was branded with the usual accusations of heresy and false teaching, of course; but if you do not get called a heretic, then you are probably not deconstructed enough yet.

Progressive revelation really does seem to be anathema to many. I once innocently mentioned it in a church leaders' meeting which included Anglicans, Methodists, independent charismatics and others with a broad range of beliefs, who used to meet regularly. I was chair of that local Churches Together group for seven or eight years and was very much involved in promoting unity by looking to encourage relationship amongst us. As I say, I innocently mentioned 'progressive revelation', and I saw the horror and fear on all their faces as if I had somehow blasphemed. I was taken aback, and they protested, "Oh no, revelation can't be progressive – we know the truth; we have the truth."

I changed my approach a little. "Okay, what you believe now – is any of it different in some way from what you believed 10 or 20 years ago?" Most of them had to admit that there were some things they believed differently. So I said, "Well, that's progressive revelation – you now know something to be true that you didn't used to believe to be true," which led to an interesting discussion and journey with them. But to be honest, what made it quite hard work was that for the most part they had an ingrained fear of 'progressive Christians'.

Theology

The second reason evangelicals fear deconstruction is that it often means church members start to realise the shaky foundation upon which their theology is built. And it really does not have a biblical foundation at all. When you look at the Bible in the context of who it was written to and how it was written, your understanding of what the Bible tells you begins to change.

I would venture to suggest that the reason so many people within evangelicalism are now deconstructing is because it is one of the primary belief systems most opposed to what God is doing in our day – revealing unconditional love and the restoration of all things. I believe that demonstrates the extent to which we former evangelicals had our theology so wrong. No wonder Arthur Burke contends that moving people out of religious institutional church structures is one of the major moves of God over the last 20 or 30 years. People are beginning to realise that the way they have been taught and the things they have believed are very different from what God is revealing to them and what they are now experiencing themselves.

I would not be honest if I said that this process is easy. It can be lonely at times, especially without someone to share your thoughts with. In the beginning, I was not sure if I could share what I was discovering, but I found that there were a few friends with whom I could, and they provided a supportive environment for my ongoing journey and growth.

All we do as a ministry (and in particular what I do online in helping, mentoring and talking to people, answering their questions and encouraging them to seek God for themselves), is really intended to support and embolden those on the journey of deconstruction. It has been so crucial to my journey and my relationship with God that I want people to feel that they can have a safe place to pursue that journey for themselves, to find the truth so that it becomes their truth.

My deconstruction journey

As I shared in an earlier chapter, the first part of my journey of deconstruction and renewal really involved the Holy Spirit in the 1980s. The Brethren and Methodist churches did not believe in the baptism of the Spirit or spiritual gifts – they were 'of the devil,' I was told. Therefore, they could not be trusted, and we should have nothing to do with them. But God had something different in mind. He challenged my view of the Holy Spirit, and eventually, I got baptised in the Spirit in the mid-80s. I was able to experience God in a different way, which changed my views in many areas.

The second part, which followed very quickly on the heels of the first, was the deconstruction of my eschatology. When I got baptised in the Spirit, God spoke to me about finding out about the Kingdom and Covenant. As I began to pursue that understanding, what I believed about the future began to change. I came to challenge the futurist interpretation of Bible prophecy, which suggests that it primarily refers to events still yet to occur in our future. Instead, I developed a different understanding, recognising that many of them actually relate to events that have taken place since the particular prophecy was given or represent current realities in our present time. What was future for them may be past or present for us.

Subsequently, and much more recently, my journey has involved deconstructing my view of who God is: penal substitutionary atonement, 'hell', the mixing of covenants, and many other subjects covered in this book that God has begun to challenge me about, mostly through conversations and experience.

Old vs New

Many people struggle with the Old Testament view of God, in which He is seen as retributive. They see God apparently doing things we are commanded not to do, and yet He did them (or at least, it was written that He did them). I do not believe He did those things at all because He does not deny Himself and He does not change. He is the same yesterday, today and forever. Therefore, it must be that we are confused because of what we have been taught about the God of the Old Testament and Jesus.

The undifferentiated Hebrew view of God and Satan means that sometimes, especially in the oldest writings, you see things said to be God's doing which clearly conflict with Christian teaching. I was taught different ways to get around this problem. But it remained a problem: how could God be good and loving when He apparently did such awful things (or told Israel to do them) in the Old Testament stories? The Old Testament was first written for and about people following Judaism, which is a different religion from Christianity. The way God is shown in the Old Testament is very hard to match up with how Christians understand God's character. Having these texts from different religious traditions in one book makes it hard for a Christian to form a clear and consistent idea of what God is like.

If we are honest and allow God to begin to challenge our thinking about what the Old Testament says about Him compared to what Jesus says about Him, I think it will begin to change and transform how we view the Old Testament and its purpose. From my perspective, I would go further, and question whether we really need it at all; it causes more problems than it solves. Would it not be better simply to listen to Jesus' voice and follow Him as He calls us to do, rather than trying to interpret and understand confusing and contradictory scriptures?

The Law implies a God who will bless those who keep it and curse those who do not. God does not curse people. God only has blessings to give because He is a good God; He is a God of love. Yet we are told that God brings curses if you do not keep the covenant or if you are not obedient, and this has shaped our perspective of who God is.

The doctrine of penal substitutionary atonement rests on the same flawed premise that God is fundamentally retributive, desiring vengeance and punishment against those who reject Him or act contrary to His Law. In truth, God is merciful. Within this erroneous framework of retribution, it is asserted that He acts in this manner because He is just and holy. This creates an artificial opposition between justice and mercy, as if one cannot coexist with the other. However, God is indeed just, and He is also holy, and neither of these attributes contradict His nature as love. Justice is a manifestation of His love; His holiness is an expression of His love; there is no conflict between them. The notion of a God who seeks retribution stands in stark contradiction to the true nature of God revealed by Jesus.

The idea that God is retributive is actually a myth – a mythology created around a Hebrew understanding of God, and an evangelical interpretation rooted in an Old Covenant view of God. This misconception seeks to reconcile an Old Covenant perspective with how the New Covenant works. In the early church, the Judaizers, who had supposedly become followers of Jesus, tried to bring everyone back under the Law. They even visited Gentile churches, attempting to enforce law-based practices on them, when they had never been under the Law in the first place. Paul, in his letter to the Galatians, expressed his shock at how easily they could forsake the grace they were born into for a Law-based system:

You foolish Galatians, who has bewitched you, before whose eyes Jesus Christ was publicly portrayed as crucified? (Galatians 3:1).

Jesus came to debunk this myth. He revealed the Father, offering a New Covenant perspective of God that was also supported by the progressive revelation previously received by many of the prophets. It is evident that although they wrote through their own filters, the prophets began to express a view of God that was very different from that portrayed in the Torah and other early books. This progressive revelation of who God really is continued with those who translated the Hebrew Bible into Greek, the most widely spoken language in that world, the Septuagint. This shift presented God in a very different light, with statements like, "God never wanted sacrifices and offerings," which directly challenged the beliefs and practices of the time, as their entire Law-based temple system relied on those sacrifices and offerings that He never wanted!

Jesus, the express image of the Father

Jesus came as the express image of the Father, and He said, "If you have seen me, you've seen the Father" (see John 14:9). This statement was a huge challenge to their belief system because they believed in one God and did not see God as one in three or three in one. When Jesus declared, "I and the Father are one" (see John 10:30), it prompted the religious authorities to want to kill Him. Jesus challenged their belief systems, which were based on a misunderstanding of God, interpreted through the system of the Law. He came to fully fulfil the Old Covenant, the Law and the Prophets. He did so by demonstrating love, and so became the fulfilment of all the promises of God. As the Seed of Abraham, He also fulfilled in the New Covenant the promise made to the patriarch that "in you, all the families of the earth will be blessed" (see Genesis 12:3 and 22:18).

"You have heard that it was said, 'Eye for eye, and tooth for tooth.' But I say to you, do not show opposition against an evil person; but whoever slaps you on your right cheek, turn the other toward him also." (Matthew 5:38-9).

So Jesus was not promoting retribution or revenge; quite the opposite. He goes on:

"You have heard that it was said, 'You shall love your neighbor and hate your enemy.' But I say to you, love your enemies and pray for those who persecute you, so that you may prove yourselves to be sons of your Father who is in heaven; for He causes His sun to rise on the evil and the good, and sends rain on the righteous and the unrighteous." (Matthew 5:43-5).

Just as Jesus was the Son of His Father in heaven, if we are to live as sons of God, we will also love those who persecute us or see themselves as our enemies. It is not justified under any circumstances to hate your enemy or refuse to forgive them. The system of forgiveness many of us grew up with teaches that we forgive someone when they say sorry. We even think God works like that. However, I am so glad that God forgave me before I ever said sorry for anything. Forgiveness came through what Jesus did on the cross, irrespective of whether I believed it or not, or whether I said sorry or not.

Jesus' words completely defied their whole interpretation of the Law, which they had used to permit or demand retribution. At least the Law limited what one could do, so if someone took an eye, you could only take an eye back – you could not take two eyes or kill them. I wish people today would at least limit the retribution they mete out and consider how anger, unforgiveness and hatred lead only to escalating conflict. We cannot demand retribution if we want to be like God. He wants us to see ourselves as one family, all equally loved by Him. Jesus modelled mercy and forgiveness, even when He was persecuted and eventually crucified. How hard would we find it to forgive someone if we were hanging on a cross, unable to breathe, having been beaten and tortured? Yet, Jesus said, "Father, forgive them."

God does hold people accountable for their behaviour, but He does so to warn them of the self-inflicted consequences of their wrong actions. If someone behaves contrary to who they truly are as a child of God and contrary to love, there will be consequences. These may be natural consequences: for instance, if you murder someone, you may be imprisoned for life or face capital punishment, depending on where you live. Did God put them in prison or kill them? No. God wants us to operate in love, which is why Jesus told His disciples, "Love one another as I have loved you." He was not just talking about loving the disciples within that group of twelve but extending that love to everyone, unconditionally.

Life, not death

As we have seen, God's judgment is not about punishment. Judgment simply means delivering a verdict, as a judge would deliver a verdict based on evidence in a court case. The evidence is that Jesus took every accusation, nailed it to the cross, overcame it, and took death into the grave. We died with Him and are resurrected with Him. Based on this evidence, God's judgment (the verdict He has pronounced) is "not guilty" for all mankind. When God delivers a verdict on our behaviour, it is not to punish us but to show mercy. His judgment is always restorative, never retributive. It is never designed to express His anger or vengeance towards us; it is always to restore us.

God does make judgments, of course. He looks at our lives and identifies some areas that are not so good. But He does this to bring life, not death. He does not condemn us to death or any kind of punishment; He reveals the truth so that we can embrace life. God is not punitive or vengeful, as He has been portrayed by many religions, including Christianity. There are many things written in the Old Testament that seem to confirm that God is a retributive God. Of course, there are also many Old Testament prophetic statements that directly contradict this, and that is the problem.

Revealing the true nature of God

Jesus came to show the love of God, not the anger of God. Yet even in the Old Testament, the true nature of God is revealed in glimpses.

The Lord is compassionate and gracious, slow to anger, abounding in love. He will not always accuse, nor will He harbour His anger forever (Psalm 103:8-9).

He may be angry when He looks at our self-destructive behaviour but He does not hate the person; He is not angry with me or with you. He is angry that we are living in lost identity and missing out on the reality of His love.

*"For I desire mercy, not sacrifice,
and acknowledgment of God rather than burnt offerings."*
(Hosea 6:6 NIV).

At last, the prophets are beginning to decree what the true nature of God is (and what the true nature of the New Covenant will be). He desires mercy, not sacrifice. He does not want us to sacrifice to Him. He wants to show us mercy; and then He wants us to show mercy too.

*The Spirit of the Lord God is upon me,
Because the Lord has anointed me
To bring good news to the afflicted;
He has sent me to bind up the brokenhearted,
To proclaim liberty to captives
And freedom to prisoners;
To proclaim the favorable year of the Lord
And the day of vengeance of our God;*
(Isaiah 61:1-2a).

When Jesus uses this text to introduce His ministry, He leaves out "the day of vengeance of our God." That was a statement made by Isaiah, arising from his own viewpoint. But when Jesus quotes it, He does not include the vengeance of God because that Old Covenant view of God as retributive was inaccurate. Jesus replaced humanity's need for vengeance with grace and mercy.

It is the year of the Lord's favour, but not the day of His vengeance. Jesus came to declare that things were now different because He is revealing the true nature of God: He has come to bring good news, to bind up the broken-hearted, to heal the fragmented, the damaged and the hurt, to proclaim freedom to those in religious captivity to an Old Covenant Law-based system that could never bring them life. He came to release those who were in the darkness of wrong thinking, believing that God was angry and retributive.

God is merciful and full of love. Jesus demonstrated that God does not seek retribution but offers mercy and forgiveness. He directly refuted the Law's directive to answer violence with violence. God commanded them not to kill, yet the Law demanded capital punishment. Jesus contradicted this in speaking with the lawyer, with the woman caught in adultery, and consistently throughout His ministry.

By your standard

"Do not judge so that you will not be judged. For in the way you judge, you will be judged; and by your standard of measure, it will be measured to you." (Matthew 7:1-2).

Jesus was warning against the wrong use of judgment for retribution: there will be a consequence of reaping what you have sown in the world, which follows a system that is not love. He was warning them not to judge others and thereby incur negative judgment from others in their own lives. He was not saying that God would make that judgment on them.

What Jesus judged was the religious hypocrisy of the scribes and Pharisees, who refused to take His path of peace and eventually used violent rebellion against the Romans. They suffered the consequences of their actions, but those reprisals did not come from God. The Romans executed judgment on Israel in AD 66-70. It was not God who executed that judgment (though the judgment of God on the system was seen in the destruction of the temple and its ritual. His judgment was on the system of Law. He judged it a failure, unable to produce life in anyone, unable to save anyone. You cannot keep the Law; you need grace).

Remember, Jesus never spoke about some future judgment at the end of the world or after death, with eternal conscious torment in 'hell' or any form of eternal damnation attached to that judgment. Jesus spoke about what would happen in that generation to those who remained in Jerusalem and would suffer in the Roman siege. His references to Gehenna, the garbage dump outside Jerusalem, were a warning of the physical, deadly consequences His contemporaries would suffer if they continued following the Old Covenant system. And when Jesus spoke of tribulation (as recorded in Matthew 24), it was in the context of the warning about the temple and Jerusalem being destroyed in that generation, not at some future time. Why did He warn them? Because He did not want any of them to go through it. He warned them as a hen wanting to gather her chicks under her wings of protection. He wanted them to escape the destruction by following Him out of Jerusalem. Figuratively, they would be following Him out of the Old Covenant and out of the system of Law, into the New Covenant. Jesus was crucified outside the city walls, and He wanted them to follow Him into the reality of the New Covenant that He was bringing.

The Great Tribulation did occur in history: it was recorded in detail by the Jewish historian Flavius Josephus. It happened, not because God is wrathful, but as a political consequence of violent rebellion against Roman rule by the Jewish zealots. The people of Jerusalem suffered those consequences as Rome ruthlessly quelled that rebellion.

God was not judging individual people; it was the system that was declared broken and unfixable. Everyone can be restored and made whole, without exception. Even those who stayed in Jerusalem and were killed and thrown into Gehenna only experienced physical death, not eternal death, and not eternal punishment.

God's kindness

When He said, "A new covenant," He has made the first obsolete. But whatever is becoming obsolete and growing old is ready to disappear (Hebrews 8:13).

The Old Covenant became obsolete and faded away completely, as the writer to the Hebrews understood. God is merciful; God is restorative. Paul experienced that mercy – and he was persecuting believers. If God was going to be retributive, it could certainly have been against Paul, who killed Christians and was there approving when Stephen was stoned. Yet, God met him. Not only that, God was actually in him, seeking to reveal that truth all along. As he noted,

God has bound everyone over to disobedience so that He may have mercy on them all (Romans 11:32).

In God's calculation, the mass of humanity is trapped in unbelief; this qualifies all mankind for His mercy (Romans 11:32 Mirror).

It is God's kindness that leads people to *metanoia*, not the fear of His anger and retribution. God's kindness leads us to change our mind and agree with Him that we are forgiven.

Do not underestimate God's kindness. The wealth of his benevolence and his resolute refusal to let go of us is because he continues to hear the echo of his likeness in us. Thus, his patient passion is to shepherd everyone into a radical mind shift (Romans 2:4 Mirror).

This emphasises the need for a radical shift in our thinking – to move away from humanism, whether religious or secular, and to embrace the mercy and kindness of God, who loves us. Yet how much preaching of the so-called 'good news' has been telling people that they are going to be saved from God's supposed wrath and 'hell', rather than affirming that God loves them, that Jesus died for them, and that they have already been reconciled to Him? Those two messages are irreconcilably different. Whilst evangelical doctrine prioritises works over grace, claiming that we must believe, repent and confess in order to be restored, God has already reconciled us and desires our full restoration without any effort on our part.

The history of the early church, including the original disciples of Jesus and those who followed for at least the first 200 years, confirms that they were not retributive or supporters of war or violence. Most of the early church fathers during this period believed that violent retaliation was alien to the true spirit of the Gospel, which was about love – turning the other cheek, loving those who persecute you and praying for them.

The main reason people believe in a wrathful God today is the assumed or asserted inerrancy of the Bible, especially when the Old Testament is read literally without regard to its context and original audience, and without the lens of Jesus, the living Word of God. The letter kills, but the Spirit brings life. Proponents of *sola scriptura*, 'Bible alone,' treat everything in the Bible as totally historically accurate, true and inerrant. This leads to doctrines based on incorrect interpretations, and to a two-faced God who is sometimes retributive and sometimes restorative, a God of tit-for-tat revenge as well as a God of love. Such a God would be fickle and hard to trust. The truth, as revealed by many prophets and ultimately by Jesus Himself, is that God is not retributive at all, but a God of grace and mercy. The restoration of all things is a recurring theme of hope throughout the Bible, although it is often overshadowed by narratives that portray God as vengeful.

God's solution for evil

To truly understand who God is, we must interpret the truth through the lens of Jesus. God is love, and there is no division or contradiction within the Trinity: Father, Son and Spirit. Deconstructing and deprogramming from false doctrines allow us to discern the truth of God's nature. Jesus came to reveal the restorative God and to reject the retributive God, who is nothing but a fiction created by human imagination. God's solution for evil is rehabilitation through refining and purification, not eternal punishment and torment. The truth that Jesus revealed is that God is merciful, His loving-kindness never ends, and His love is eternal because God is eternal.

Unfortunately, the term 'Christian' has become associated with a negative image of God, which is why some, like myself, prefer to identify as disciples or followers of Jesus rather than as 'Christians'. The retributive God of Noah's flood, the Canaanite conquest and wholesale slaughter is so repulsive to many that they have discarded faith in Jesus outright on that basis alone. A religion based on forgiveness through blood sacrifices is rightly seen as incompatible with a God who is love. Such a double-minded theology is toxic and is rejected by the world. It is time to discard this false image of God and embrace the truth revealed by Jesus – of a loving Father who is merciful, restorative, and endlessly pursuing us with unconditional love.

I invite you to join me in an encounter with God who is Unconditional Love.

Activation #16:
Embrace Unconditional Love

I would encourage you to embrace that place of peace and rest, embrace the reality of entering into a place of intimacy by meditating in a place of rest.

> Close your eyes and begin to think,
> And fix your focus and your thinking on Jesus,
> on the Father,
> on God as love.
> It might help just to breathe slowly,
> and begin to slow down your breathing,

and slow down your thinking,
and come to a place of rest.

Be comfortable, get relaxed,
And begin to think about
the unconditional love of the Father for you, His child.

Feel that love,
that love poured out upon you,
that love filling you,
that love within you,
that love flowing.

Be still and let God begin to love you unconditionally,
removing any fear;
any fear of God being angry or vengeful,
any mindsets you might still have.

Allow Him, as the Truth,
to remove those false narratives
of a vengeful God,
to reveal a merciful God.

Let God's mercy triumph over every wrong thinking,
any fear-based thinking,
any wrong beliefs about who God really is.

Be still and allow the truth that God is love,
that God is joy, that God is peace,
that God is the truth and the life,
that God is a God of limitless grace
and triumphant mercy.

As God speaks those words to you of who He is,
invite that flow of love,
that flow of joy and peace and grace and mercy.
Let it fill you.

See it flowing like rivers of living water
in your innermost being.
Begin to drink from that fountain of love.

Drink it in as you drink deeply.
Drink it in deeper and deeper and deeper,
that it will flow in you as a mighty river of love,
flowing through your spirit,
through your soul,
into your body,
being focused in the innermost part of your very being;
energising you,
strengthening you,
encouraging you,
filling you with acceptance,
affirmation, appreciation, approval,
loving you unconditionally.

As you see and feel that river of love flowing in you,
release that love out,
release it through you.
Let it be rivers flowing through you,
touching other people.

Maybe think of those that you would like
the love of God to touch,
maybe family members,
workmates, people you know,
that the love that's in you will touch them,
that you will expand
your spiritual boundary around them,
that they will have a safe place
to explore the love of God.

Rivers of love,
flowing from your innermost being,
touching people's lives
as you demonstrate unconditional love,
as you choose to forgive,
as you choose to release,
as you choose to bless
those who might be persecuting you;
as you choose to demonstrate mercy and grace
in the way you live,

in how you speak,
in how you act,
and how you think.

Be filled to overflowing with that amazing,
amazing, wonderful love of the Father,
that He loves you unconditionally,
because you're His child.

You're in a safe place.
Let Him speak to you words of affirmation,
let Him encourage you,
let Him reveal to you the truth of who you are.

Spend a few moments listening to His voice
as He speaks the truth,
as He reveals your true identity as a son of God,
as He affirms you.

Part III

Immortality

17. Embrace Immortality

Love conquers

Almost everyone who is a Christian believes in immortality from a spiritual perspective because they expect to be with God in heaven forever when they die. Yet if it were true that immortality comes about only after you die physically, that would be somewhat ironic. I believe our immortality is strongly linked to the unconditionally loving nature of God. He loves me unconditionally, so He does not want me to die or experience any break, any interference in that love, because love conquers death and all its consequences.

The atonement view of the early church fathers was primarily that of Christ's victory over death. When they saw what He did on the cross, they saw Him conquering death – not only His own death but our death, and indeed, death itself. When the Father brought Him out of death in the resurrection, He was bringing the whole of mankind out of death, out of lost identity, back into life; and with the ability to perceive the reality by seeing that truth.

A covenant with death

Christians have long been deceived into making a covenant with death, in which they embrace and accept it. The notion that death opens up the heavens is totally opposite to the truth, but that is the expectation I was brought up with. I was taught it was 'promotion': when you die, you go to heaven, you see God; and all the pains, all the sorrows and all the problems of this world will disappear 'in the great by and by'. The whole concept of 'crossing Jordan' and singing songs about going to heaven – that was the spiritual environment I grew up in, so death was something that was to be accepted – and even (with some reservations) to be welcomed.

Many believers have been deceived into embracing death as their saviour, rather than Jesus. In their thinking, if they are going through difficulties in this world, death will set them free from those struggles. And in a way, it does. But the truth is that we can be free without having to die, because Jesus died to set us free. To portray death as being the end of suffering, toil, hardships and labour is a human theological perspective that totally obscures the truth. Jesus did not come so that we could die and go to heaven; He came so we would not have to die. Jesus overcame death so we could live in the abundance of resurrection life, not welcome death as a friend. He never taught that we should accept death; He came to overcome it once and for all.

For the law of the Spirit of life in Christ Jesus has set you free from the law of sin and death (Romans 8:2).

The law of the Spirit is the liberating force of Life in Christ. This leaves me with no further obligation to the law of sin and death. Spirit has superseded the sin-enslaved senses as the principal law of our lives (Romans 8:2 Mirror).

Let's come out of agreement with the spirit of death and come into agreement with the Spirit of Life in Christ Jesus. That is something we can choose to do. I encourage you to think, reflect, and ask God to reveal what you are coming into agreement with. What thinking do you agree with? What mindsets, beliefs, doctrines or theology do you agree with? Are the things you currently agree with in alignment with the spirit of life or with the spirit of death? Any aspect of your life that is not aligned with the principles of abundant life is surely up for re-evaluation.

Let's check what agreements we might have made (even unwittingly) and what agreements we are living in, so that we can be set free to come into agreement with 'the liberating force of Life in Christ', which will bring about immortality. In fact, it has already brought about immortality, it is just that we need to embrace it. Everything changes when we receive, embrace and agree with this liberating force of life in Christ because what it liberates us from is death. It overcomes death in us so that we are free to experience abundant life now.

For the wages of sin is death, but the free gift of God is eternal life in Christ Jesus our Lord (Romans 6:23).

That was a verse often quoted in my early Christian experience, and the implication was that the wages of sin being death was about 'hell' and punishment. But it does not say that; it just says that the wages (or consequence) of sin is death. And the free gift of God is eternal life in Christ Jesus our Lord. How? Because He overcame death. Because He was resurrected out of death and brought life to all mankind.

For since by a man came death, by a man also came the resurrection of the dead. For as in Adam all die, so also in Christ all will be made alive (1 Corinthians 15:21).

Everyone who came after Adam, everyone in Adam's line, has died. But it also says that everyone will also be made alive in Christ. The same 'all.' Because Jesus, as the last Adam, has overcome what the first Adam did in bringing death into mankind's experience. No-one in the second Adam's line needs to have that experience at all.

Overcoming death with life

What is death? You could define it as the absence of life. God is our life. In Him we live and move and have our being. Therefore, we can think of death as the absence of God and the absence of light. Jesus came to deal with that.

When I saw Him, I fell at His feet like a dead man. And He placed His right hand on me, saying, "Do not be afraid; I am the first and the last, and the living One; and I was dead, and behold, I am alive forevermore, and I have the keys of death and of Hades (Revelation 1:17-18).

He is the living One, and because He is alive forevermore, so are we. What do you think He did with the keys of death and *Hades?* He unlocked them; He unlocked being hidden in lost identity to reveal the reality of truth and life. The wages (or results or consequences) of sin, which is lost identity, are death. And death is the ultimate lost identity. Death is losing sight of God and of our identity as sons. Death is being in darkness, hidden from the light and the truth. Death is not seeing our true identity: *'Hades'* literally means 'unseen.' We have all been caught in that place where we could not see our true identity and destiny, but Jesus has made it possible for us to see that reality; and not just see it but come into it and experience it fully, so that we do not have to embrace death in any shape or form.

Jesus overcame death; He took the keys of death and *Hades*. We died with Adam; we died with Christ. We were buried and resurrected and made alive with Jesus. Our lost identity is now unveiled and revealed in Jesus, who came to seek and to save those who were lost, in lost identity. He came to seek and save those who did not know who they really were.

Do you not know that all of us who have been baptized into Christ Jesus have been baptized into His death? Now, if we have died with Christ, we believe that we shall also live with Him. we have become united with Him in the likeness of His death, certainly we shall also be in the likeness of His resurrection (Romans 6:3-5).

The life we live with Christ is immortal life, but we need to embrace that. We died with Him. He died on our behalf. He died for all of mankind to heal mankind's wound of lost identity.

But now Christ has been raised from the dead, the first fruits of those who are asleep. For since by a man came death, by a man also came the resurrection of the dead (1 Corinthians 15:20-21).

Christ is the first fruits of everyone who was dead before. And when He rose from the dead, He opened the graves, and eventually, all who were dead became alive. They awoke. They were awakened to the truth. They were no longer asleep. That is the reality. Spiritual death and spiritual resurrection are already achieved for us in Christ through what He did on the cross and how He came out of the tomb.

This whole process is complete, finished, and never has to be done again.

Paul writes in Galatians 2:20, "I have been crucified with Christ." This was his conviction because he had experienced that reality; Jesus died for each of us and represented all mankind by dying our death on the cross, including each of us in Himself. By the same token, Jesus has also included each of us in Him, in His life, in His resurrection life. We are included in His death, and we are also included in His resurrection. We are included in His abundant life.

Life and immortality

For He must reign until He has put all His enemies under His feet. The last enemy that will be abolished is death (1 Corinthians 15:25-26).

for it behoveth him to reign till he may have put all the enemies under his feet - the last enemy is done away - death (1 Corinthians 15:25-26).

What is the last enemy? The last enemy that will be abolished is death. When does that happen? When Jesus overcame death by being resurrected and resurrecting mankind. The last enemy is done away. Jesus has abolished death. Death is swallowed up in victory. This is the victory of the Cross. "O death, where is your victory? O death, where is your sting?" There is none. But the question is when did death lose its sting, its victory, for us? Because a lot of people would absolutely agree that death has been abolished, but they only apply it to the fact that if they were to die, they would go to heaven and live on in the spirit. They do not apply it to their physical life. I believe it happened when Jesus overcame death and that it applies to us now, not just sometime in the future.

[God] who saved us and called us with a holy calling, not according to our works, but according to His own purpose and grace, which was granted to us in Christ Jesus from all eternity, but has now been revealed by the appearing of our

Savior Christ Jesus, who abolished death and brought life and immortality to light through the gospel (2 Timothy 1:9-10).

This has been brought to light now. Being saved and being called is nothing to do with us, but according to His own purpose and grace, which was granted to us in Christ Jesus from all eternity. Everything necessary for our salvation, for our holy calling, is nothing to do with our works but was granted from eternity. It was already a done deal, but has now been revealed to us. It has been revealed by the appearing of our saviour, Christ Jesus. This is why every eye, ear, tongue and knee will bow, because every eye can see Him: He has appeared. And He abolished death and brought life and immortality to light through the gospel.

This is true good news, for us to embrace and to experience. We were already granted that grace before everything even started, from all eternity, so that we would be able to come into this immortality; for that truth, that light, to be revealed and for us to see it, embrace it and experience it.

He rescued the integrity of our original design and revealed that we have always been his own from the beginning, even before time was. This has nothing to do with anything we did to qualify or disqualify ourselves. We're not talking religious good works or karma here. Jesus unveils grace to be the eternal intent of God. Grace celebrates our pre-creation innocence and now declares our redeemed union with God in Christ Jesus (2 Timothy 1:9 Mirror).

We were always His own; we were only lost from our own perspective. God is not careless; He did not lose us. We chose to walk away from Him. All we like sheep have gone astray; we all walked our own way. But we have been brought back to what we were in God from the beginning. We have been declared the righteousness of God in Christ, not because we did anything, but because He chose to make us the righteousness of God in Christ because in reality that is how He has always seen us. We had lost sight of how He sees us, and saw ourselves through the filter of our own life experience and works. Most people sadly do not know this truth, so they do not know what Jesus has already done and what is already theirs. They have not yet seen it and therefore they have not even desired it.

Everything that grace pointed to is now realised in Jesus Christ and brought into clear view through the gospel. Jesus is what grace reveals. He took death out of the equation and redefines life; this is good news indeed (2 Timothy 1:10 Mirror).

This is why we have responsibility to present a gospel which reveals the whole truth of who God really is and what Jesus has done. Representing God as a cosmic child abuser (as Steve Chalke memorably put it) who would kill His own Son is not 'bringing into clear view' what Jesus has done. It is not revealing what God has done in Christ in reconciling the world to Himself, not holding anything against them. And it has categorically not demonstrated that He has redefined what life really is by taking death out of the equation.

That redefined life is immortality. That is the good news; that is what is to be brought into clear view. Even for many of us who have had a knowledge of Jesus, an experience of Jesus and even a relationship with Jesus, the reality of immortality has been obscured and hidden under the covering of death and an acceptance of death as inevitable. Jesus has abolished death; and with death, all that it implies: the results or wages of sin, which is our lost identity, wickedness and evil. That has all been abolished; death is abolished. That is why we need to be free from this whole deception and from our continued embracing of it.

To those who by perseverance in doing good seek glory, honour, and immortality, He will give eternal life (Romans 2:7).

There are things here to seek for which are already ours: glory, to be clothed with our true identity; honour, recognised in our sonship as made in the image of God, not for what we do but for who we are; and immortality. If we embrace the reality of that, He will give eternal life, life that comes from the source of eternity.

Put on the imperishable

For this perishable must put on the imperishable, and this mortal must put on immortality. But when this perishable puts on the imperishable, and this mortal puts on immortality, then will come about the saying that is written: "Death has been swallowed up in victory. Where, O Death, is your victory? Where, O Death, is your sting?" The sting of death is sin, and the power of sin is the Law; but thanks be to God, who gives us the victory through our Lord Jesus Christ (1 Corinthians 15:53-57).

It is for us to embrace what God has done by accepting it and figuratively putting it on like clothes. "Death has been swallowed up in victory." Now that is the truth of what Jesus did on the cross, but until we put it on, it is not true for us because we have not yet seen it as the truth. When we see it as the truth, embrace it and receive it, then death is swallowed up in victory for us. When we embrace the reality of immortality, we do not need to die.

For we who live are constantly being handed over to death because of Jesus, so that the life of Jesus may also be revealed in our mortal flesh (2 Corinthians 4:11).

Our day-to-day experience continues to exhibit that even in the face of death, our association with the death Jesus already died remains the inspiration of His life made so clearly visible within us. This is in such contrast to the circumstances that we are often faced with (2 Corinthians 4:11 Mirror).

They were living in perilous times, being persecuted, constantly faced with the possibility of death, of being killed or martyred. So, how can God's life be revealed in our mortal flesh? I believe by doing what Jesus told us to do, by eating His flesh and drinking His blood in communion. Communion will bring about immortality in our lives if we embrace the reality of drawing on the source of life it contains. Embracing His life will overcome death in our flesh. Eternal life in our bodies counteracts death, and we receive communion as God's life in us so that we do not have to die.

Church history says that people tried to kill John a number of times and could not do it. I believe that was because he embraced and saw the reality and the truth of life in Jesus, and received that life in himself. Some even contend that he has never died and is still actually living today.

We may be faced with death all around us, and with evidence that seems to confirm that everyone dies. Yet we have a revelation of the reality of what Jesus' death accomplished: we have already died with Him and been resurrected to new life with Him, and that life is clearly visible within us. It is revealed as in us; the life is in us, and we need to embrace it.

For indeed, we who are in this tent groan, being burdened, because we do not want to be unclothed but to be clothed, so that what is mortal will be swallowed up by life (2 Corinthians 5:4).

If we put on the right clothes, wear the right identity, know the truth and embrace it, then anything which is mortal, which has the possibility of dying, will be swallowed up by life. Abundant life in Christ will overcome physical death. This is not just talking about dying and going to heaven, which is how people have been taught to interpret these Bible verses. They think we will have eternal life because we will go to heaven, but first they expect to physically die. People are conditioned to believe in dying, but I believe we need to have a realisation of not dying, that we do not need to be conditioned by death but by life. Our expectation can be an abundance of life which has already overcome death.

We are not complaining about our bodies, even though we are often aware of its frailties. Instead, we yearn to be overwhelmed with life. We know that every evidence of death, even in our bodies, will dissolve into life (2 Corinthians 5:4 Mirror).

I love that: every evidence of death, even in our bodies, will dissolve into life. Embrace that, receive it, align with it, agree with it, and come into the reality of that truth because God really does not want you to die physically.

Everyone around me is dying

The belief in immortality is a powerful message that God is revealing and bringing out over and over again. More and more people are starting to embrace it, but it is a huge challenge because we see death around us all the time, and it is hard to stay strong in the midst of that.

As I was first preparing this material, in the space of one week, three people close to me died. One was Chris Carter, a friend I hung out with online most weeks during the pandemic. I got to know him really well; a lovely guy. Another was Anna Wingate from Seattle, with whom I had been in touch since 2013. I visited and did conferences there with Anna, staying with her two years ago. She believed in immortality in life, and yet, she died. Both were struck down with cancer very quickly. My mum also died the same week. She was 91, and in her case it was somewhat of a relief because she was unable to get out of bed and was sleeping all the time.

Three times in one week, I was faced with the deaths of people I know and love. Not long after, two more good friends I had known for many years also died just a few months apart. Now, just as this book goes to press, another good friend of mine, Lindy Strong, has passed away. Lindy was a true ambassador of heaven and a forerunner of the restoration of all things message. She had a ministry of healing and wholeness – and revealing immortality – yet she had cancer three times. The third time, three years ago, she was given only weeks to live and told to go into a hospice. She did not accept that prognosis. She rejected it because at that time her assertion was, "My Father does not want me to die now."

I could be intimidated by all that: "How can I proclaim a message on immortality when everyone around me is dying?" But I am not going to be intimidated, even if I do not have the answers to the questions people are asking. Why did Chris, Anna and Lindy die, despite so many people believing for their healing and restoration, and even having themselves engaged heaven? God has not told me, and I am not going to hypothesise. However, I can engage with them in the cloud of witnesses, where they are glorified in light. Would I rather they were here with me on earth? Absolutely. But the reality is that they are where they are. I do not know why, but their deaths have not shaken my trust in God being a good God nor my belief in immortality. God is bringing immortality to light in this time, and He wants us to embrace the fact that we do not need to die.

I do believe that immortality has to be contended for. Having embraced it, we need to stand against anything contradictory to it. If you have been shaken by anything like that, I would encourage you to go back to the truth of who God is. Go back to what I am sharing in these closing chapters and do not allow what you see with your natural eyes shake your trust in who God is and what He has done. It is like Peter getting out of the boat when Jesus called him to walk on water. He was walking on water, but then he started to look around, saw the wind blowing, the waves, and he began to sink. Let's keep our eyes fixed on Jesus, the author and finisher of our faith; keep our eyes fixed on Jesus, the Way, the Truth and the Life.

The quality of eternity

There are many aspects of immortality I could share with you, but I want to stick with my personal journey to understand and experience immortality. I would not want to live forever in a body that was not capable of doing everything I am called to do. I would not want to live forever if I am going to be sick. I want to live forever in health and wholeness. My personal journey so far in this has been about experiencing the reality and the abilities of immortal life, because immortality is not just about not dying, but that we will enjoy the quality of living from eternity today.

He has made everything appropriate in its time. He has also set eternity in their heart, yet so that man will not find out the work which God has done from the beginning even to the end (Ecclesiastes 3:11).

God has placed something in our hearts that is designed to draw us back to our eternal position and identity in Him. But we cannot find out about it? No, we cannot find out about it in our own strength or through the tree of the knowledge of good and evil. But we can see the reality of it because it has been brought to light through Jesus and the good news of what He has done for us. We cannot think of immortality as the 'Fountain of Youth' or some eternal elixir of life. This is only accomplished through our inclusion in Christ, in His resurrection life.

The Journey to Immortality

I have been on a journey from healing to health to immortality. I began to learn how to cooperate with my body in union – spirit, soul and body – to bring about health and wholeness. I had to be deprogrammed from being tethered to the expectation of death. Now I have begun to experience living in multi-dimensional and non-linear reality (of which more later), which is what immortal life is all about.

When I was brought up in the Methodist and later the Brethren Church, there was little belief in healing. They might pray for someone's healing but would add, "if it be Your will, Lord," I suspect not really believing it would be. They certainly did not lay hands on the sick, so I had no expectation of healing. Things changed when I was baptised in the Spirit. I began receiving healing through prayer and supernatural ministry. For example, I had a chronic back condition that made it impossible to sleep lying down. However, in 1993, while engaging with God and laughing in the Spirit, I was healed instantly and never had a back problem again.

My theology at that time was that healing was part of God's kingdom – the future breaking into the present – but it was not guaranteed. When I was diagnosed with Meniere's disease (causing tinnitus, deafness and debilitating motion sickness), I was not healed immediately, despite all the prayers I received and healing meetings I attended. This prompted me to explore every Bible verse I could find related to healing, health and wholeness.

I discovered that healing was eternal, accomplished by Jesus on the cross. He took my sin (which I now understand as lost identity) and sickness, and dealt with them. I accepted that reality and recognised that Jesus, who revealed the Father, was my healer. Jehovah Rohi is the Lord who heals. I read numerous books on healing, mostly focused on faith, and eventually, in a worship conference, I experienced a miraculous healing. My ears popped open, and I could hear perfectly. From that day, I never needed to take medication for Meniere's disease again.

I came to understand that health is the norm for a child of God, not just repeated healing but not getting sick in the first place. This changed my whole perspective and I began to live without sickness or disease. Despite numerous injuries from being careless, especially with power tools, I learned to respect my body and take better care of it. I realised that spirit, soul and body were designed to be whole and one. My behaviour needed to reflect that understanding, so I determined to use proper equipment and engage in safer practices to show my body that I was serious about looking after it.

Whenever I had an accident, I would apologise to my body and seek accelerated healing, often seeing quick recoveries without lasting scars. This reinforced my belief that while accidents may happen, we do not have to suffer long-term consequences. God wants us to actively embrace the reality of immortality by applying unconditional love, aligning ourselves with immortality, renewing our minds, and deconstructing any thinking aligned with death.

I believe that involves spirit, soul and body coming together in union and oneness, living in a state of immortality. In one sense, we are all alive and therefore in a state of immortality right now. Let's maintain that state of life in Christ and not entertain death in our future. I communicate and fellowship in communion, receiving life from God to live in health and experience accelerated self-repair and healing.

I have experienced progressive revelation that goes from healing to health to immortality, linked to communion. This is not just a ritual but a state of being. My understanding of communion evolved from taking it daily to receiving life from God, eradicating sickness, disease and genetic issues. I made my communion declarations for physical health and wholeness available on our website[14]. Eventually, I began to renew my mind through communion to embrace the reality of who I am as a child of God.

The Father revealed that every time I ate or drank, I could receive life from God, bringing wholeness and eradicating death from my being. I focused my thoughts and intentions on life. The Father also revealed that every time I breathe, I am receiving life. This continual state of communion and flow of eternal life creates a state of being in union with God.

How precious is Your lovingkindness, O God!
And the children of men take refuge in the shadow of Your wings.
They drink their fill of the abundance of Your house;
And You give them to drink of the river of Your delights.
For with You is the fountain of life;
In Your light we see light.
(Psalm 36:7-9).

"Whoever drinks of the water that I will give him shall never thirst; the water that I will give him will become in him a well of water springing up to eternal life." (John 4:14).

This river of life, this living water, this energy flows within us, and connects us to immortality. As our mind is renewed to the truth of our immortality, our consciousness expands. Immortality is not just something we have; it is who we are. We are immortal; let's embrace immortality.

---

[14] You can find it at freedomarc.blog/teaching-series/communion-prayer

As we go into a brief activation, I encourage you to ask the Father to show you if there are any areas of your thinking in which you have agreed with death, any covenants that you have entered into with death, any thoughts of expecting to die. Ask Him to reveal whether you really only envisage immortality as meaning that you will go to heaven rather than not die physically; and whether you have any negative mindsets, belief systems or any other issues around this subject.

Activation #17
The Spirit of Life

>Close your eyes,
>and come to that place of rest.
>
>Focus on Him.
>Focus your thoughts,
>your intentions.
>
>Get your body into a place where you're at rest,
>where you're relaxed;
>breathe in deeply, slowly,
>and hold it;
>and breathe out.
>
>Breathe in deeply,
>and hold it.
>Breathe out.
>
>Come to a place of love, unconditional love.
>
>Breathe in unconditional love.
>Breathe in the life of God;
>breathe in life, the Breath of Life.
>
>Times of refreshing come from the presence of the Lord. That 'times of refreshing' means 'to breathe easily again,' to breathe in life.
>
>Be still and breathe in life.

And I just ask, Father
you'd reveal to every person,
that you would reveal to them any areas of their life
any mindsets, belief systems,
which are still connected and tethered to death;
where they are still tethered to time
being a factor in aging,
that they are getting older every day,
where they have a wrong relationship with time.

Any mindset,
unveil and reveal that truth:
areas that they need to come out of agreement with.

Come out of agreement with the spirit of death
and come into agreement with the spirit of life in Christ,
the abundance of life,
the eternal, immortal life.

Breathe it in.

And as He shows you any mindset or belief system,
surrender it, renounce it, give it to Him;
to renew your mind,
to deconstruct,
to pull down those pillars in your thinking
which may be aligned to any aspect of death.

Stay in that place
and for a few minutes
just allow Him to reveal that,
to unveil that truth
to show you that truth.

As you let go of any wrong mindset or belief system,
as you hand over death,
receive life.
Breathe in life.

Think about, within you, a fountain of life
a fountain of living water

that you can take and drink;
drinking from the river of life
flowing out of heaven
flowing into your spirit
flowing through your soul and body,
rivers of living water.

Drink.
Drink deeply.

And as you drink –
drinking in life and energy,
the very life of God...
drink it in –
let it saturate every fibre of your being
every atom, every particle, every cell;
restoring your mitochondria,
restoring the ability of your cells to communicate
and bring about restoration and health and wholeness.

And if you have any area of sickness
in your physical body right now,
drink and apply that living water to that area.
See life, light, energy, spirit
touching that area;
touching your heart,
touching your liver,
touching your kidneys;
touching your skin,
touching your eyes,
touching every area of your physical body.

Be surrounded in unconditional love.
Be absolutely saturated
in the light of life,
in the life of immortality.
Embrace it
let it touch every area of your being:
mind, emotions, body

immersed, saturated in life
immortal, eternal life.

Continue to drink.

18. Jesus Abolished Death

My experiences have revealed who God really is, showing His loving nature and that He is my Father. He loves me, and that is why I am convinced of the truth of immortality. God loves all His children and creation equally and unconditionally, and He wants all of us to be in a relationship with Him that never ends.

It is vital that we are deprogrammed from being tethered to death to experience immortal life. Culture and religion program us to expect death as the end or as a 'promotion' to heaven. We need our minds renewed to be untethered and freed from faith in death. Death does not rescue us; Jesus rescues us. Death does not save us; Jesus saves us. Death does not give us entrance into heaven; Jesus gives us entrance to heaven. He is the door through which we enter; and we can enter into it now. Death was originally the consequence of sin, of lost identity.

How difficult it is

How difficult it is to believe in a judgmental, vindictive, hell-casting God! He came in the flesh and allowed religious zealots to murder Him to demonstrate His love, forgiveness, mercy and unwillingness to be separated from mankind. God has passed judgment, and the judgment is that we are justified, righteous, forgiven and no longer separated.

Most people have no problem with the concept of eternal life from the spiritual perspective of going to heaven after death, although the Bible actually never specifically promises that. You can perhaps infer what happens if you die, but the Bible does not say, "If you die, you will go to heaven if you believe in Jesus." It does record Jesus saying, "If you believe in me, you have eternal life and will not perish." In other words, you will not stay lost – that is what "perish" actually means. Yet the idea of immortality, meaning not dying physically at all, causes problems for many people because we have all come to believe we are going to live eternally with God in heaven. What the Bible says is that God is going to live eternally with us: He will come and dwell with us, not invite us to dwell with Him. This changes the dynamic and explains why the restoration of the universe is necessary: God will dwell with us in this restored creation.

Renewing our minds

Many have not even considered the concept of not dying physically at all. That does not correspond with their reality, but I believe God is revealing this reality so that we can have our thinking renewed, embrace immortality, and not die physically. Most people are conditioned to expect physical death, and of course, they have no evidence that anyone has not died, from a historical perspective. There are some examples in the Bible of people not dying – Enoch and Elijah were two, and Adam had many children before he and Eve took us on the path of independence. Some of those children did not follow Adam as father; they followed God as Father, went through the fiery sword, and embraced the tree of life. They are still alive in that realm, often called hooded ones or ancient ones, and have roles within creation and towards the rest of mankind. They have turned up in my life several times, especially when I had important decisions to make.

So most people expect everyone to die, as that has been the norm in the past. But this concept needs to change. Some say there are desert fathers or mystics who are hundreds of years old. There was a man named Sadhu Sundar Singh who wrote several books about encountering the Maharishi of Mount Kailash in the Himalayas. This Maharishi had been alive for several hundred years and was still functioning in that place. I imagine he still is. Some say the Apostle John never died. Chris Reed, President and Executive Director of MorningStar Ministries, had a vision of John living in a cave[15]. John told him he would be seen again publicly in the future. That would be interesting, though many might not believe he is John. If

---

[15] 'Is the Disciple John Alive? – Chris Reed on the Elijah List' https://youtu.be/G5T259mERYU accessed 01/08/2024

someone is 2,000 years old and has not died, it would certainly challenge people's views on the necessity of death.

Immortality is our birthright. Man was created immortal, but sin ushered in the deception of mortality. Jesus came to set the record straight. Through His death, we have immortality restored. When we die with Him, we are raised to immortality. Well, we have all died with Him, so have we realised that truth and embraced it?

[God] who saved us and called us with a holy calling, not according to our works, but according to His own purpose and grace, which was granted to us in Christ Jesus from all eternity, but has now been revealed by the appearing of our Savior Christ Jesus, who abolished death and brought life and immortality to light through the gospel (2 Timothy 1:9-10).

Being saved and called with a holy calling was granted to us because of what God desires through His purpose and grace. Who is the 'us' in this passage? It includes everyone, not just Timothy and those to whom he probably read this letter. It includes everyone who was in Christ before the foundation of the world (and that is everybody). This grace was granted to us in Christ Jesus from all eternity. It happened before we were created, born, and even before the world was established; it was guaranteed from the beginning. Before time began, it was already agreed that God would manifest our identity as His sons, and He was committed to ensuring that happened through His purpose and grace.

But it has now been revealed. He accomplished His purpose through what Jesus did on the cross. Life and immortality have been brought to light through the gospel – and that is truly good news. Now, I have read the Bible many times throughout my life, but I never fully grasped the significance of these two verses until the last four or five years. I must have read them before, and even preached on them, but I never truly understood the importance and reality of what they are saying about immortality. Like many others, I used to think it was about going to heaven when I died. Jesus warned us of an enemy who seeks to rob, kill and destroy, and declared that He came to give abundant life. I believe that abundant life refers to the life of immortality, and it is something we can embrace now.

The bread of life

"Truly, truly, I say to you, the one who believes has eternal life. I am the bread of life." (John 6:47-8).

Jesus compared Himself to the manna that the Israelites ate in the wilderness, which sustained them but did not prevent their eventual physical death:

"This is the bread that comes down out of heaven, so that anyone may eat from it and not die. I am the living bread that came down out of heaven; if anyone eats from this bread, he will live forever; and the bread which I will give for the life of the world also is My flesh... This is the bread that came down out of heaven, not as the fathers ate and died; the one who eats this bread will live forever." (John 6:50-51, 58).

He was talking about Himself, emphasising that eating 'this bread' means not dying physically as those in the wilderness who ate the manna had died. Jesus demonstrated that when we partake of His body and blood and remember Him, we receive transforming life for our mortal bodies.

As I previously described, through daily communion and making intentional declarations, I developed a transformative practice of receiving spiritual life and power, which evolved to become a constant state of being. This led me to a profound understanding of spiritual DNA transformation, in which the blood of Jesus continuously purifies and realigns my genetic material with my true divine identity. I would speak creative words to my DNA to release the supernatural abilities of God, triggering the ability to see in the realm of the Kingdom, to move in the realm of the Kingdom, and to transform matter. When I said these things, I was engaging in the realm of the Kingdom, seeing into that realm, and (in a limited way) doing the things I was declaring.

But there are other abilities: to be non-linear, multi-dimensional, able to engage other dimensions, able to create (not just transform), and to transrelocate, and I have also experienced something of these. By declaring them, they too became my reality. This process unlocked my full sonship potential, embracing the unconditional love of God and living from the flow of the Eternal Source in an intimate relationship with the Way, the Truth and the Life Himself. Embracing abundant life and immortality means living in God's light, love and spirit.

If the spirit of Him who raised Jesus from the dead dwells in you, He who raised Christ Jesus from the dead will also give life to your mortal bodies through His Spirit who dwells in you (Romans 8:11).

The 'if' in that verse is used to introduce a logical premise rather than a condition: it is a declaration of truth. The Spirit is in us, energising our mortal bodies, leading to immortality. The Spirit gives life, light and energy to our mortal bodies.

Our innermost being

This spiritual life is often expressed in scripture in terms of the breath of God and the rivers of Living Water, to illustrate the flow of life and energy within us. To put on immortality, we need to focus this flow of living energy. We have gateways in our spirit, soul and body, as well as energy gates within us. Living energy flows from heaven into our spirit, then into our soul, and finally into our body; uniting spirit, soul and body. Jesus described this as welling up from within our innermost being, where the river of Living Water, symbolic of life and energy, flows and becomes a fountain of life within us.

"Whoever drinks of the water that I will give him shall never thirst; but the water that I will give him will become in him a well of water springing up to eternal life." (John 4:14).

According to Jesus, living water flows in us when we drink and reconnect to the Spirit as the source of immortality. We can actively engage this, rather than passively look forward to it happening. This water represents the source of eternal life and immortality within us.

"He who believes in me, as the Scripture said, from his innermost being will flow rivers of Living Water." (John 7:38).

By consistently drinking from this heavenly source, we open ourselves to the reality of immortality. At the core of our being lies the Merkabah, an energy matrix that serves as the focal point where our spirit, soul and body unite with Father, Son and Holy Spirit. This is the source of the living waters, a wellspring of limitless energy, light and life. The River of Life, originating from God's throne and flowing through the Tree of Life, streams into our core. As it reaches the Merkabah, it is distributed throughout our being via seven energy gates or seals. This continuous flow of living energy transforms us, bringing union to our spirit, soul and body, and enabling a state of constant communion with God.

In our innermost being, where there is union, rivers of Living Water begin to flow with energy. It is a little like a hydroelectric turbine, where a large reservoir of water is focused into small channels that drive a turbine, producing electricity. Similarly, this river focuses in the Merkabah at the core of our being and is then distributed, producing energy and life. Rivers flow from our innermost being, creating a field of energy around us. This energy field is what brought healing through Peter's 'shadow', which was really the energy field around him. The energy of living light within us concentrates in the Merkabah, giving us access to eternal life and enabling us to communicate with and access multi-dimensional realities through inner portals.

Within the Merkabah, there are portals of energy that give us access to travel and receive communication within our innermost being. Our consciousness expands as our mind is renewed to the truth of our immortality. As we begin to believe the reality of this truth, our ability to live from that state of being increases.

Now may the God of peace Himself sanctify you entirely; and may your spirit, soul, and body be preserved complete, without blame [in the presence] *of our Lord Jesus Christ* (1 Thessalonians 5:23, amended).

We are preserved entirely complete and without blame in His presence (not 'at His coming'), which produces life energy from the Spirit that flows within us.

There are many systems within the physical body, such as the blood, nervous, lymphatic and hormonal systems. It is entirely reasonable to suppose that God has created us with an energy system to generate and distribute all the energy we need for ourselves and to engage with creation as sons.

In 2010, God gave me a lesson about quantum physics, energy, string theory, vibration, frequency and harmony, which led me to appreciate the unified quantum field that fuels everything. We are all connected to that quantum energy field. It consists of vibrating strings of living light energy. In the Chamber of Creation, I engage with these living light beings, which we call 'Quantum Lumens'. These smallest particles of energy, vibrating strings of light, are the building blocks of all matter. By engaging with this energy, we can draw on it to produce all the energy we need for all that God intends for us, including immortality.

Sound and light are energy on the same spectrum, used as biblical metaphors for living energy. The vibrating strings are the voice of His power that holds all things together (Colossians 1:17 and Hebrews 1:3). The grace of God, or vibrating strings of light energy, are the still-vibrating words that spoke creation into being. When we speak with the authority of the voice of God, living light responds to us creatively.

We can learn the process of speaking with the authority of the voice of God. By embracing and engaging His heart in the Cradle of Life, His thoughts, heart and intentions are revealed to us. We come into agreement and resonate with those thoughts and intentions, becoming a frequency, a sound, a voice of God. As oracles, we can speak creatively, and light responds to us, forming reality around us.

That energy field is often called Zero Point Energy. It is called zero point because technically nothing should be existing in a vacuum. When scientists created a vacuum and measured it, they found there was energy in it. They were not sure where it was coming from, but knew that if they froze it down to absolute zero, nothing should be moving, and there should definitely be no energy within the vacuum. However, when they did so and measured it, there was still energy there. That is Zero Point Energy, the energy that is energising this physical realm from a non-local realm or quantum field. We can draw energy from this field and focus it within our innermost being.

All matter and all energy particles – atoms, their nuclei, electrons, and their components – are all blinking in and out of this quantum or spiritual realm, the quantum field, at a very fast rate, in the smallest particle of time that can exist scientifically, Planck's constant (one twenty thousandth of a billionth of a second). Unless God tells you that this is true, as He did me, you are never going to know that some of your cells are in that realm and then coming energised out of that realm back into this one. We are engaging in another realm, picking up energy in a process that is designed to effectively mean that we have a limitless supply.

Scientists say that this energy is so powerful that one sugar cube amount of Zero Point Energy could power 400 billion galaxies. It would not take the size of a single grain of sugar to power our own galaxy. This is immense power, and God has created the universe and all of creation to operate within this field. There are those who are working at harnessing Zero Point Energy to create travel engines, space travel, and all these sorts of things. This is the stuff of science fiction (in the Stargate series, Zero Point Energy powered gateways, creating wormholes used to travel between planets, and into other dimensions. I believe that this is actually feasible, because I have travelled through a few of them).

Energy portals

If we have access to this power source, how do we open the seals or portals to engage this energy? The Merkabah, figuratively described in Ezekiel 1:4-26 as a chariot (see the next chapter), gives us access to open these portals. We all have gateways within our body, spirit and soul. We have energy gates within us. There are gateways between heaven and earth, portals under the earth, and gateways between dimensions. There are north, south, east and west gates, which we have been engaging. There are everlasting doors or gateways from heaven into the earth. We have access to all of these gateways, but we have to learn how to navigate and use them appropriately and correctly. Some people have tried to open those gateways inappropriately and illegitimately, creating problems for the earth. But now the sons of God are beginning to administrate gateways between the solar system, the planets, different dimensions, to bring about the restoration of all things and creation's freedom.

The energy fields produced by our body, heart and consciousness, can be measured. Heart energy extends about 10 feet (3 metres) or so. Brain energy – consciousness – produces a field of around 10-12 inches (25-30 centimetres). Our body also produces energy fields of frequency. All these energy fields interact with the quantum unified energy field which extends throughout creation. When we learn how to activate our senses, we can engage it and feel and sense creation itself. We can access the portals or intersection points between dimensions; we can energise them and travel through them. All this is being revealed, and something we are now starting to do as sons of God.

There are seven energy fields or gateways within each of us. Complete health and immortality are achieved when these fields are balanced, vibrating at the correct frequency, and energised. There are portals or energy gates within us that maintain the balance of energy when they are open and flowing. This is why we need to embrace and engage with how to focus living light or rivers of Living Water to energise our whole being.

I have seen how Nancy Coen spikes with energy when she is connecting to these energy gates within her. To avoid that, I learned to dissipate the energy into a field around me rather than actually getting too much at once. Heaven operates on a logarithmic scale, not a linear one. It is not addition; it is not multiplication; it is exponential. The seven seals or gateways release exponential amounts of energy as they are activated from heaven.

For example:

> Gate One: $1 \times 2 = 2$
> Gate Two: $2 \times 2 = 4$
> Gate Three: $4 \times 4 = 16$
> Gate Four: $16 \times 16 = 256$
> Gate Five: $256 \times 256 = 65{,}536$

That is a sizeable jump, is it not? It only gets more astonishing:

> Gate Six: $65{,}536 \times 65{,}536 = 4{,}294{,}967{,}296$

Four billion, two hundred and ninety-four million, nine hundred and sixty-seven thousand, two hundred and ninety-six. Now imagine what happens when the seventh gate is fully activated and flowing.

> Gate Seven: $4{,}294{,}967{,}296 \times 4{,}294{,}967{,}296 = 18{,}446{,}744{,}073{,}709{,}551{,}616$

Eighteen quintillion, four hundred and forty-six quadrillion, seven hundred and forty-four trillion, seventy-three billion, seven hundred and nine million, five hundred and fifty-one thousand, six hundred and sixteen.

That represents far more energy than you could ever possibly think of, imagine, or ever want to use. As we increase and activate the energy within the core of our being, it can distribute all the energy we need.

Our consciousness also performs logarithmically. When we come into union, when we operate each with our consciousness in agreement with others, then one can put a thousand to flight and two can put ten thousand. It is exponential. Let us say someone operating at a low level is measured at 80. How many people operating at 400 would be the equivalent of 5 billion operating at 80? Not as many as you might imagine. That is why agreement is so important. It is why union and unity are vital when we come to embracing these realities: being at one with the Lord, my spirit, soul and body in union being joined to the Father, Son and Spirit, in one spirit with Him. Virtually limitless creative energy is available to us to live immortally.

The Merkabah is a sacred geometric shape, related to various other concepts such as Metatron's Cube and the Tree of Life. If we learn to activate it, and use it practically, life energy flows from the very glory of God's presence within us. His light, the weight of His presence, His glory; it flows through our spirit gates, through our soul gates, through our body gates, until it is energised and activating all of our energy gates. Thus we will always have all the energy we need to enable us to do all that we see the Father doing.

Gateway of First Love

I would encourage you, when you are looking to activate this, to visualise opening up the Gateway of First Love so that the river begins to flow. Ezekiel describes the river flowing under the East Gate of the temple, becoming ankle-deep, knee-deep, waist-deep until it is out of our depth and flowing. It brings life wherever it goes, and I believe this is what it illustrates.

We are the Temple of the Holy Spirit, with God living in us. As we visualise opening up our gateway of First Love and embrace that life energy of love, joy and peace – the presence of the Father, Son and Spirit in us – it begins to flow like a river of Living Water in us. We drink it, we partake of it, it fills us, and it flows through us. Then you begin to see that living spiritual energy flowing in you and through you, flowing through the gateways of your spirit, flowing through the gateways of your soul, and flowing into the gateways of your body. You will begin to see it activating energy gates, seeing wheels spinning within wheels, which is Ezekiel's description of the Merkabah spinning. The gateways within us are also known as chakras in some circles, which is just a Sanskrit word for 'spinning disc of light energy'. This creates a powerful flow of life force within the body that energises the Merkabah, activates it from rest like a hydroelectric turbine, and then distributes that energy into our being so we can live as sons of God.

As we discover our identity as the sons of God, it is an amazing journey. I discovered healing, health, and eventually immortality, as my mind was deconstructed and renewed, my consciousness expanded, and I began to accept the reality of who God says I am. Unconditional love is a relationship with the Eternal Father. He wants us to enter into that state of rest and being where we are totally trusting in His goodness, in His love, kindness, faithfulness, and loving-kindness. I believe His intention is that we live an abundant life of immortality.

But as always, we need to experience it. That is why I finish each chapter with a short activation.

Activation #18
Energised by Unconditional Love

> And again, I would encourage you
> to close your eyes
> come to a place of rest
> where you begin to feel and sense
> that you are loved,
> you are accepted,
> you are approved of.
> He unconditionally loves you.

Begin to slow down your mind,
slow down, relax your body.
Slow down your breathing.

Begin to breathe deeply.
Breathe in through your nose, and hold it,
and then slowly release it through your mouth.
Breathe in,
and gently breathe out.

Come to that place where you are breathing in
the unconditional love of God.
You are breathing in life,
you're being energised,
you can feel unconditional love
flow through your whole being.

In that place of stillness and rest,
God is loving you,
unveiling and revealing the truth of who you are.
Be still and embrace that.
Come to that place of stillness.

In that place,
I'd encourage you to picture Jesus
knocking on the door within you,
knocking on your first love gate.

Picture that door having a handle on your side.
You choose to open that door,
and as you open that door,
beyond the door is a well and a fountain,
and that water begins to flow,
and you can drink.
Drink Living Water,
Drink, receive that energy,
drink it in,
partake of it.
Drink deeply.
You are engaging Father, Son and Spirit

and their life,
their abundant life.

That river flows through you,
a river of life,
its flowing energy filling your spirit,
flowing through your spiritual gateways.

And I want you to go with the flow.
Think of it as:
it's gone beyond ankle-deep,
knee-deep, waist-deep,
and it's flowing, bringing life wherever it goes.

And you are flowing with it:
you are flowing with the stream,
and it is flowing through your spirit,
flowing through your soul,
touching your soul, your mind,
your emotion, your will,
your imagination, your choice.
And it's beginning to engage
in your innermost being.
And it comes and flows where you are in union –
spirit, soul and body –
with Father, Son and Spirit, in oneness
to that place where there is light,
there is the Merkabah,
there is this inner source.

And it begins to activate,
and it begins to energise
and it begins to increase
in activity and energy.

It's flowing.
That energy generates rivers flowing.
They flow to each of your seven energy gates,
from top to bottom,
and each gate is beginning to energise.

To begin with, it is energised partially,
giving you just enough energy that you can handle.
But as you learn to generate and focus
and intentionally engage that flow,
it can activate all of the spiritual connection
you need in the spirit,
in your crown.

It can engage in what's known as the third eye
so you can engage
and have all the spiritual insight you need
to be able to see, and discern and engage.

It can flow through your words
as living words of power, as an oracle.
It can flow out from the different energy gates –
from your heart,
from each of those seven gates –
until you begin to feel activated.

Draw on that immortal, living energy,
to touch the cells of your body.
If you've got sickness in any area of your body;
if you've got disease in any area of your body;
if you've got any part of your physical being,
your emotional being –
any area which needs wholeness,
which needs health –
just see those rivers flowing,
touching every cell
touching every aspect of your physical being,
energising it,
bringing life, bringing health, bringing wholeness.

And as that energy is forming an energy field,
let it flow around you,
let it create a field of living energy
which will touch other people with life,
which will touch other people with healing
and health and power.

Live every day
within an energy field of immortality,
of abundant life.

See, and feel, and sense living light energy
illuminating your mind,
activating every aspect of your being;
bringing you to that place now
of oneness, of wholeness, of union,
embraced in the *perichoresis* of Father, Son and Spirit,
who are around you.

You are in the circle of their life and light,
drawing from that unified field of energy,
drawing from life,
living abundantly.

Continue to practise training your senses so that you can discern and open the gate every day. Flow with it, starting from ankle-deep and increasing to knee-deep, waist-deep, and beyond. As you flow and practise generating and drawing on this energy, it will increase, and you will be filled with living energy.

Just keep practising. Draw on the life of God: He is our source of life; He is abundant life; He is immortal life. We are drawing from life itself: the Way, the Truth and the Life. We are drawing from light and love and Spirit, who is God Himself.

19. The Chariot of Ascension

For this perishable must put on the imperishable, and this mortal must put on immortality. But when the perishable puts on the imperishable and this mortal puts on immortality, then will come about the saying that is written: 'Death has been swallowed up in victory.' The sting of death is sin, and the power of sin is the law (1 Corinthians 15:53-56).

Through what Jesus did, He overcame every aspect of death by dying so that we died with Him. The result of that is resurrection life. I want to share more truth about our core or innermost being, known as the Merkabah. I discussed this in the last chapter, but I want to delve deeper into it. This is the focal point of the rivers of living water, abundant immortal life, where spiritual energy is distributed in us. The Merkabah is our access to limitless grace and living light energy.

Understanding and Activating the Merkabah

What is the Merkabah? How do we activate it and use it practically? I know some of you might find this topic strange and perhaps beyond your comfort zone. Please use discernment when researching the Merkabah online and elsewhere, as you will likely find all sorts of mystical New Age and religious concepts that can obscure the truth with layers of deception. Be aware that although the words used may be the same, the reality behind them may not always be. The truth is often hidden by deception, which is why we need spiritual discernment.

There are many other terms you might find, such as sacred geometry, the sephiroth, and Metatron's cube, which may be confusing or perhaps enticing. And I would also not advise studying Jewish mystical books like the Kabbalah if you are looking for truth. Jesus is the Truth; you do not need to find truth in an old religion that ended when Jesus removed its power and its temple was destroyed. I encourage you to keep your focus on the Father, and on Jesus, who is the Way, the Truth and the Life. As Jesus reveals through the Spirit, the Spirit of Truth will be our guide on this journey of discovery.

Always take everything back to the Father. Please do not just accept what I am saying; take it back to the Father to get firsthand revelation, not just information. I am sharing the revelation and experience I have, but you need your own firsthand experience and revelation that you can enter into.

The chariot of ascension

Merkabah (sometimes spelled with an 'h' on the end and sometimes not) is originally three words, not one. Often in Hebrew or Greek, several words are combined to form another word. These three words are *mer*, which means a light that rotates within itself; *ka*, which means spirit, referring to the human spirit; and *ba*, which means the physical body, although it can also refer to the concept of the reality that the spirit holds. This foundational concept connects us to physical reality. The word *Merkabah* is used 44 times in the Hebrew books of the Bible, mostly translated as 'chariot' – and indeed the word means 'a vehicle' in very ancient Hebrew. Sometimes it is translated as 'a vehicle of light' or even just 'a wagon'. It can refer to both physical and spiritual chariots, and the exact translation depends on the perception of the translator in each instance.

"Behold, he goes up like clouds,
And his chariots like the whirlwind;
His horses are swifter than eagles.
Woe to us, for we are ruined!"
(Jeremiah 4:13).

For behold, the Lord will come in fire
And His chariots like the whirlwind,
To render His anger with fury,
And His rebuke with flames of fire.
(Isaiah 66:15)

In both the above verses, 'chariot' is a translation of the word *Merkabah*. The Merkabah is also referred to as the throne of God, which is said to be a four-wheel chariot driven by four living creatures, the *chayoth*. Each of these creatures has four wings with four faces: man, lion, ox and eagle. These are associated with our nature within the order of Melchizedek[16].

There are three orders of angels described in association with the Merkabah in Ezekiel: the *chayoth* (living creatures), *ophanim* (wheels within wheels), and the *seraphim* (the burning ones). The *chayoth* are often connected with the cherubic nature of man, carrying the image of God in the four faces that represent the order of Melchizedek: the lion, ox, eagle and man (or the king, oracle, legislator and priest, the four functions we have within the order of Melchizedek).

"For the altar of incense, refined gold by weight; and gold for the model of the chariot, even the cherubim that spread out their wings and covered the Ark of the Covenant of the Lord." (1 Chronicles 28:18).

These instructions given to build the temple linked the chariot with the cherubim and the Ark, creating a connection between our position and God's position within His four faces, within His name, and within our heavenly position of being in Christ.

The Merkabah is the spirit body surrounded by counter-rotating fields of light, the wheels within the wheels; spirals of energy that transport the spirit body from one dimension to another. The Merkabah can be thought of as the chariot of ascension. In ancient Egypt, the Merkabah was referred to as rotating light that would take the body and the spirit from one world to another. It is often portrayed pictorially as two equally sized interconnected tetrahedrons of light within a common centre, where one tetrahedron points up (the mountain of the house of the Lord in Zion) and the other down. This geometric, symmetrical form is called a stellar octangular or star tetrahedron. They overlap and inter-react. Some friends at a conference in Seattle gave me a beautiful scarf representing the Merkabah, which is pinned up in my office.

---

[16] See *Engaging the Father*, Chapter 15.

In this simplified diagram, the Merkabah is represented by two intersecting triangles, symbolising heaven on earth, our position as sons on earth, and God's position in heaven as the Father. They are interconnected with positions, portals and connecting points. They also form other sacred geometric shapes, Metatron's cube and the seed of life, in the centre of it. But do not miss the point: it is not what it looks like that matters, but how it functions; and how we can engage it practically in our lives to generate all the energy we need for health, wholeness and life.

The Merkabah is connected to the energy field of a human being. We all have energy fields. These energy fields can have a low frequency, leading to a lesser quality of life, sickness and disease. The Merkabah is connected to our genetic code and development, our eternal identity: it brings together the eternal with the physical to reveal the reality of who we always were in God. The Merkabah is connected to the physical body as well as the spiritual, which is why it is important that we operate in oneness and union of spirit, soul and body.

Eternity in our hearts

He has made everything appropriate in its time.
He has set eternity in their heart (Ecclesiastes 3:11a).

I believe God has placed the Merkabah within us as the convergence point of time and eternity. It is the centre of our innermost being, enabling us to connect with both the spiritual and physical realms, capable of manifesting the reality of immortality. This eternity in our hearts is where the finite and the infinite intersect, revealing our true origin from God's perspective – the culmination of His amazing thoughts about us, reflecting how we were fearfully and wonderfully made in His image.

The Merkabah is also connected to our state of being: designed to be at rest, living in the frequencies of love, joy and peace in harmonious balance. This is where we are one, living loved, loving living and living loving, which releases immortal energy and abundant life. Limitless energy is connected to the balance between body, soul and spirit in wholeness and oneness, releasing the blessing or empowerment of immortality. Immortality is difficult when we are fragmented, broken, divided: not whole in union of spirit, soul and body. God is doing a work of transformation in our lives to reveal the truth of who we are so we can know that union. It requires a surrender of the soul and an inside-out flow from spirit to soul to body, not outside-in from body to soul to spirit. Everything needs to flow from the inside out, from our connection point with Father, Son and Spirit within us.

Structure and function of the Merkabah

The structure of the Merkabah consists of layers of living light, quantum or Zero Point Energy, intertwining in a way that forms a light matrix, seen as a tiny double tetrahedron convergence in our innermost being. As it is activated, it begins to spin, become energised, and larger, more spherical in appearance. It spins so fast in light that you cannot see what it would be if it were still. That is when it begins to function fully in us. The Merkabah interacts with the unified quantum field also known as the ether, which exists around the body and in all space. We can connect to everyone and everything in this way.

The Merkabah acts as a transducer of Zero Point Energy, extracting and bringing abundant energy into the body. I believe the ability to draw and extract from Zero Point Energy is going to be released to the sons of God as a limitless energy source, enabling us to operate independently of any grid or other conventional power source. What happens in us is a picture of what will happen in all creation.

The Merkabah has several uses:

Protection: The Merkabah generates energy that can protect us from hostile entities, physical assaults and harmful electromagnetic fields. It creates a shield around us generated from within.

Travel: The Merkabah can be used to transport the body, soul, and spirit from one place to another – translation and transrelocation – using the energy from within to move us around.

Healing and Regeneration: The Merkabah helps regenerate the soul and physical body by generating abundant life within. The energy it brings promotes healing, interacting with our subtle energy fields. Scientific discoveries about meridians and energy flows, once seen as quack medicine, are now more widely accepted as fact. Our connection to the unified field through the Merkabah furthers abundant life and health.

The Merkabah works through frequencies of intention, focusing love, joy and peace to bring rest and access to abundant life energy from within God, who is within us. Through meditation and learning to draw on that flow, we can be filled with love, joy and peace, coming to a place of rest and stillness. We can learn to train our senses, engaging with the flow of energy from rest, and allowing it to energise spirit, soul, and body, creating a powerful energy field around us.

This is like Ezekiel's picture of the temple (representing our body) with God's presence within and the flow that comes through the gateways of our body – ankle-deep, knee-deep, waist-deep – until it is flowing plentifully and freely. Its flow brings life wherever it goes, making salt water fresh and bringing life to all it touches. We, made in the image of God, are intended to produce energy and life wherever we go, uniting with creation to set it free into the freedom of the glory of the children of God.

The Merkabah also connects us to the grace of God, the living light within everything that helps us communicate with other people, angelic beings and creation itself throughout multiple locations and dimensions – all because we have this in us as a connection point.

The Merkabah operates as a communication device by the principle of quantum entanglement. My spirit can be anywhere within the universe, anywhere within the dimensions, and I, in the soul, can be instantly connected to that reality. Information can be communicated to me, and I can engage there. Wherever my spirit is, my soul (my conscious awareness) can instantly be there, because neither distance nor dimension is an issue with quantum entanglement. I am one, even if my spirit is in one place, my soul in another, and my body in another. I am one but together in this place, instantly connected: my soul can be where my spirit is.

An extension of this use of the Merkabah is broadcasting. Individuals (and corporate bodies) can communicate by broadcasting or radiating energies to others and into other realms and dimensions. I have reached out from my innermost being to engage people in the spiritual realms in many different ways. I have made connections in the spirit realm and the physical realm. I did not really know what I was doing initially, but God then showed me that the energy within me enabled me to do this when released from my innermost being. It was energised within the Merkabah, which has portals that connected me to other realms and dimensions, and particularly to people I was trying to reach and connect with in this realm.

Our frequency, and the frequency of sonship through the broadcasting of this frequency by the Merkabah within us, flows through multiple portals designed to connect to the multiple dimensions of Heaven and different dimensional realities. These dimensions are beginning to pick up the frequency of our sonship, and are beginning to connect and communicate, seeking help. We need to ensure that the frequencies we are broadcasting are those of love, joy, peace and rest. We can focus the energy of intentional conscious choice through the portals across dimensions, engaging with angelic beings, the Father, the Son, the Spirit – and anything connected to us – by choosing to engage through our innermost being. This is not through our mind, but through our being one, generating energy and thought from within. Thus the Merkabah is part of how we are designed to operate as multi-dimensional beings; and I will go into that much more in the next chapter.

Developing sensitivity and joy

The Merkabah can be developed or enhanced by drawing energy from heaven, bringing it to earth through our body as a gateway, through our first love gate, through the very presence of Father, Son and Spirit in us. Conscious, intentional grounding allows the flow of spiritual energy from the River of Life into and through the body, which is both cleansing and energising. It is a flow of living water designed to bring about the abundance that God intends us to live in.

It is important to develop sensitivity through practice. Learning to use the Merkabah will increase our sensitivity to different sensations, physical and spiritual, as we tune into distinct frequencies and energy fields. I can sense particular energy fields around me; I can connect to those energy fields. I can sense what is in the physical and the spiritual realm. With practice, we can learn to walk into a room and feel and sense the atmosphere:

But solid food is for the mature, who because of practice have their senses trained to distinguish between good and evil (Hebrews 5:14).

Joy is associated with engaging and activating the Merkabah, our innermost being. Jesus said that His joy is in us so that our joy can be full. Those who are operating with improved health and higher energy are likely to be happier people. Living with an attitude of gratitude generates joyful energy, usually expressed in some positive, helpful way to others or to creation. We are designed to be joy generators. I know this can all sound a little theoretical, but it becomes more than a theory when you put it into practice and learn how to focus this divine energy as abundant rivers of living water flowing.

New abilities are associated with the Merkabah. They are not new from God's perspective, but they may be new to you. The Merkabah, aligned with intentional conscious choice, can catalyse spiritual abilities such as telepathy, telekinesis, pre/post cognition, creativity, and more. We can express these abilities because we are made in the image of God. They develop with maturity in sonship and as we assume our position and responsibility as sons. When we know who we are, our identity and our position in God, that enables us to use those abilities appropriately with wisdom and in love.

Convergence and rest

The Merkabah is a hub to access energy portals that enable the convergence of the eternal now of God's heart perspective with the positional heavenly governmental position we hold in Christ, bringing a manifestation of heaven on earth. We need to see God's eternal purpose, the 'now' of God in His heart, incubate that within, and activate it within the Merkabah. We are a convergence of time and eternity, heaven and earth, manifesting through our physical being and who we actually are.

Rest is coherence, a measure of the pattern of the rhythm of the heart. If you look into HeartMath, you will find that the rhythm of our heart in rest is about coherence (independent of the amount of heart rate variability or HRV). This reflects an orderly, harmonious synchronisation among various systems in the body such as the heart, respiratory system and blood pressure rhythms. Our being is designed to live in harmonious rhythms, not discordant ones. Discord often arises when we are not operating in union as one. Our body or soul may be predominant, but we need our spirit, soul and body completely in union and oneness to bring us to a place of health, wholeness and immortality as our whole being operates coherently in union together. Coherence is the state when the heart, mind and emotions are in energetic alignment and cooperation. We can be at rest in union, wholeness and oneness with God, with ourselves, with others and with creation. Everything was designed to be one, not separate or apart.

Jesus conquered death

Immortal life includes factors of both quantity and quality. It is not just about endless life but the quality of life we can have, with God's original intention restored, fully realising the comprehensive possibilities that come from being made in His image and likeness.

Jesus conquered death so we can live in the newness of Resurrection Life. Immortal life does not necessarily mean we function in this earthly realm forever; we may have different dimensions to our destiny. Some of us, like Enoch and Elijah and others, may transition to another state or realm, and their whole being will be transformed or transfigured by the light and energy of immortal life into that realm. I do not know all the details of that, but it relates to our transformed state, our being clothed in glory – this living light we were created to embody. It reflects our true identity in Him, the essence of who we are, and how we are designed to express that light. Our spirit has always been intended to live in that spiritual dimension around us, and now God wants to transition us back into the estate that we fell from and come back into that reality once again.

Immortality is multi-dimensional and non-linear in nature. As we mature in sonship, as Adam would have done if he had continued to follow the path of the Tree of Life to an ascended state, we will discover the ability to reconnect to the eternal now, to become non-linear, multi-dimensional, free from the limitations of time and space. Unconditional love will eventually lead to our body being transfigured and our mind renewed into a fully expanded state of conscious awareness: that consciousness is the true knowledge of who we really are. We will live in the full knowledge of our identity as sons of God in a state of rest, a state of being and not doing. Everything flows out of rest.

Visualising and activating energy gates

We can learn to visualise opening up the Gateway of First Love, embracing the life energy of love, joy and peace within us as rivers of living water flowing in us, filling us, flowing through us; a flow of living spiritual energy in and through us. We can open our gateways to the flow, purposefully surrendering to that flow, not resisting it, not trying to control it, but flowing with it consciously and intentionally. We can begin to come to that place when we are at one: spirit, soul and body. When we have fully surrendered our soul and been made whole, we are no longer out of sync or imbalanced. In this state, we can consciously activate our energy gates, visualising the wheels spinning within them, creating a powerful flow of life force energy throughout our body. This energises the Merkabah, activating it from rest, allowing us to access our full potential as sons of God. It enables us to operate with light and sound, engage our creative choices, and transcend the limitations of the lower frequencies we may have been trapped in.

Co-creators with God

Ultimately, God wants us to become ascended fathers, creative beings. God has given us the ability to create: we are made not just to be co-heirs but co-creators. A number of times, I have chosen to create something. My journey with this began unexpectedly, at the Father's prompting, around 2011-12. Standing at the edge of the universe, I heard Him say, "Let your creativity flow." I really did not know what I was doing, but in response to His words a surge of creative energy emerged from my innermost being and a galaxy was formed. This experience served as a forerunner to many similar occurrences in my life. Often, I would agree to act on His prompting without fully understanding the process, only to discover the significance of my actions much later. Over time, I have gained a deeper understanding of this creative ability and what started as an unfamiliar process has become a conscious skill. Now, I can intentionally engage in this type of creation, making use of all I learned from these earlier experiences. This pattern of saying yes, acting in faith, and only later comprehending the process has been a recurring theme in my spiritual journey.

When I first released a blue light to call people to sonship, I just said, "I release a blue light." Now I know how that energy was released from my innermost being, and I have done that a number of times. One of the most recent was when some Guardians within a courtroom in Heaven asked me to create more Guardians because more were needed. I checked it out with the Father, and He said, "Why wouldn't you release creativity in this way?" I said, "Okay," but He knew I was still hesitant. "You know how to do this. It's like what you've done every other time you've been creative." So I engaged my intention, aligned with the Father's heart, with the request that they made. From my innermost being, I chose to create a number of Guardians, and then referred them to the council of Guardians, who assigned them out to dimensional portals in the cosmos in various different constellations.

I shared this experience with a few others, and they were eager to try it themselves. When they did, their approach was more detailed and imaginative than mine: they described their creations with vivid colours and intricate details. My focus was simply on releasing the creative energy from within. The important takeaway from this is that we all have the ability to create – it is not limited to just me or the way I operate in it. All of us can do it. I am no different than you as a son of God. You have within you the creative power of Father, Son and Spirit, just as I do. Through your willingness to say yes and focus that intention, you can begin to engage your choice to create the reality.

All of us are designed to be able to use and focus this energy within us. When we pray for someone and lay hands on them for healing, where does the energy come from? It comes from aligning with what the Father is doing. We draw and refocus energy from the life of God. It all originates from the Spirit. It is not my independent action; rather, it is the river of life being directed into someone's DNA, into their body. This refocusing of creative energy heals them and brings them into wholeness.

Perhaps for now you just lay hands on them, and you hope for the best, and sometimes that works because God is always gracious and merciful. It worked for me, when I had no idea what I was doing. But now I do know what I am doing, I am very careful to only do anything when I know it is the Father's heart and intention. None of the things that we can do are party tricks we perform just because we can do them. Jesus only did what He saw the Father doing, so let us make sure when we operate in these things, that we operate in love, in rest, and in humility; and operate out of the Father's heart, to only do what we know the Father is showing us to do. In that way, we are never going to seek attention or take any glory for ourselves. Our purpose is aligned with the Father's heart and His intention. We are just cooperating and working together with Him to bring about His heart's desires through who we are as creative sons of God. He wants to reveal to you the full power of your creative ability as a son so that you can begin to participate in bringing freedom and restoration to creation.

Activation #19
Energise the Merkabah

> Close your eyes.
> Start breathing slowly.
> breathe in slowly
> and breathe out slowly,
> breathing in the very breath of God,
> the life of God,
> focusing your thinking on God who is love.
>
> And as you're breathing in,
> let love flow, flow and flow into you,
> flow around you, flow into you,
> and let it rest upon you so you can be still.
>
> Let God love you,
> And feel and sense
> the unconditional nature of that love,
> where you can be still and know that He is love.
>
> You can be still and know that He is love.
> Be still and know that He is joy.
> Be still and know that He is peace.
> Be still and know that He is truth,
> and light, and life,
> and limitless grace and triumphant mercy.
>
> It may take a little bit of time sometimes
> to slow down your thinking and focus on love.
> Come to that place of love.
>
>> [And as you're doing that,
>> I'm just going to release some sounds,
>> and these frequencies.
>>
>> I want to encourage you
>> to let the frequency and sound
>> of the intention of love
>> touch your physical, emotional,
>> and spiritual being.

> Let this sound go around you,
> and in you, and through you
> generating energy, frequency.]

Jesus is knocking on that door within your first love gate,
you can picture that door, picture Him knocking.
Beyond that door is a well;
choose to open the door
and drink from the well, from the fountain.
It's living water.
It's flowing as a frequency and an energy of life.
And as it begins to flow,
flow with it as it forms a river.

Choose to flow with it
as these waves of energy
begin to flow within your innermost being;
that river flowing through the gateways of your spirit,
flowing through your soul,
just beginning to converge in the core of your being,
the Merkabah,
which begins to energise.
Energy forming, spinning, increasing,
flowing from you
as rivers of living water,
energising each gate.

Energising your crown,
your ability to connect to heaven.
Energising your spiritual insight,
knowing truth and revelation.
Energising what you think
and what you say when you speak;
speaking with the energy
of the voice of God as an oracle.
Energising your heart,
feeling and releasing love,
unconditional love.

Each of those seven gates,
the creativity, feelings
deep within your innermost being,
the gut instincts, the knowing,
energised, connecting you to creation, the root
grounded with that unified quantum field.

You are connected,
you can become spaghettified,
every atom of your being can be connected to creation.
Feel and sense creation.
Feel and sense your sonship touching creation –
broadcasting, communicating, beyond yourself,
through those portals within your innermost being.

You may want to travel along that portal,
you may want to send a message,
an intention of love to someone in particular.
Focus that intention of love
and let it travel through that entanglement you have
with someone that you carry in your heart,
to touch them with love.

Limitless energy
generated from your innermost being,
flowing around you,
creating an energy field –
a field of light, a field of love.

You can choose to stay in that place.
If you are engaged, feel free to stay there.

This is not something that is just a one-off, but something that we need to develop. We need to practise day after day, practise generating flow; so that we can learn to become sensitive, and learn to focus these things in our lives, and through our lives to others and out into creation itself.

20. Transcending Time and Space

Limitless grace, triumphant mercy

Unconditional love is expressed through limitless grace and triumphant mercy. These are phrases that God spoke to me over and over again: limitless grace, meaning it will never, ever run out; and triumphant mercy, which triumphs over man's version of justice (and injustice) and man's version of judgment. It triumphs over it all.

Grace, in this instance, is the divine enabling power of God, and it is limitless in empowering us to have a relationship with Him. It knows no boundaries, no limitations; in fact, it has no limits at all. Triumphant mercy overcomes every obstacle, every hindrance, every barrier to our relationship with the Father, including those in our own thinking and the alienation of our own mind. We may have been taught that we are separated from God, but we never were.

Mankind has been made immortal in the image of God. Many doctrinal positions maintain that God is angry, that God punishes, that God sends people to hell forever to torment and punish them. Such theology distorts any idea of immortality. It has even been suggested that God made us immortal so He could punish us forever; so that we would never die and would always have to endure excruciating pain. That is not the nature of our loving Father. Let me say again, Penal Substitutionary Atonement is an invention, a total deception. I encourage you, if you have been brought up with that view, do not embrace it anymore. Embrace the truth of who God really is and what Jesus really did in demonstrating God's love and removing the power of death over us, to give us abundant life.

No end of days

Our origin is eternity; the origin of our immortality is in God, outside of time and space, within God Himself. Eternity is within our hearts, accessible to us because we were always designed to live an immortal life.

I thank you, God, for making me so mysteriously complex.
Everything you do is marvellously breathtaking.
It simply amazes me to think about it –
how thoroughly you know me, Lord.
(Psalm 139:14 TPT).

This is a wonderful passage, one of my favourite Bible readings in the Old Testament, from The Passion Translation. We will struggle with it if we see ourselves through the lens of our own past rather than how God sees us. "Oh no, God knows me; He knows all the bad." But God does not see anything bad. He sees how He made you, how marvellous you are, how wonderfully complex you are, made in His image. He made each of us who we are, gave us our true identity, which is why we need to engage with Him to find that truth.

You even formed every bone in my body
when you created me in the secret place;
carefully, skillfully you shaped me
from nothing to something.

You saw who you created me to be before I became me!
Before I'd ever seen the light of day,
the number of days you planned for me
were already recorded in your book.

Every single moment you are thinking of me!
How precious and wonderful to consider
that you cherish me constantly in your every thought!
O God, your desires toward me are more
than the grains of sand on every shore!
When I awake each morning, you're still with me.
(Psalm 139:15-18 TPT).

Now, some might read verse 16 and say, "Ah, there is a defined number of days that you planned for me; therefore, immortality cannot be possible." Yes, there is a defined number of days: no end of them. So when I read that, I just think, "How wonderful! There's no end of days, and they're all planned for me to enjoy in relationship with God."

These verses are a wonderful expression of that relationship. God wants us to know about it so that we can truly experience His amazing love and the reality of who we are as sons of God – and that there are no limitations in knowing who we are.

The fact that God loves us unconditionally means He never wants to be out of relationship with us. He does not want us to die and experience any break in that relationship. We have immortal life energy flowing within us through the Merkabah, able to help regenerate the soul and the physical body. The energy it focuses contributes to healing as it interacts with each person's subtle energy fields by raising their frequency. Much sickness is a result of low emotional and mental frequency – fear, worry, and anxiety – which lowers our frequency and makes it easier for us to become sick. But when we are living in abundant health, the energy field within us raises our frequency. The frequencies of love, joy and peace bring us into a place of health. Our whole immune system functions more efficiently when we are living in an attitude of thanksgiving and gratitude.

Revelation of the Merkabah

The healing effects of the Merkabah help prolong life, and connection to the unified quantum field promotes abundant life in immortality. We are drawing life out of the life of God. Effectively, this works as we learn to focus the frequencies of intention, converging love, joy and peace to bring rest and access to the abundant life energy from God within us. We drink from Jesus, the source, and have rivers of living water flowing from the core of our being – rivers of the Spirit, life, energy and light.

As we have seen, this living light energy flows to the Merkabah, our innermost being, where it is focused and distributed to our seven energy gates to give us limitless energy and abundant life. That is also connected to the Sephiroth or the Tree of Life, which has a geometric shape associated with the energy gates, bringing a balance between spirit and soul which in turn brings wholeness to our body. It is pointless if we function only in the spirit without any outward working in the soul, and equally pointless if we only operate in the soul and not in the spirit. We need the correct balance for both, on earth as it is in heaven. This equilibrium allows our body to come into the same wholeness our spirit and soul are living in.

The Father has spoken to me a great deal about the Merkabah. To begin with, I did not understand everything He said (and to be quite honest, I still do not understand it all) but I believe that what He said is true. There will be a journey of discovery and revelation before I can know and experience the full reality of it all. As I share some of the things the Father said, you too can embrace them as truth if you choose to, and seek Him for the revelation.

"Son, the Merkabah has multiple levels of revelation and application that will open up with the maturity of sonship. The first level for most people is as the Chariot of Ezekiel, which moves their heavenly throne dimensionally. The application of energy linked with the gateways that some call chakras is another level; and entering through portals as gateways is another level of revelation to experience."

The more we begin to mature in sonship, the more we will begin to understand and function in these truths. At that point I did not know that I could enter into portals inwardly. I was actually already doing so, but I did not understand how I could choose to do it. He told me there was a connection to "governmental positions within the Tree of Life and Metatron's Cube in light". I did not understand, but it prompted me to pursue the Tree of Life and how it related to the seven energy gates and the Merkabah within me. As I pursued that revelation, and engaged with it, He opened it up for me to begin to understand. Metatron's Cube appears in the centre of the Merkabah in the image, in a sacred geometric shape. I have looked to engage with it, but I am sure there is much more to experience.

Intentionality

"Using Limitless Grace energy to create and choose reality, drawing from the unified quantum field, is not a common revelation but will come with expanded consciousness."

When God said this to me a few years ago, I was bewildered. "What is the unified quantum field? How can I choose reality from energy that I don't even understand?" But the Father was teaching me how to begin to choose reality based on the revelation of His heart. As I learned to do that, it expanded my consciousness, my awareness and the way I thought. Quantum physics, as I discovered, reveals that the observer chooses the reality; and I began to understand that reality responds to my observation or my choice. I now have many testimonies of intentionally choosing something when I have needed to, enabling me to do what some people might call miracles. Really, they were just me choosing a reality aligned to the Father's heart rather than any other reality aligned to my own thinking or that of other people. The intentionality of choice is really important; we have to intentionally choose to do something and focus on it.

"Son, the activation of your energy gates and fields by intentionality isn't going to happen randomly or haphazardly; you have to choose and focus. This is the first step towards the ability to generate and direct thought energy as a frequency."

He said a good deal about frequency, vibration and resonance. Everything in creation is made up of frequency energy, which we perceive as matter when it is vibrating at particular frequencies. The Father was saying that as I learn to activate the energy gates within me, and to activate the fields of energy around me (rivers of living water flowing through my innermost being, from within me and out through the gateways of my body), I am learning to create energy fields in which I can live: a place of peace, rest, life and abundance – and that is a frequency.

Look deeper

"Son, look deeper into the sacred geometric image and use this knowledge to increase your thought energy and creative ability."

When the Father said that, once again I did not know what He meant at all. I knew of the image because I had it behind me in my office as a big picture. When I looked at it, I began to ask, "What am I looking at? What does this mean? How does this relate to me and my thoughts?" The more I did that, the more the Father began to show me that the knowledge of dimensional connections and portals within the Merkabah actually meant I could use my thought energy in a creative way. Then He took me on a journey to show me how I could brood within the Cradle of Life within His heart – a place where I could come into resonance and agreement with Him. Then I could go through a process of becoming His voice, creatively speaking as His voice, and light would begin to respond to me.

But when He first talked to me about this, I did not know any of that. I set my heart on it, pondered it in my heart, and treasured it in my heart, even though I had no real clue what it was all about. But that treasuring, that incubating, that being pregnant with something allows it to grow, and as it grows in you, it begins to manifest and be birthed.

Bounty

"The unified quantum field can be the connection between your consciousness and creation through the Elementals that are connected to the living light strings of our grace."

Now, again, that is a mouthful (and a mindful). I thought, "Okay, unified quantum field, consciousness, creation, Elementals, living light strings of grace. Wow!" Then I began to receive revelation about the Elementals, beings that God created for us to connect with creation. We think of them as earth, fire, air and water – and also ether, which is the field in which we can engage with them. We can learn to interact with and connect with all of them, so that light begins to outwork in our life towards creation.

"Son, engage the Elementals through the Merkabah by your consciousness, not just in physical locations, so you can connect to all dimensions or realities to restore hope."

I am on a journey with engaging things dimensionally, but this helped me because I have seen Elementals in the dimensions as well as on earth. We can connect to the elements, and with the trees, the earth, the plants and so on. I have done quite a lot of gardening recently, tending, and cultivating the trees, and growing fruit and vegetables. I have begun to connect my conscious choice to them for favour, blessing and bounty. As a result, I have had plentiful harvests because I am engaging with creation on an elemental level, in a sentient way, in my thinking.

We have a cherry tree at the front of the house, but we were not getting many cherries from it, and the blackbirds would eat most of those that did grow. I set my heart to engage with the cherry tree, and I communed with it through the Elementals, in a sense of connection, so that I could communicate my desire for the tree to produce an abundance of cherries – "more than enough for all our needs, and an abundance for every good deed." That way, the neighbours could have some, the blackbirds could have their fill, and we would also have plenty for ourselves. And indeed, we had an abundant harvest of cherries. I planted runner beans and started harvesting them in July. I was still harvesting them well into October. I believe God wants to reveal how we can begin to connect with creation in a very positive light, just as Adam and Eve did in the Garden. We are here to tend and cultivate the earth, and therefore receive a bounty – not to strip it bare or abuse it, but to cooperate and work with it.

Babel-like towers

"Son, the Merkabah can be the connection to the dimensions, but it also has the ability to broadcast intentional thought energy to the Babel-like towers you have seen."

The Tower of Babel was a communication system designed to connect to the heavens and to other dimensions. It was broadcasting the negative frequency of our lost identity. When God opened those dimensions for me to visit and engage with, I met some beings who wanted help. When I engaged with them, they wanted to know how they could be set free and come into freedom and restoration. They were feeling our energy, the energy of sonship, and they were drawn to it. As they began to reach out, God opened the door for me to connect with them.

When I went to several of their dimensional places to engage with them, I saw that there were Babel-like towers in each of them that were created to connect to our dimensional reality for communication. I disrupted that communication and broadcast into those dimensions the truth of God's love, the truth of freedom, truths that would counteract all the negative frequencies they received from our lost identity. I broadcast the true frequencies of our full identity as sons of God. Again, this has been a journey and a process to come into this reality.

"Son, use this ability to send love letters as messages of hope and freedom dimensionally."

I have been doing that. I have been engaging the Earth Shield and the dimensions. It is part of what I do, part of who I am, to communicate God's love – not just on Earth but out into every dimensional reality.

Photonic strings of grace

"Creation does not distinguish between the frequency of sound produced by the voice, by a crystal bowl, or in your mind as you think the sound."

Now, again, this was something I had been exploring, using crystal singing bowls and other means of generating frequencies, focusing intention and seeing healing as a result. But what the Father was showing me here – and what He will show all of us – is that creation does not distinguish between those sounds: whether we speak, produce a frequency and release an intention, or think.

"All frequency-generating methods have the same effect at a quantum level, where photonic strings of grace and living light will respond to your sonship mandate."

Again, I have come to appreciate the truth of this. I did not understand it at first, but as I continued to pursue it, I began to learn more and more about how to use my mind, my intention, and to focus my thinking.

"Son, this is the function of oracles and legislators."

Remember the four faces of God in regard to the order of Melchizedek: man, lion, ox and eagle (priest, king, oracle and legislator). When we are an oracle (in other words, when we speak from the heart of God with the voice of God), we can then legislate and bring that authority into manifestation. The oracles of God's heart resonate with us at a motivational level. I do not want to be an oracle of my own thoughts or a legislator of my own ideas; I want to resonate with the Father's heart, with the oracles of His heart, with that passion, that burning desire, that overwhelming love, that deep compassion, that intense joy. These are the oracles of His heart: when I engage with creation, when I engage with dimensions, fallen beings, and people, I choose to resonate with those oracles and to be motivated by their rhythm and frequency. I want to demonstrate and be a reflection of the Father's heart, resonating with it and carrying that essence of love.

Pentatonic energy fields

"The hearts of our sons produce pentatonic energy fields by design to generate the oracle frequencies to connect with creation."

Again, when I first heard that, I thought, "What on earth is all that about?" I am not a musician and had no knowledge of pentatonic scales or pentatonic energy fields. I had no idea, but I treasured it, and I began to pursue it. I googled a little bit and found that pentatonic musical scales, which are five notes, always sound harmonious. If you play just the black keys on a piano, that is a pentatonic scale.

For someone like me, who is not a musician, that meant I could have five crystal bowls tuned to a pentatonic scale; and when I played those crystal bowls, it would always be harmonious. Then I asked, "Father, what are the actual frequencies of the oracles of Your heart?" And He showed me what those frequencies were. In fact, He showed me several different sets of frequencies, but the one I was most drawn to was this minor key pentatonic scale:

Passion	A4 = 444 Hz
Burning Desire	C5 = 528.01 Hz
Intense Joy	D5 = 592.67 Hz
Deep Compassion	E5 = 665.25 Hz
Overwhelming Love	G5 = 791.12 Hz

I played the five notes on my crystal bowls, recorded them, and fine-tuned them in Audacity, the free sound-editing software we use. I tuned the recordings to the frequencies He showed me, so that when I played them, they would be powerful in bringing about the outworking of the oracles of His heart – to demonstrate His passion, His burning desire, intense joy, deep compassion and overwhelming love.

"That is why the pure of heart can see beyond, and why life flows from the heart."

The central energy gate within us is our heart. The crown connects to the spiritual realm; the root connects to the creational realm; and our heart is connected to God within us. The heart here is not the physical organ, and not only the soul: it is the union of soul and spirit, our innermost being. When we are pure in heart, life flows.

"Son, this ability to choose and create reality has been limited to the unconscious and subconscious. This ability has mostly been lost by the conscious mind."

Thus, we tend to keep creating the realities in which we have been birthed and have experienced in the past. As the ability to consciously create reality is being restored, we will find ourselves increasingly able to choose a different reality from that which we are programmed to live in by our past. If we keep operating out of what we remember from past experiences, we will keep creating the same reality and going around the same mountain again and again. But when we begin to choose new creation realities, this restored ability will enable us to live and operate in a completely different way dimensionally.

"A heart motivated by the selfishness of the do-it-yourself path – the tree of the knowledge of good and evil – will only create more chaos if it accesses these abilities."

This is why we lost these bandwidth abilities: we were using them selfishly. Only as our hearts are renewed, restored and made whole, and as we begin to operate from the heart of God, will the fullness of these abilities be released to us. That is why we need to be mature.

"A pure, undivided heart resonating with Love's oracles is the only way to bring about restoration at both a creational and dimensional level. Son, guard your heart and focus on developing the pentatonic frequencies and energy fields around your being and spheres."

He was referring to my spheres of authority. So, that is what I began to do. I started to learn how to engage my heart with the pentatonic frequencies. I played them on the crystal bowls, intentionally engaging them, and began to create energy fields around me from what was developing. Those energy fields were the oracles of the Father's heart.

I want people around me to feel God's passion for them, His burning desire for relationship with them, His intense joy when He thinks of them, His deep compassion, and overwhelming love.

"Blessed are the pure in heart, for they shall see God." (Matthew 5:8).

"For the mouth speaks out of that which fills the heart." (Matthew 12:34).

Therefore, we need to make sure that what fills our heart is good. Let us examine our hearts and ensure they are being restored, made whole, healed, and focused on choosing intentions aligned with those of the Father.

"My son, give attention to my words;
incline your ear to my sayings.
Do not let them depart from your sight;
keep them in the midst of your heart.
For they are life to those who find them
And health to all their body.
Watch over your heart with all diligence,
For from it flow the springs of life."
(Proverbs 4:20-23).

When we engage with the heart of the Father face to face, heart to heart, and mind to mind; when we engage with the cradle of life; His thoughts and intentions begin to shape us. If we keep them within our heart as the central motivation for all we think, feel and do, they will bring life to those who find them and health to their whole body.

This is a statement of immortality: we need the reality and truth of God's heart in our heart, at the very core. That will bring life and health. The springs of immortal life flow from the core of our heart, and our heart is the centre of the energy gates connected to the Merkabah, flooded with energy from Heaven, which is then dissipated into our body, energising us for life.

As long as we keep our heart, spirit and soul in union, in oneness with the Father, Son and Spirit – not separated – that life flows. We need to focus, to give attention to what He says, to His truth that He reveals. I am not just talking about the Bible here, but the words He speaks to you, to me, because as Jesus said, "My sheep will hear my voice, and they will follow me." Let's make sure we are focusing on the things that God has said to us.

The eternal quality of life

Immortality is not just about transcending time and space, or the quantity of life – never dying – but about the eternal quality of life. We originate from the eternal realm, which means we have eternal abilities that can be outworked in time and space while transcending their limitations.

Who would want to live forever if they were miserable or limited? I certainly would not want to continue living if I did not have my full cognitive abilities, the capacity to think, feel and act. I want a fully functioning spirit, soul, body, mind, emotions and will, so that I can be a true demonstration of what a son of God is. I want to live in the full power of eternal life, in the full power of immortality, in a fully restored way that embraces non-linear and multi-dimensional perspectives, a new reality of renewing my mind to operate from a completely different framework. It includes not being controlled by time, not being limited by space, but being free and untethered from those limitations so I can live as a multi-dimensional, non-linear being. This is the quality of eternal life we are called to embrace and live from now.

As we mature and ascend higher, we will discover that we have creative abilities far beyond anything we could have imagined or thought. We have the ability to live multi-dimensionally, not just in heavenly realms and on earth. We can engage and travel dimensionally, even in time. All this is part of the eternal aspect of our lives as sons of God, part of our immortal life, our eternal life. Let's be willing to embrace and come into the fullness of it.

TRANSCENDING

A few years ago, we shared a meme on social media: "Information flowing from your future possibilities is waiting for you to see, observe, and call it into being." God calls things that are not as though they are; that is how He created. We can begin to engage the heart of the Father, and He will reveal His heart for our future, creating possibilities that we can then focus on, see, observe and call into being. These exist as possible timelines or streams.

I do not believe in multiple worlds or multiple versions of myself; I believe I am created to be one. However, I do believe in multiple possibilities of timelines that I can choose from. I can choose multiple versions of those timelines, and they can all be good, or I can choose a future based on my past, which may not be so good. Therefore, I need to be mindful of where my information is coming from: whether it is flowing from engaging in the *perichoresis* (the circle of relationship) between Father, Son and Spirit, within the Eternal Now. This allows me to feel, sense, and know the heart of God for myself and for creation; and then I can begin to call it into being by choosing that reality for my life and for the spheres of government and authority in which I live as a son of God.

God is teaching us how to do this – to see through His eyes, know His heart, and begin to shape the future into that reality. That is what we are called to do as co-heirs and co-creators. It is astounding when you think about it, and I am still in awe of what God has spoken to me about. Even though I do not understand everything, I treasure it, and I believe that the reality will come about as I fully embrace it.

Ultimately, I believe we are all in a creative process that God is using to take us beyond being merely human[17]. He is restoring humanity from lost identity back into mankind made in God's creative image. We are becoming God-like, as sons of our Heavenly Father who is limitless. Our experiences

---

[17] I recommend my friend Justin Paul Abraham's excellent and very readable book *Beyond Human* which develops this theme in much greater depth.

of this will challenge and change our views of life, our mindsets and our belief systems.

My experiences have revealed the unconditionally loving nature of God, our Father, and that is why I am so totally convinced of immortality, inclusion and restoration. God loves all of His creation and all of His children equally and unconditionally, and He wants us to know that reality for ourselves.

[God], who has saved us and called us with a holy calling, not according to our works, but according to His own purpose and grace which was granted us in Christ Jesus from all eternity, but now has been revealed by the appearing of our Savior Christ Jesus, who abolished death and brought life and immortality to light through the gospel (2 Timothy 1:9-10).

Put yourself into that scripture. The grace of God, the divine enabling power of God, the living light of God, was granted to you in Christ Jesus from all eternity; but now it has been revealed to you by the appearing of our Saviour Christ Jesus, who abolished death for you and brought life and immortality to light through the gospel. Now that truly is good news.

I know this chapter may not have made much sense to you, and introduces many concepts that I am still trying to fully understand myself. I am aware that you might be thinking, "What on earth is all that about?" Feel free to go back over it, and reflect on what the Father said to me; but most importantly, ask Him about these things for yourself. Meditate on what He tells you, and engage your heart with it.

Activation #20
Spheres of Authority

> I encourage you
> to come to a place of rest.
>
> Get into a comfortable position.
> Close your eyes,
> Begin to relax.

Begin to rest.
Start focusing your thinking on the Father,
on the Son,
on the Holy Spirit.
Start to breathe very slowly.
Breathe in, and breathe out,
very, very slowly.

And as you are breathing in,
consciously focus on breathing in
the unconditional love of the Father.

Breathe it in, hold it, and breathe out.
Let it energise you,
let it fill you,
let it flow through you –
filled with unconditional love.

Breathe it in,
so you can truly know who God is, as love.
Embrace it.

Slowly dial everything down
to that place of rest.
Focus on Father, Son and Spirit within you.

Choose to open the gateways
of your spirit, soul and body.
As you choose to open that gateway of first love,
to embrace Father, Son and Spirit,
consciously choose to drink from the Source.
Drink from the Fountain,
drawing from the life of Jesus,
the Way, the Truth, the Life.

Drink deeply into your innermost being,
so that rivers of Living Water,
rivers of life,
rivers of light energy
start to flow through the gateways
of your spirit, soul and body.

Let that river flow to your innermost being,
to your core,
the union of Father, Son and Spirit,
and your body, soul and spirit,
where it meets within the Merkabah
and is focused.
Let that river begin to focus and build and energise.

And then see that river
flowing to your seven energy gates,
and begin to activate your crown.
Activate each of those energy gates.
Let it activate your heart,
and let each one be energised with life.

If you need insight,
if you need to be able to see
in the realm of spiritual things,
that it would open that gateway;
the eyes of your heart would be enlightened.

If you need to speak wisdom, truth, love,
that your voice gate will be activated:
the very energy
causing you to speak life.

Each of your gateways energised with life,
abundance.
And as you're filled,
filled to capacity,
see that river flowing from your energy gates outwards,
creating fields of energy around you,
fields of life.

So that wherever you go,
you have life in abundance,
that your shadow can heal,
that you can focus that energy to bring life.
It will turn salt water fresh.
You are creating life around you, flowing,

energising each of the spheres
you are called to engage:
those spheres of family,
those spheres of work,
maybe those spheres of church,
those spheres of different aspects of your life.
You are creating energy and life for those fields,
energising them.

You can live in that bubble
of energy, of life in abundance.
Begin to rest in that energy,
in that love,
in that life,
filled and flowing with amazing,
living, flowing, life energy
from the source of Life,
who is Light and Love and Spirit.

Be filled,
be flowing,
be energised.

Feel free to stay in that place as long as you like. It requires practice to focus your intentions and your thoughts; but the more you do it, the better you get at it, and the more your senses become attuned to it.

21. Time Miracles and Immortality

Because God loves us unconditionally, He never wants us to stop experiencing that love here on this earth and we do not have to die physically. Immortality is about the eternal quality of life and the abilities that His life confers, our capabilities and capacities as sons of God. He wants to reveal who we truly are as His sons and for us to fully explore and understand the astonishing extent of the creative capacity we have. Discovering the truth of our identity as sons of God comes from an intimate relationship with our loving Father. It cannot come from intellectual knowledge or any other way: it stems from the Father and from the Father's heart.

Non-linear, multi-dimensional

On my journey, the Father eventually revealed that I could function non-linearly and multi-dimensionally. To come to that knowledge and truth, and then outwork it, is something I believe God really wants us all to embrace.

Non-linear and multi-dimensional perspectives of reality require a renewal of the mind in order that we can operate from a different framework. We are not taught, nor are we accustomed to thinking non-linearly or multi-dimensionally. Therefore, there needs to be a shift to enable us to do so. We can be untethered from the limitations of time and space and become free to live as multi-dimensional beings. That is the quality of eternal life. As we mature and ascend higher, we will discover that we have creative capabilities and abilities far beyond what we could ever imagine. We have the ability to live multi-dimensionally, not restricted to one dimension or even to living in dual realms, but to live and function multi-dimensionally.

For a number of years, from 2012 to 2016, I thought living in dual realms was the pinnacle to which I could ascend. I was living in heaven; I had been living in heaven since 2012 in the spirit, engaging there with my soul daily. But the Father called me to go 'beyond beyond,' and that concept began to take root in my heart. As usual, I did not really understand what

He meant at the time, but I embraced it, and He began to unveil and reveal it to me. For me, 'beyond beyond' was to experience multi-dimensional realms of existence; I began to go into other dimensions and engage there, and found I was able to exist multi-dimensionally as well.

Expanding consciousness

The Father took me one day into my own mind and showed me how my mind was constructed – all the pillars and frameworks of my thinking – and went on to lead me into a lengthy process of deconstruction. But He also showed me some areas of my mind that were behind closed doors. They were not locked, but I was restricted from connecting to them by what seemed to be a great gulf. The Father asked if I wanted Him to bridge this gulf, and I agreed. As the bridge formed across the gulf, we walked across.

I looked at the Father, expecting Him to open the door, but He looked at me and said, "Are you going to open the door?" So, I chose to open it, and as I did, the door opened. Suddenly I could see a whole way of choosing future possibilities. I saw every possibility that existed at that moment, which was confusing because I did not know which one to choose. The Father reassured me that they were all good, as I was coming from His heart. That gave me confidence that I can choose my reality without fear, knowing I will not get it wrong.

After that encounter, I had the opportunity to choose a reality because it had made me late for a meeting at work. I had a choice: to phone and say I would be late, or to rush, or to choose the reality that I get there on time no matter what? I chose the latter, and I began to live in suspended time. I was in a bubble – I took a shower, and went down to the kitchen, the clock on the wall was ticking past the time I should have been at work, but my watch remained still. I tested this reality by doing several other things before walking to work. On the way, my watch started ticking again, and I arrived on time. My mind had expanded, my consciousness had expanded, and I believed it was possible. I chose that possibility, and it came to be.

Do you remember that meme I mentioned in the previous chapter? "Information flowing from your future possibilities is waiting for you to see and observe it and call it into being." When we stop thinking linearly, minute by minute, we see all the possibilities that we can engage in within the next second. As sons, we are called to align with the Father's heart without restrictions or limitations.

Cooperating with Time

In my walk with God, He kept giving me more and more opportunities, and that required me to rule over time to accommodate them because I could not fit them into my already busy natural schedule. I had to create a schedule that allowed me to expand half an hour into a day or half a day and then contract it back. This enabled me to accomplish everything I needed to in that half hour or hour. This is how I began to increase my capacity to do all that God was calling me to do as a son.

I began to travel in time, engage in heavenly missions, and experience being translated in time and space, whether in spirit, spirit and soul, or through cognitive experiences that I could remember. There were encounters where I was meditating, and suddenly, I found myself somewhere else, ready to minister to someone in a different location or time. These experiences initially took place within our time period and space but later expanded to other places in creation, and even into the past. I became more active in making myself available for these adventures, and I became aware that God was using me to answer people's prayers by ministering healing or helping them in some way.

Time is also a being, whom I have met many times when engaging in heaven. I believe we can all engage and cooperate with Time as a being who wants to help us connect with the things that Time has to offer in everyday life. We can travel back in time when untethered from our restricted and limited mindsets. We need to understand the relationship between time and immortality if we are to live in an immortal state. God spoke to me about this several times.

"Son, your encounters with Time must become widespread as our children need to cooperate with Time and not be subject to it."

I encountered Time as a being many times during ascensions, and a correct relationship with Time was restored. I began to engage with Time, and Time helped me understand things from the past that I needed to know in the present in order to act effectively. This relationship developed in a very positive way.

Time (the being) spoke to me about changing my vocabulary towards time. It was because Time was for us, not against us, and wished to cooperate with us. It will be helpful to evaluate what we say about time and think positively, not negatively, when we consider time. We need no longer say things like, "I don't have enough time," because that is untrue. It may seem true from a linear, single-dimensional way of thinking, but when we start to think like sons of God, we need never think we do not have enough time. Time is there to serve us, and we can make time – not by curtailing our other activities, but by expanding the time we have to do more.

Quantum moments

We need to be untethered from the restrictions of time and learn to cooperate with Time creatively. Time can be expanded, contracted or suspended. I have done all three at different times in my life when it was necessary for particular reasons. I do not do it lightly; it is something I do to fulfil God's purposes. Each quantum moment of time, which is the smallest particle of time, contains all possible particles of time. This means that any one quantum moment of time can be expanded and contracted as necessary.

In one such quantum moment, I could expand that moment into six months, do six months' worth of activities, and then contract it all back into that moment. I would have the memory of six months' worth of work, yet no time would have passed. I have done this when God asked me to accomplish things that would have taken months of continual effort. I expanded a moment, did what was needed, then contracted it back and retained the memory of it.

Time wishes to be part of the restoration of what we call history, so we can be free from the negative effects of the past in our own lives and in creation itself. Time gives us insight and understanding of history and its effects. When we are doing something legislatively or authoritatively as sons of God, we can have insight into past events that are affecting the present: we can undo what was done and so nullify its consequences in our present, which then positively impacts our future.

Time is creative and collaborative, allowing us to access all of history by engaging through the Eternal Now. I have engaged in this process several times and have many testimonies of its effects. By making myself available to God's leading, I have been used to minister in different times and places, helping people and affecting history in ways I never imagined possible.

A friend, not an enemy

Time desires a positive relationship with us that enables us to function fully as sons of God, where there is always enough time to be all we are destined to be. There is always enough time, when I choose to operate with that mindset and belief system in nonlinear thinking. Time wants to be our friend, not our enemy. We never have to think about being too busy or not having enough time.

The Father said, "Son, it's important for our children to exchange their entire relationship with Time and work together in union with Time." The Father showed me that I could live nonlinearly and choose realities that were not restricted by time.

Personal Experiences

As I have said, I have many testimonies of time suspension, time travel, and similar phenomena.

The first time it ever happened to me, I was in the car. I was running late, but it did not really matter because I was just hanging out with a couple of friends for the day. I drove around a corner and found myself seven miles further down the road than I had been. I had missed out a whole sequence of villages in which traffic was always slow-moving. I arrived just before I was due to meet my friends. I did not think much of it at the time, but God was showing me what was possible. On the way back, I retraced the exact same route, and it was seven miles longer than on the way there. When He shows you what is possible, you treasure it in your heart, plant it as a seed of testimony, and water it with the River of Life.

One day, I needed to apply that testimony to my present by choosing a reality in travel. I was taking my youngest daughter to the main line railway station to catch a train. The trip usually takes around 45 minutes. We set off in the car, and a mile out of town we became stuck in traffic, and sat in the queue for 25 minutes before it started moving again. Two minutes before the train was due to leave, we still had about eight miles to go. Not unreasonably, my daughter was quite anxious, but I had to put that aside and choose my reality. We arrived at the station just in time, and she caught the train.

I have also chosen realities for flights where I could have potentially missed connections. For instance, I was travelling by plane from Hanover to Brussels and then to Bristol. Despite the first flight being delayed by over an hour, I chose the reality that I would make my connection. I visualised warping space so that the distance we travelled was less than it would have been otherwise. The flight attendants, who had seemed uneasy, suddenly started smiling and making sure we knew about our connections. We landed after being in the air about 40 minutes for a flight that should have taken an hour and 40 minutes. I managed to get through security and make the connection, even helping another passenger (who seemed bemused at the prospect that we might catch our connecting flight after all) along the way.

These are just a few of my experiences which show that we can choose to be at rest and not let negativity, fear or anxiety dictate our actions. By recognising our authority to engage with time, we really can contract or expand it as needed.

Evolution of My Journey

My journey has continually evolved since 2010 when I first engaged heaven in a consistent way. My soul was tethered to my spirit, and I would go into heaven every day in spirit and soul, then return to earth. By 2012, after separating and reintegrating my soul and spirit, I found I could dwell in that realm. My spirit has been continuously aware of that realm ever since, living in dual realms of heaven and earth, my spirit and soul always connected, quantum entangled, regardless of distance in space or time.

As I said earlier, I felt I had reached the pinnacle. I had a greater capacity; there was a deep sense of connection; things were flowing from my spirit and my soul all the time. And then in 2017, God took me into this nonlinear thinking: multiple realms and dimensions, all in multiple quantum moments of being. That could not have happened back in 2010 or 2012 because I was not ready for it. Now, with increasing understanding and experience of these things, I have discovered that at the core of my innermost being – my spirit, soul and body in union – is the connection between the heavenly realms dimensions and creation, where there are portals for both communication and travel.

I can engage inwardly anywhere in creation. I do not have to travel externally, go through a portal, or get into a spaceship. I do not have to go into the realms of heaven externally either, although it is open, and we can go that way if we choose. I have access within, so I only have to think to be there. I think myself to anywhere I have been or anywhere that God has intended me to be, and I am there, instantly connected, because my spirit engages it and my soul connects to my spirit. Whenever I am travelling in the spirit, it happens, and I am there. Our spirits and souls are quantum entangled; they are connected in a realm where there is no time to disconnect us. We are one: spirit, soul and body in union and oneness with Father, Son and Spirit. All the created realms are connected within me (and within you) through being connected to that Kingdom within us, or heaven within us, whichever way you want to put it. We were made to be quantum entangled in union with God, ourselves and creation, and that connection is what is being restored.

Embracing Our Identity

The Father said to me, "Son, our sons are beginning to rise up to be seated in their positions of responsibility to steward the restoration of all things in the realms and dimensions of creation." That is happening. Perhaps you have recognised that it is happening with you; it is happening with a growing number of people. We are beginning to realise who we are as sons, what our identity is, what our position is, and that we have been given responsibility as sons for creation – to creatively co-labour with Jesus to bring restoration to creation.

"The knowledge that you are designed to be immortal is vital to your mature sonship. As the restrictions and limitations on the minds of the sons of God are removed, consciousness is awakened and expanded, and creation responds to your sonship identity and frequency even more."

This is happening too. The more you are who you are intended to be, and the more you know your identity from the vast sum of His amazing thoughts about you, the more the frequency of your being engages creation; and creation begins to respond to you and connect with you. As our consciousness expand, we learn to access all the different types of brainwaves so they can function simultaneously. Usually, we only function in beta waves, problem-solving mode, because our eyes are open and we are looking around, thinking, "How do we fix this problem?" When you focus on your other capacities, you can draw on alpha waves. These are slower and can be used to shut out beta waves, allowing us to meditate with our eyes closed and shut out the world if we like.

Alpha waves are creative and can come from your soul, solving problems or coming to solutions because you are drawing on the creativity with which you are made in the image of God. Often, when trying to solve a problem, especially in the workshop, I draw on my experience and remember techniques or tools I can use. However, sometimes when I do not know how to proceed, I slow down my thinking, focus creatively, and draw on my alpha waves to find a solution. Sometimes it just comes into my mind, or I go to sleep with the issue and wake up with the solution.

Theta waves are where my spirit communicates with my mind. My spirit operates at a different wavelength from my soul and can interject into my mind with solutions from heaven, potentially from the library room of heaven, which holds an infinite number of books. Some solutions to my problems come through the Holy Spirit providing knowledge or words of knowledge. We need to learn to tune into the capacity we have even within our own thinking and consciousness, to function through not just beta waves but also alpha, theta, delta, and gamma waves, which operate at higher levels of creativity and draw information from another realm into our mind.

We can draw from various sources – our conscious thoughts, through the Merkabah, or where we are seated in heavenly places – and learn to choose and create reality in alignment with God's heart. God had a heart intention and desire; He created thoughts, then words, and spoke them into being, calling things that were not as if they are. We can do the same, if only we will stop thinking, "I can't do that. It's impossible." Nothing is impossible for God, and nothing is impossible for the sons of God if we are aligned with His heart.

Restoring Humanity

*I said, "You are gods,
And all of you are sons of the Most High."*
(Psalm 82:6).

We are all in this creative process that is taking us beyond being merely human, restoring humanity from its lost identity into mankind made in God's creative image. We need to return to how God created us, to become God-like as sons of our Heavenly Father. We are not God; I did not create the universe. I was part of the creation of the universe, being part of God, but I am not God, and neither are you. God is God. But we are His sons, and we need to embrace our full potential as sons of God.

His desire is that we enter into more and more of the truth of who we really are as His sons. We are getting glimpses of it, and in the final chapter we will explore the multi-dimensional reality of sonship, how we can learn to live multi-dimensionally, and I will share some of my experiences in this regard. God wants us to experience and enter into these truths and the truth of who we really are from His perspective. We are all made in the image of God, and we all have that potential.

We need to enter into that state of rest where we come to rest in the reality of who we are. Rest is a state of being where we are totally trusting in the Father's love, His goodness, kindness, faithfulness, and the loving-kindness of God. Rest is where there is no fear, worry, doubt or unbelief in our life because we are in a totally trusting state with God our Father. We have the abilities to choose realities that align with Him. He wants us to come to that place where we engage in the possibilities and have the restrictions removed from our minds, so we can fully embrace immortality and the quality of life that goes beyond our current abilities.

The following activation might perhaps help to remove some of the restrictions about time in your mind. You might make yourself available, and God might take you to experience something in history that you could be involved in. If that is not where you are right now and you want to do something else, that is perfectly okay. Be led by whatever God leads you to do, and that might be something different from what is in the text and on the recording. God will encounter you and you will be able to experience what He desires for you.

Activation #21
Removing Time Restrictions

Let's come to a place of rest
where we can begin to live loved.

> I encourage you to close your eyes,
> And as you close your eyes,
> begin to tune out
> of all that's around you.
>
> Relax – physically relax.
> You might want to find a comfortable place,
> lie down, just relax,

Start to focus on your breathing.
Breathe in more slowly and deliberately.
Breathe in that slow, deliberate breath and just hold it,
and breathe it out.
You can breathe in through your nose,
and breathe out.
Be slow, deliberate,
thinking, focusing your attention
on the Father, on Jesus.
Start thinking about God as love.

> God is love,
> God is unconditionally loving.
> Breathe in the unconditional love of the Father.
> Breathe it in slowly,
> breathe it in and rest.
> Unconditional love is flowing through you.
>
> You're surrounded in a cocoon of unconditional love,

as God just begins to love you
and show His amazing love for you.

Be still so you can know who you really are,
as the Father reveals it to you.

Slow down,
picture that open door in your own heart,
where you can engage
in intimacy with Father, Son and Spirit.

Begin to see the River of Life flowing within.
Begin to see love filling you,
every part of your physical being,
every particle of your body,
every part of your soul.

Just see that flow of energy,
of immortal life,
of abundant, living energy filling you,
flowing into you;
focused in the core of your being,
energising those portals within the Merkabah,
energising the energy gates.
You have all the energy you need.

Come to that place where you begin to abide and rest
in that innermost being,
that union of Father, Son and Spirit
with you, body, soul and spirit.
Rest there for a few moments,
in that love.

And as you are there,
open up your heart,
open up your mind,
open up the realm of possibility.

Father, I ask that You remove restrictions
of time, thinking, linearity,
from each of those who are asking right now.

Begin to remove the restrictions.
Remove the impossibilities in their minds.

Open up their hearts,
that they might enter into
the Eternal Now of Your presence,
enter into that place of Father, Son and Spirit.

Make available to those who desire it
the ability to be used in history.
Take them from the Eternal Now of Your presence
And use them in the past
to fulfil Your purpose in history.

Be open to go
wherever it is the Father wants to take you right now.
Be open to that.

22. Unlocking Our Identity as Sons

There is no death

In the way of righteousness there is life,
And in its pathway there is no death.
(Proverbs 12:28 NASB).

In the way of righteousness there is life;
along that path is immortality.
(Proverbs 12:28 NIV)

We have been made the righteousness of God in Christ. Along that path is immortality. Then why is there still death? It is because we believe and expect there to be death. We empower death in our lives because we give it the legal right by believing in it. We have been conditioned to believe in it because everyone says, "one day, you are going to die," and we condition children from an early age to accept that as true. We need to change that. Jesus fully identified with our lost identity so that He could completely undo what Adam did.

Jesus said to them, "The sons of this age marry and are given in marriage, but those who are considered worthy to attain to that age and the resurrection from the dead, neither marry nor are given in marriage; for they cannot even die anymore, because they are like angels, and are sons of God, being sons of the resurrection." (Luke 20:34-36).

That is a Bible passage I have not spoken about very often. Jesus was comparing 'this age' (which was the Old Covenant age) to the New Covenant age. People take 'that age' to mean when you have gone through death and are in heaven. It does not say that, and that is not what it means. Look beyond the question of whether you should be married or not; Jesus is talking about covenants, New and Old. The resurrection from the dead happened to bring in the New Covenant. God offered marriage to Israel in the Old Covenant; they rejected it. In the New Covenant, God has offered marriage again, and Jesus has brought us into that marriage relationship: we are the bride (and now the wife) of Christ.

The important part to focus on, in the context of a discussion on immortality, is that if we believe and know that we have been made worthy; if we believe and know that we are sons of the resurrection, then we can know that we do not have to die anymore because we are like the immortal angels and are sons of God. Again, I must have read this so many times, but I never saw it because I was stuck on the issue of marriage. We have already attained the New Covenant age and the resurrection from the dead, so we cannot even die anymore. Meditate on that, embrace that, take the truth of that, chew on it, and receive the revelation that you do not need to die anymore. In fact, you cannot die, because you are a son of the resurrection, a son of God.

Do you believe this, Martha?

Jesus said to her, "I am the resurrection and the life. Those who believe in me will have life even if they die. Everyone who lives in me and believes in me will never ever die. Do you believe this, Martha?" (John 11:25-26 NCV).

Resurrection and life are implicit within the very name of God, I AM. You might read 'even if they die' and think, "if you believe in Jesus, you will have eternal life after you die." That is absolutely true, but there is something more here. "Everyone who lives in me and believes in me will never ever die." Now again, I must have read this so many times, but I never saw that last part because I was conditioned to see what I always saw, and it just passed me by, as it does for many of us when we read the Bible. Things that do not compute, things that contradict our paradigm just pass us by.

Again, focus on this, meditate on it, embrace it: "Everyone who lives in me and believes in me will never ever die." So, if you believe in Him, you will have life, even if you die; but if you believe in Him and live in Him, you will never die.

Where I am

We can see how this is outworked in another passage of Jesus' teaching, in one of my favourite chapters in the whole Bible:

IDENTITY AS SONS

John chapter 14. I have meditated on this chapter so many times in my life to perceive the reality of what it is truly saying, and the revelation that God gave me through meditating on this has totally overturned the conventional way of looking at it for me.

"If I go and prepare a place for you, I will come again and receive you to Myself, that where I am, there you may be also." (John 14:3).

Now, most Christians interpret this as Jesus going to heaven to build a mansion or a house for us to live in. Then at the 'Second Coming' He will take us to be with Him in heaven. But that is not what that verse says, and that is not what Jesus was intending. Peter had previously asked Him where He was going and He said, "Where I go, you cannot follow Me now; but you will follow later." (see John 13:36). Where was He going? To the cross, to His death.

It is not that Jesus was going to prepare a place for us – the word 'for' is not in the original Greek. A better way of looking at this is, "If I go and prepare you to be a place..." He was going to the cross to prepare us to be a dwelling place of God. He would come back to them after His resurrection, as we shall see in a moment, "so that where I am, you will also be."

Consider that phrase, 'where I am.' Again, think of 'I AM' as the name of God. Where was He? Verse 10 gives us the answer, and it was not a physical place. "Do you not believe that I am in the Father, and the Father is in Me?" Where He is (in the Father), they would also be. Jesus was going to the cross, to the grave, to be resurrected, to come back again to enable us all to have God dwelling in us and for us to dwell in Him.

"On that day you will know that I am in My Father, and you are in Me, and I in you." (John 14:20).

Jesus told them when it was going to take place. "On that day" – the day of resurrection. If we really had to wait until we go to heaven one day when we die to know that we are in the

Father, and the Father is in us, and we are in Him, that would be a very poor gospel. But we do not have to wait because the day of resurrection came, and Jesus was resurrected.

So when it was evening on that day, the first day of the week, and when the doors were shut where the disciples were, for fear of the Jews, Jesus came and stood in their midst and said to them, "Peace be with you." And when He had said this, He showed them both His hands and His side. The disciples then rejoiced when they saw the Lord. So Jesus said to them again, "Peace be with you; as the Father has sent Me, I also send you." And when He had said this, He breathed on them and said to them, "Receive the Holy Spirit..." (John 20:19-22).

This is when Jesus 'came again' to the disciples as He had promised. When He breathed on them and said, "Receive the Spirit," they were resurrected with Him. Now they knew exactly what Jesus had meant when He said, "On that day, you will know" (not by intellectual knowledge but by experience) "that I am in My Father, and you are in Me, and I am in you."

This is the true dynamic of the gospel, yet this passage has been so adulterated as to put it off to the distant future when, in context, it is very clearly referencing the cross, the resurrection, and Jesus breathing on the disciples. They were refreshed by the presence of God when Jesus came to them, and remember, that word 'refreshed' literally means 'to breathe easily again'. They were now breathing the life that God had implanted in them in the Spirit. Wonderful, amazing truth.

Put on immortality

For this perishable must put on the imperishable, and this mortal must put on immortality. But when this perishable puts on the imperishable, and when this mortal puts on immortality, then will come about the saying that is written: 'Death has been swallowed up in victory. Where, O death, is your victory? Where, O death, is your sting?' (1 Corinthians 15:53-4).

This is a real possibility for all of us because Jesus has already done it for us. He went into the grave, and He came out having overcome and abolished death, and brought life and immortality to light. So then, as mortals, we put on what He accomplished for us in the grave, which is resurrection life and immortality, because death has no victory over us. Death can only continue to have victory over you if you believe it has. So why give any legal right for the lie of the enemy to be working in your life? You do not need to die.

Let us embrace immortality and clothe ourselves in the glory of our true identity that God always intended us to have. Let us embrace that identity, that truth of that glory, the essence of who we are as sons of God. Psalm 8 describes it:

What is man that You think of him,
And a son of man that You are concerned about him?
Yet You have made him a little lower than God,
And You crown him with glory and majesty!
You have him rule over the works of Your hands;
You have put everything under his feet...
(Psalm 8:4-6).

"Well, that is talking about Jesus." Yes, but are we not in Jesus? And actually, all of us were made a little lower than God, and all of us were crowned with glory and majesty, it is just that we lost sight of that reality. We were created to rule and govern creation. Creation eagerly anticipates the unveiling of our true glory as sons; it awaits the moment when our authentic identity is fully revealed, and for that revelation to bring about the renewal and restoration of the entire created order, of all things.

For the eagerly awaiting creation waits for the revealing of the sons and daughters of God... that creation itself also will be set free from its slavery to corruption into the freedom of the glory of the children of God (Romans 8:19-21).

Embracing our immortality is essential for realising our true identity and helping all of creation achieve the freedom God always intended for it in the restoration of all things. This is part of a transformative process that elevates us beyond mere humanity into mankind made in God's image. As sons and daughters of our limitless Heavenly Father, we are becoming more like Him, allowing us to reach our fullest potential.

Scroll of destiny

I have heard some people teach that God has plans for us that include all the bad things that happen in our lives. I have been asked about this several times, particularly the idea that we agreed to a scroll of destiny containing all the bad things as well as the good, before coming to earth. This could include sickness, pain, abuse, trauma, sorrow, and even death itself. However, this notion is in total contradiction to the unconditional love of God, and I absolutely reject it. That completely misrepresents who God is. God, our loving Heavenly Father, never intended anything bad to happen in our lives, including death. All His thoughts about us are good; His intentions for us are good.

"For I know the plans that I have for you," declares the Lord, "plans for prosperity and not for disaster, to give you a future and a hope." (Jeremiah 29:11).

It is a mistake to believe that God is sovereign and therefore everything that happens must be His will. He gives us freedom to make our own choices, and the consequences of those choices are not always what He wants for us. Mercy can even overcome many of those consequences if we embrace it. God is love; God is good.

Our scroll of destiny is the record of who we are created by God to be. It reveals our identity and how we are designed to outwork God's desire and intention in our lives. The scroll of our life is the record of what we do as sons of God. This is not about sin because we are new creations in Christ. We are not sinners; we are saints; we are made righteous. Still, there may be a disconnect between the scroll of our destiny – God's desire for us – and the things that we actually do.

I believe that God created us to be the people He wanted us to be, and though we are born into a world that somewhat distorts that, His original desire and purpose are encoded within the DNA of our spirit. Our spirit can reform that image into our whole being when spirit, soul and body come into union.

There are several Bible verses that talk about scrolls.

Then I said, "Behold, I have come;
It is written of me in the scroll of the book.
I delight to do Your will, my God;
Your Law is within my heart."
(Psalm 40:7-8).

This was obviously referring to Jesus, but it also refers to us. Jesus came to do only what He saw the Father doing. He did not come to be under some external law but to live by the love of the Father that was in His heart.

For You created my innermost parts;
You wove me in my mother's womb.
I will give thanks to You,
because I am awesomely and wonderfully made;
Wonderful are Your works,
And my soul knows it very well.
(Psalm 139:13-14).

Is that true for you? It might have been true for the psalmist, but does your soul know it very well? Your spirit knows it, unquestionably, but does your soul? Is there a disconnect between your spirit and your soul? That disconnect needs to be unified so that spirit and soul can become one, operating together in harmony rather than in a disconnected understanding. That psalm continues:

My frame was not hidden from You
When I was made in secret,
And skillfully formed in the depths of the earth;
Your eyes have seen my formless substance;
And in Your book were written

All the days that were ordained for me,
When as yet there was not one of them.
(Psalm 139:15-16).

As we have seen, some people interpret this to mean that there is a set number of days ordained for us, and then we die. It does not say that; it just says 'all the days.' From God's perspective, there is no end to the days.

How precious also are Your thoughts for me, God!
How vast is the sum of them!
Were I to count them, they would outnumber the sand.
When I awake, I am still with You.
(Psalm 139:17-18).

Here, the psalmist is inspired to share and reveal an amazing understanding of who we are and who God made us to be. We can come into that knowledge, know the truth of it, and let it manifest in our lives.

Not a list

We are His workmanship, created in Christ Jesus for good works, which God prepared beforehand so that we could walk in them (Ephesians 2:10).

Our scroll is not a list of instructions or tasks we must complete. Rather, it is a revelation of who we are that empowers us when we are at rest in being who we are. These are not works to earn our salvation or God's favour and blessing because we are good and try to be obedient. Instead, these good works naturally flow from the fact that we are created in Christ Jesus. We are His workmanship, and God has already prepared who we are so that we can live out that reality and express it to the world.

These good works are in perfect alignment with our identity as sons of God. They are not a prescriptive list of things we need to do; rather, they reveal who we are. When we simply rest in being ourselves, that will naturally enable us to live out who we are in this world, reflecting our Father God. The outworking of our eternal identity and redemptive gift will reflect His heart and unconditional love. He gave us this eternal identity because He wanted us to be like Him. We are made in His image and likeness, but we are all unique: each of us is a facet of the multifaceted God whom we love.

We will see the things that the Father is doing aligned with our identity. The Father will not show us things that align with someone else's identity. If we are focused on what others are doing and trying to do the same, we can miss our own calling by pursuing what I have called an alien destiny[18]. If we rest in who we are, we can outwork the things that are aligned with us. Jesus only did what He saw the Father doing. He had a relationship with the Father; He was in the Father, and the Father was in Him. They were working together in relationship, and that is what sons of God are designed to do.

Purifying my scroll

So our scroll is not filled with a list of prescriptive good works, but is a revelation of who we are and how we have been made, our redemptive gifts and our identity. It is a revelation of the Father's heart and desires, enabling us to cooperate with Him. It is not a guarantee but an opportunity to collaborate with the Father as a son. We have all missed opportunities, and we have all had mixed motives. So, what happens if the scroll of our life does not match up with our scroll of destiny as it is supposed to? This is what happened to me.

For no one can lay a foundation other than the one which is laid, which is Jesus Christ. Now if anyone builds on the foundation with gold, silver, precious stones, wood, hay, or straw, each one's work will become evident, for the day will show it because it is to be revealed with fire, and the fire itself will test the quality of each one's work. (1 Corinthians 3:11-13).

The scroll of our life is the record of the outworking of our new creation life in Christ. It is not a record of our lost identity

---

[18] See https://freedomarc.blog/2017/05/15/228-alien-destiny/

because that is completely gone. God has no record of our lost identity, and we can forget about that too. Instead, it is a record of our life as a son. The wood, hay and straw represent the things we may have done with mixed motives, or the things we may not have seen and therefore did not do.

I was on the Father's lap on the throne of grace, enjoying His amazing love. Then, the Spirit of the Fear of the Lord passed by, and the Father asked if I wanted to see my scroll. I said, "Oh yes, I want to see my scroll" (though I probably regretted it a few minutes later).

The Spirit of the Fear of the Lord brought out the scroll, sealed front and back, and gave it to me. I was led to something resembling a cave, which appeared like a lion's mouth. As I walked in, I felt somewhat uncertain and really quite fearful, even trembling. I stood before the Father, who looked at me with eyes full of love and fire. He asked me to open the scroll. When the scroll opened, I saw all the wood, hay, straw, gold, silver, and precious stones. There was no condemnation, guilt, or fear – only mercy. The fire of love from God's eyes consumed all the wood, hay and straw, leaving only the gold, silver and precious stones.

On the reverse of the scroll were all my missed opportunities. Again, I felt no condemnation from God, no disapproval, only love. His fire consumed all those things, so my scroll had no record of them in my life.

Immortality and sonship

Our scrolls, containing the immortality and sonship identity that God desires for us, reflect His wish for us to enjoy eternal life, not death. Immortality is not just about endless life in terms of quantity but also about the eternal quality of life and the abilities that life unveils, our abilities as sons of God. God has uniquely and wonderfully made us to be His sons, and He did not intend for us to die. His intention was for us to have an ongoing, continuous relationship that would never end.

We can only discover the truth of our identity as sons of God within that relationship with our loving Father. It is not something we can strive for or work towards. If your identity comes from what you do, then when you can no longer do it, you will not know who you are. However, if your identity comes from who God says you are, then no matter what you do or do not do, you remain the same person.

God has ensured that we will be restored to that face-to-face relationship with Him that Paul described in Ephesians 1:14. For now, we are in a transitional phase, moving into the full reality of everything God intended, which includes our immortality.

Nonlinearity

On my journey, the Father revealed to me my capacity for thinking and functioning in a nonlinear way, and for multi-dimensional living. Nonlinearity and multi-dimensional perspectives of reality will renew our minds to operate from a completely different framework. I could never have imagined how this would expand my consciousness, enabling me to perceive reality from an entirely different perspective. We can become untethered from the limitations of time and space, allowing us to live as multi-dimensional beings.

We live in a physical dimension, necessary for our physical bodies. However, we also know that we can think outside of that restriction, dream and imagine beyond the limitations of the physical realm. This creativity has given rise to works of science fiction that go far beyond what we can physically perceive. We also have a spirit that can dwell in and explore spiritual dimensions. The physical body is an earth suit, created to occupy this physical dimension, but we do not need to be restricted by it. Our spiritual bodies are designed to occupy the spiritual dimension and to clothe our physical bodies in glory, light and energy, enabling us to travel and experience other dimensional realities.

As we mature and ascend higher, we will discover creative abilities far beyond what we could have imagined. We have the potential to live not just in dual realms but multi-dimensionally. I began by being in dual realms of heaven and earth – my spirit was in heaven while my body and soul were on earth, quantum connected through entanglement. What I was doing in heaven related to earth and vice versa, but initially, I was in one place here and one place there. Eventually, I began to travel and exist in more than one place in both dimensions. This dimensional and time travel became something I realised I had the ability to do. My mind expanded, allowing me to perceive that I was capable of being in multiple places at multiple times, doing multiple things simultaneously.

I wrote in my journal, "I am, therefore I exist in manifoldness like my Father, in nonlinear quantum moments that are the fulfilment of my destiny." Remember, a quantum moment is not a second, nor even a microsecond; it is a moment within which all moments exist, across time and all dimensions. Thus, you can live from a perspective of expanded moments.

I have shared testimonies of contracting and expanding time. This is a way of being, a way of thinking that embraces what that means. I cannot claim that I understood it all at the time, but I began to experience it and realised that my capacity for understanding was growing. I was fulfilling my destiny in both the spiritual and physical realms, which were entirely connected. In those moments, I began to see all the things that I was doing and became aware of the amazing scope of who we are as sons of God – our capacity to become nonlinear, multi-dimensional beings unrestricted by the limitations of time and space. I am within I AM; therefore, I am in multiple places, doing multiple things simultaneously.

Journey to nonlinear understanding

I was engaging in the Eternal Now some time before my mind was deconstructed and I gained the capacity to think nonlinearly, though initially I could only do so in the spirit. Eventually, I could engage it consciously because my ability had expanded to rest there without trying to figure it out. Had

I, at that stage, attempted to understand living in the Eternal Now, it might have threatened my sanity. I did not; I set aside my desire to understand and embraced the experience, which began to change and expand my thinking to accommodate what would have been too much for me to bear.

God continued to reveal things to me, and although you may not understand all the terminology, everything I list here involves places where I have had encounters with the Father, the Son and the Spirit. These encounters happened in time, sometimes expanded time from a heavenly perspective, where hours here equated to days and weeks there, but they all occurred sequentially, one after the other, as I learned to function as a son in the realms of heaven. It took ten years or more to learn all these things one after another. I share my linear journey in the *Engaging God* programme[19], to help people embark on their own journey to discover who they are and express that as sons of God.

Quantum entanglement and multi-dimensional living

Quantum entanglement is the term I use to describe the connection between my spirit and soul in different dimensions, as well as my connection to God in every dimension. In quantum physics, when two particles (such as a pair of photons or electrons) become entangled, they remain connected even when separated by vast distances. Similarly, my spirit and soul can be in two completely different places, both in distance and in dimension, and I can be instantly connected without any time difference. What I am doing there can affect what I am doing here, and vice versa.

I can choose to engage my soul, my mind and my consciousness with where I am and what I am doing in that realm (or those realms). However, I do not often choose to engage it that much because I do not need to; I am at rest, and therefore, I am content to be seated in heavenly places, doing all those things effectively without needing to know. Yet, I do

---

[19] Engaging God is a modular subscription resource. Find out more and get a free trial at eg.freedomarc.org/free-trial

know all the places I am in and all the things I am doing because I have been there previously and learned how to do them.

And He raised us up with Him and seated us with Him in the heavenly places in Christ Jesus (Ephesians 2:6).

Paul's statement is true whether you know it or not, whether you are aware of it cognitively or not; it is the truth because it is something God has done for us. We are seated with Him in multiple heavenly places, and we can become aware of that at any time by engaging our spirit and soul together, because we are connected and entangled within the core of our being. This connection enables us to be seated or enthroned in multiple places, increasing in number and levels of authority as we mature in sonship.

This is a state of abiding, of dwelling, in all of these realities simultaneously. In each, things are happening that contribute to my life, unrestricted by time or space. I am engaged with the Merkabah, the Tree of Life, and the seven energy gates, which are receiving life flowing through them. I can expand my spirit to engage these realities, and I often do whenever I feel led to connect with someone. I can do it consciously; for instance, if I were to speak at a conference, I could extend my spirit around the conference room and open myself so that people could experience and engage with me. When I speak in such a dynamic, people can feel and draw from me the things they want me to discuss, which is why I often go off on so many tangents in a live setting. I am engaging with people's spirits, and I am drawn by their desires and needs, which guide what I share.

I am also quantum entangled multidimensionally with the Eternal Now, dwelling in that space outside of time and space, the Cradle of Life within the heart of the Father. In that place, I brood and come into agreement with the Father's desires, creating a resonance within me. As I vibrate with the frequency of His heart, I can then engage with the sound of many waters, the waterfall, which has been of great significance to me for many years. In that place, I resonate with His voice, and it becomes my voice. I become that frequency, the voice of His authority: I speak what He has shown me is His desire and His heart. Behind that waterfall lies the Chamber of Destiny, where Enoch has assigned me many quests. When I brood and come into resonant agreement, I become a voice; and then I enter that Chamber of Destiny to see where I have permission to outwork what I am doing. I can then engage the Chamber of Creation, where light responds when I speak, forming reality around my life. All of this occurs in another quantum moment, and I am in all those places right now, continually brooding, because I only want to do what I see the Father doing.

I am quantum entangled with the Eternal Now, the Throne of Grace, the Judgment Seat, the altar of fire, the fire stones, and the thrones upon which I am seated, in another quantum moment. This is another outworking of my governmental authority in sonship. The Eternal Now involves engaging with God in the present moment, outside of time and space. I love the Throne of Grace: it is a place where I can engage my entire being in openness, honesty and transparency, without fear of retribution. I can be completely honest about any struggles or issues in my life and take them to the Judgment Seat, where the fire of His eyes purifies my scroll. I can be on the altar of fire, where the fire purifies my heart and motives. The fire stones are nine stones, eventually becoming twelve, which are steps of ascension into sonship, revealing my sonship through revelatory experiences. I dwell in that place, seated on many thrones, operating in my governmental sonship. All of these things are happening simultaneously, and I am there all the time. All I need to do is engage, and I can bring my conscious awareness to each of those places. This is a significant increase in the capacity we all have for sonship.

I am quantum entangled with the Eternal Now, the Court of the Upright, the Cloak of Mystery, the Dark Cloud, Wisdom's Heights, and the Consuming Fire of God's Love in another quantum moment. This is where I engage with the restoration of all things mandated on my life. I am engaged with God's heart, the Court of the Upright, and with the person of Wisdom. I am also engaged with the Cloak of Mystery and the Dark Cloud, where I can minister to fallen angelic beings to help them come into a place of restoration. I engage with Wisdom's Heights and the Consuming Fire of God's love, where people need to be rescued out of the fire because they do not yet understand the love of God. This is a continual process; it is not something that I have to consciously keep doing. This is who I am, and therefore, I am continually involved in the restoration of fallen angelic beings and any other things that God has placed on my heart. It always starts with the Eternal Now. I do not do any of this just because I want to; I do it because the Father's heart is revealed, and I respond to His heart, outworking who I am as a son of God.

I am quantum entangled with the Eternal Now and the 'beyond beyond' dimensional antechamber, where I engage with other dimensions, the constellational portals, which are access points to other dimensions out in the constellations, and many other dimensions in another quantum moment. Part of my destiny and identity involves engaging with other dimensional realities and helping in their restoration. Again, I feel led and called to do this, but I do not have to do it consciously and cognitively all the time. This is where I dwell. The Father opened up an opportunity for me to engage with dimensional beings seeking help, and I continually maintain a position to provide assistance to them. I can access different dimensional realities through the constellational portals, and this is part of who I am.

I am engaged with the Eternal Now, the Father's garden, the seven elemental thrones, and creation in another quantum moment. From the very beginning of my engagement with the Father in His garden, He opened up the possibility and experience of engaging with creation when I was spaghettified and connected to the whole of creation in an instant. That was probably the first quantum moment I ever experienced. It was beyond my ability to understand, but I felt it. I felt creation's groan, its longing and desire for the sons to be revealed, and it stirred me. Ever since, it has been the desire of my heart to see creation restored. I engage with the Father's garden, dwell in the pools and waters there, and engage with the seven elemental thrones, which connect me to the beings that God has given to help us connect with creation. I feel and engage with creation, sharing its desire for restoration. There is so much more to all of this. I am only scratching the surface, but there is so much more to our role in sonship in bringing creation into freedom from its corruption into the freedom of the glory of the children of God. If we do not know the fullness of our glory, our true identity, we will be limited to what we can do on earth or in heaven. But we are called to be multi-dimensional beings, immortal in both quantity and quality.

When I experienced this reality, my heart was filled with joy, and I sank deeper and blissfully into rest. But at the same time, I was so excited by this revelation that I could hardly contain myself. Can you imagine, in a moment, God showing you all that I have just described? It was mind-blowing, yet somehow I was able to retain and believe what He was revealing, and from that I understood the reality of who I truly am.

The Father said, "Son, see how easy it is to just be." That was a profound and challenging statement. When this happened to me, it did not feel easy! It was overwhelming, yet at the same time I was at rest. In that sense it is easy to just be. "This is just a glimpse of what it is to be 'I AM that I AM,' which you will ascend to when you become ascended fathers."

I do not know if you will have access to all these places and dimensions, but no doubt you will have access to others, because you are you, and I am me. I am expressing what I have discovered is possible for me, but please do not try to copy what I am doing: find your own set of dimensional realities to engage with. Find where you are quantum entangled; mature and grow by learning to do things from a linear perspective if you feel you need to. I was taught how to do this linearly so that I could teach others how to do it linearly, which is why the *Engaging God* programme is as it is. However, I do not believe you necessarily have to follow a linear path. You can fully engage with this multi-dimensionally through your intention and choice of being a multi-dimensional being of immortality. Do not be limited to just the thought of being a good son. God desires us to become co-creators in an ascended state of fatherhood. Do I fully understand that? No, but it is in my heart, and I know that this is His intention for us.

"Son, learn to become aware of multi-dimensional reality, but always stay in rest, living in love, joy and peace within. Be balanced by the tree of life, in the union between your spirit, soul and body."

I always anchor myself within that core of my being, ensuring that spirit, soul and body are equally in union and harmony. I do not place more value on the spirit or soul than the body; I value every part equally. The tree of life brings balance, so that we do not become overly focused on spiritual matters or get too caught up in the physical world around us. We are balanced and in harmony, one with the other.

As you expand your spirit's boundaries, practise expanding your consciousness to become more aware of the dimensional realities you are mandated to govern. I have done this. It is not something I do all the time, but it is something I am aware of, and I rejoice in and am grateful for all of it. All you learn to do as a son, made in His image with creative abilities, will equip you to become an ascended father in the ages to come.

"Son, the true authority of a son is realised through surrender, not service, so abandon yourself totally to just being."

That is why I do not focus on the doing; I focus on who I am. This is who I am. This is who you are. This is who we are. We are called to embrace this level of expanded awareness and consciousness, freeing us from the limitations of being earth-bound – or even heaven-bound.

Activation #22
Seated in Heavenly Places

    Close your eyes
and begin to get into
a place of rest, relaxing.
Turn off any agenda
you might have
and just come to a place of rest.
Start focusing on love;
you are going to be living loved.
He is going to express His love to you.

Focus on your breathing
and begin to slow it down.
As you slowly breathe in
and slowly breathe out,
you are drawing in that life,
the love of God.
You are breathing in His love;
it is touching every particle of your being.
As you breathe in,
love is being absorbed into your whole being:
spirit, soul and body.
So breathe.
Focus your whole attention
on breathing in that amazing, unconditional love.

Begin to centre your whole thought,
your whole desire,
on intimacy and relationship with love.
Let God's love touch every part of your being.
If you need physical healing,
let the love of God, the energy of love,
touch you in the place you need it right now.
If you need emotional healing,
if you need mental healing,
if you just need a touch of that love of God,
focus it into that area that you need it right now.

Be still
so you can know the amazing love flowing through you,
through your whole being.

He is loving you,
embracing you.

Some of you need a hug;
you need the Father's hug,
His arms of love around you.
You can rest in His arms of love.

Some of you need
to engage the throne of grace right now.
You just need to sit on the Father's lap,
let Him hug you,
hug Him, put your head on His chest
and feel the comforting rhythm of His heartbeat.
And while you are there resting, surrender.
Cast all your burdens onto Him.
Anything you are worried or concerned about,
give it to Him.
Share your heart with Him.
Anything you may be even afraid of right now,
give it to Him,
because in this place of amazing, unconditional love,
the Father desires to meet your need
with His grace and His mercy.

Some of you just need to stay in that place
and let Him comfort you.
Let Him encourage you.
Let Him strengthen you.
Let Him heal you.
Let Him make you whole.

For others, you may feel you want to go further.
You are in a safe place.
Just begin to think that heaven is open,
that you have access through Jesus

to engage the Father,
to engage His heart.

Maybe right now He wants to take you
into the Eternal Now,
to take you into the place of nonlinear reality
within the *perichoresis* of relationship.
If that is you,
set the desires of your heart upon it
and ask the Father
to take you into that Eternal Now dimensional realm
so you can just be.
Do not try to figure it out or ask questions.
Just embrace what you feel and what you experience.

Some of you, I feel,
need to engage the light of love,
that place of heart to heart, face to face,
where you can look into His eyes
and know His love at a deeper level.
Let Him affirm you,
affirm your identity,
affirm the reality of who you really are.
That He will speak to you right now
some of the vast sum of His thoughts about you.
Open your hearts
and begin to listen to what He shares
in that realm
where you can experience that vast sum of thoughts
maybe one or two or more.
Be open to listen and embrace.

For some of you, you desire to see
where you are seated in heavenly places.
Maybe you desire to see
that multi-dimensional perspective of who you are.

If that is you,
just ask the Father to open up that realm
whether you can see, feel, perceive –

maybe it is even beyond your capacity –
but it will begin to expand your consciousness.
Just open your heart
and let Him show you
what you need to see,
what you need to feel in this moment,
seated in heavenly places.

We ask You, Father,
to expand our consciousness,
expand our awareness,
expand our capacity,
so we will begin to realise
that we are multi-dimensional beings,
sons of the Living God.

Just rest in that place.
Stay in that place of rest.

Whatever you are experiencing right now.
know that you can live loved,
free from guilt, free from shame,
free from condemnation.
You can love living,
enjoying the joy of life.
You can live loving,
be merciful,
choosing to live, forgive, release,
and engage in loving others
as you have been loved.
Rest in love, in joy, and peace.

You are an ambassador of unconditional love
to a world desperately in need
of knowing they are accepted and loved.

We have a message,
an ambassadorship of reconciliation,
of restoration, of love.

Let us embrace that.

Further resources

Books

Mike's previous books are all available from local and online booksellers and as ebooks from our website.

My Journey Beyond Beyond (2018)
The Restoration of All Things (2021)
The Eschatology of the Restoration of All Things (2022)
Engaging the Father (2023)
Into the Dark Cloud (2024)

For more details, visit

    eg.freedomarc.org/books

Other media

Access All Areas: get access to everything you see on our website: event recordings, ebooks, teaching series, and the entire Engaging God programme, with a monthly subscription at eg.freedomarc.org/aaa

Engaging God: our self-paced monthly subscription programme for the Joshua Generation. For your two-week free trial visit eg.freedomarc.org/subscribe-to-engaging-god

Patreon: partner with us at patreon.com/freedomarc to join Mike for monthly group Zooms and other benefits.

Mike's YouTube channel: new videos are normally posted daily. View and subscribe at freedomarc.org/youtube

Sons of Issachar blog: shorter written articles and videos drawn from Mike's teaching and online conversations. Read and subscribe at freedomarc.blog

Social media: follow Freedom ARC at

    freedomarc.org/facebook
    freedomarc.org/twitter
    freedomarc.org/instagram
    freedomarc.org/pinterest

Bible Versions

Unless otherwise noted, scripture quotations are taken from the (NASB®) New American Standard Bible®, Copyright © 1960, 1971, 1977, 1995, 2020 by The Lockman Foundation. Used by permission. All rights reserved. www.lockman.org

Other versions referenced:

AMP: Scripture taken from the Amplified Bible, Copyright © 2015 by The Lockman Foundation. Used by permission.

AMPC: Scripture taken from the Amplified Bible, Classic Edition. Copyright © 1954, 1958, 1962, 1964, 1965, 1987 by The Lockman Foundation. Used by permission. www.lockman.org.

JBP: The New Testament in Modern English by J.B. Phillips. Copyright © 1960, 1972 J.B. Phillips. Administered by The Archbishops' Council of the Church of England. Used by Permission.

KJV: King James Version (Public Domain).

Mirror: The Mirror Bible. Copyright © 2017, 2021 by Francois Du Toit. Used by kind permission of the author. All rights reserved.

MLT: Modern Literal Translation New Testament. © Copyright 1999, 2016 by G. Allen Walker, Co-Editor.

NCV: New Century Version. The Holy Bible, New Century Version®. Copyright © 2005 by Thomas Nelson, Inc.

NIV: Holy Bible, New International Version®, NIV® Copyright ©1973, 1978, 1984, 2011 by Biblica, Inc.® Used by permission. All rights reserved worldwide.

NKJV: Scripture taken from the New King James Version®. Copyright © 1982 by Thomas Nelson. Used by permission. All rights reserved.